Praise for

Growing Up Getty

"A brisk and sympathetic chronicle of the man [J. Paul Getty] and his many descendants. Add this to Anderson Cooper and Katherine Howe's *Vanderbilt* and Tina Brown's *The Palace Papers*, and we may have a new pandemic escape genre on our hands: the scionography."
—*The New York Times Book Review*

"Reginato's meticulously researched and beautifully written account takes the reader deep into the lives of the charismatic and elusive clan that comprises the 'House of Getty,' piercing the myths that have surrounded some of its protagonists for decades and introducing us to others for the first time."
—Sara Gay Forden, *New York Times* bestselling author of *The House of Gucci*

"What a wonderful journey into the lives of one of America's most fascinating dynasties. A must-read."
—Laurence Leamer, *New York Times* bestselling author of *Capote's Women*

"A fascinating, and sometimes revisionist, take on the quasi-mythic figure of J. Paul Getty—and an impeccably researched tracing of the lives of his descendants: the people who grappled, in astonishingly diverse ways, with the strange fate of belonging to a modern dynasty."
—Laura Thompson, *New York Times* bestselling author of *The Six* and *Heiresses*

"A first-rate look at one of the world's greatest and most misunderstood dynasties. Engrossing, illuminating . . . exhaustively researched, and elegantly written. Taking us reassuringly by the hand, James Reginato leads us on an absorbing stroll through the funhouse hall of mirrors that is the Family Getty."
—Christopher Andersen, #1 *New York Times* bestselling author of *Brothers and Wives*

"The Gettys' eccentricities are on full display, delightfully so."

—*San Francisco Chronicle*

"Reginato's meticulous research and personal interviews create a sweeping portrait of arguably the United States' greatest industrial dynasty and extracts the untold stories behind the sensational headlines. . . . Reginato argues that Getty spawned not just a dynasty but a betterment of society, as the current generation of Gettys are aligned with the times. . . . This narrative captures a sensitive and influential family who, at its heart, values togetherness . . . verdict: A rapturous biography for casual readers."

—*Library Journal*, starred review

". . . [an] entertaining chronicle of the illustrious dynasty's four generations . . . engaging in its cinematic depictions of the family in their element: the Getty patriarch surrounded by priceless antiques in luxurious Sutton Place, Paul Jr. and Talitha Getty smoking up with a carnival of 1960s cultural icons in the Palais de la Zahia, Billy and Vanessa Getty's glittering Napa Valley wedding. The result offers the approximate pleasure of thumbing through a century of society pages."

—*Publishers Weekly*

"In a captivating narrative, Reginato, writer at large for *Vanity Fair* and a contributor to *Sotheby's* magazine, brings readers up to date on the state of the Getty family. . . . A fresh and engaging look at a complex and elusive American family."

—*Kirkus Reviews*

"This fascinating exposé moves the narrative onto the current generation, from dress designer to the stars, August Getty, to leading environmentalist Anne G. Earhart."

—*Bury & West Suffolk Magazine*

Growing Up

Getty

Growing Up

Getty

*The Story of America's
Most Unconventional Dynasty*

JAMES REGINATO

G

GALLERY BOOKS

NEW YORK   LONDON   TORONTO   SYDNEY   NEW DELHI

G

Gallery Books
An Imprint of Simon & Schuster, Inc.
1230 Avenue of the Americas
New York, NY 10020

Copyright © 2022 by James Reginato

Excerpts from "The Getty" from "California Republic" from
THE WHITE ALBUM by Joan Didion. Copyright © 1979 by Joan Didion.
Reprinted by permission of Farrar, Straus and Giroux. All Rights Reserved.
Getty Diaries © J. Paul Getty Trust. Getty Research Institute, Los Angeles (2010.IA.16)
Getty Family Papers © J. Paul Getty Trust, Getty Research Institute, Los Angeles (1987.IA.09-01)
Helen Ann Rork quotes: Getty Research Institute, Los Angeles (1986.IA.48-06)

All rights reserved, including the right to reproduce this book or portions thereof in any form
whatsoever. For information, address Gallery Books Subsidiary Rights Department,
1230 Avenue of the Americas, New York, NY 10020.

First Gallery Books trade paperback edition April 2023

GALLERY BOOKS and colophon are registered trademarks of Simon & Schuster, Inc.

For information about special discounts for bulk purchases, please contact Simon & Schuster
Special Sales at 1-866-506-1949 or business@simonandschuster.com.

The Simon & Schuster Speakers Bureau can bring authors to your live event.
For more information or to book an event, contact the Simon & Schuster Speakers Bureau
at 1-866-248-3049 or visit our website at www.simonspeakers.com.

Interior design by Michelle Marchese

Manufactured in the United States of America

1   3   5   7   9   10   8   6   4   2

Library of Congress Cataloging-in-Publication Data

Names: Reginato, James, author.
Title: Growing up Getty: the story of America's most unconventional dynasty / James Reginato.
Identifiers: LCCN 2021058317 (print) | LCCN 2021058318 (ebook) |
ISBN 9781982120986 (hardcover) | ISBN 9781982121006 (ebook)
Subjects: LCSH: Getty family. | Children of the rich—United States—Biography. |
Millionaires—United States—Biography. | BISAC: BIOGRAPHY & AUTOBIOGRAPHY /
Rich & Famous | BIOGRAPHY & AUTOBIOGRAPHY / LGBTQ+
Classification: LCC HC102.5.A2 R44 2022 (print) | LCC HC102.5.A2 (ebook) |
DDC 305.5/234092 [B]—dc23/eng/20211213
LC record available at https://lccn.loc.gov/2021058317
LC ebook record available at https://lccn.loc.gov/2021058318

ISBN 978-1-9821-2098-6
ISBN 978-1-9821-2099-3 (pbk)
ISBN 978-1-9821-2100-6 (ebook)

Contents

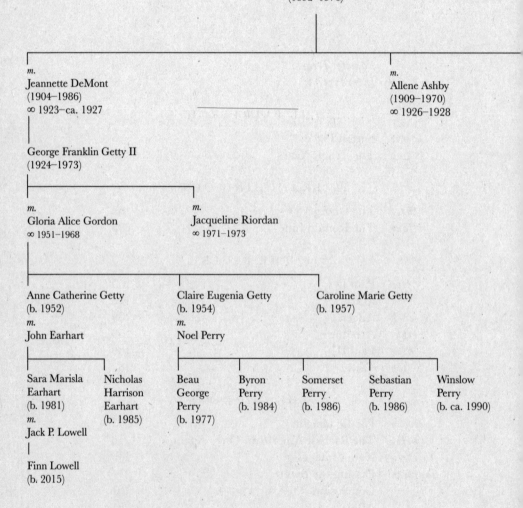

Jean Paul Getty
(1892–1976)

m.
Jeannette DeMont
(1904–1986)
∞ 1923–ca. 1927

George Franklin Getty II
(1924–1973)

m.
Gloria Alice Gordon
∞ 1951–1968

m.
Jacqueline Riordan
∞ 1971–1973

m.
Allene Ashby
(1909–1970)
∞ 1926–1928

Anne Catherine Getty
(b. 1952)
m.
John Earhart

Claire Eugenia Getty
(b. 1954)
m.
Noel Perry

Caroline Marie Getty
(b. 1957)

Sara Marisla
Earhart
(b. 1981)
m.
Jack P. Lowell

Nicholas
Harrison
Earhart
(b. 1985)

Beau
George
Perry
(b. 1977)

Byron
Perry
(b. 1984)

Somerset
Perry
(b. 1986)

Sebastian
Perry
(b. 1986)

Winslow
Perry
(b. ca. 1990)

Finn Lowell
(b. 2015)

❧ THE GETTY FAMILY ❧

PART ONE

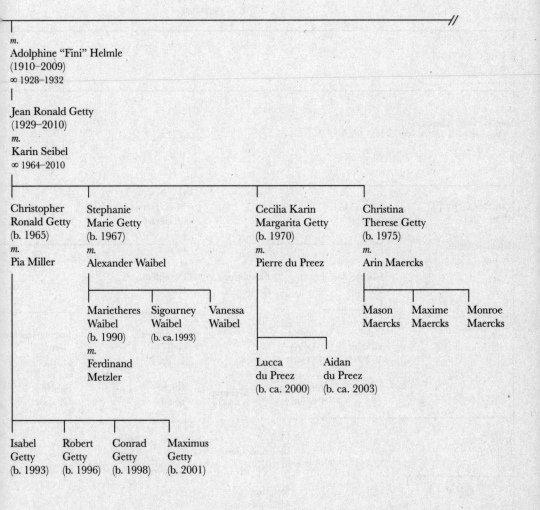

m.
Adolphine "Fini" Helmle
(1910–2009)
∞ 1928–1932

Jean Ronald Getty
(1929–2010)
m.
Karin Seibel
∞ 1964–2010

Christopher
Ronald Getty
(b. 1965)
m.
Pia Miller

Stephanie
Marie Getty
(b. 1967)
m.
Alexander Waibel

Cecilia Karin
Margarita Getty
(b. 1970)
m.
Pierre du Preez

Christina
Therese Getty
(b. 1975)
m.
Arin Maercks

Marietheres
Waibel
(b. 1990)
m.
Ferdinand
Metzler

Sigourney
Waibel
(b. ca.1993)

Vanessa
Waibel

Mason
Maercks

Maxime
Maercks

Monroe
Maercks

Lucca
du Preez
(b. ca. 2000)

Aidan
du Preez
(b. ca. 2003)

Isabel
Getty
(b. 1993)

Robert
Getty
(b. 1996)

Conrad
Getty
(b. 1998)

Maximus
Getty
(b. 2001)

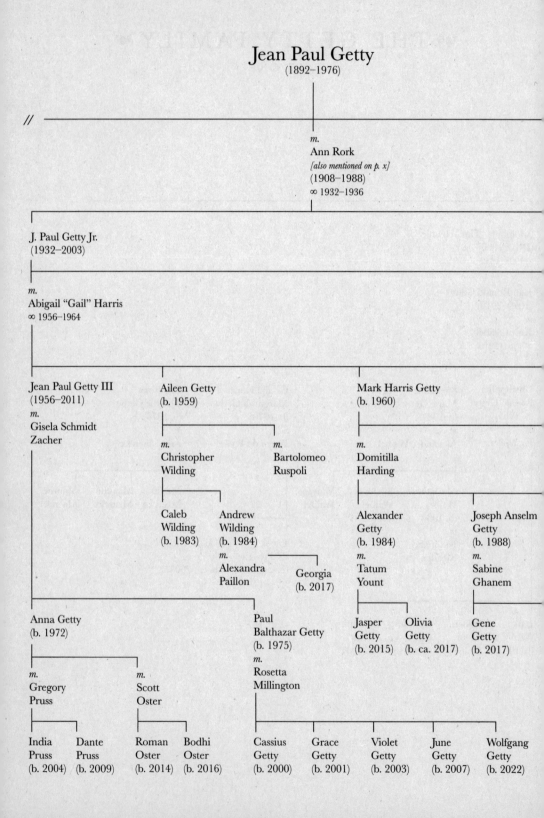

Jean Paul Getty
(1892–1976)

//

m.
Ann Rork
[also mentioned on p. x]
(1908–1988)
∞ 1932–1936

J. Paul Getty Jr.
(1932–2003)

m.
Abigail "Gail" Harris
∞ 1956–1964

Jean Paul Getty III
(1956–2011)
m.
Gisela Schmidt
Zacher

Aileen Getty
(b. 1959)

m.
Christopher
Wilding

m.
Bartolomeo
Ruspoli

Mark Harris Getty
(b. 1960)

m.
Domitilla
Harding

Caleb
Wilding
(b. 1983)

Andrew
Wilding
(b. 1984)
m.
Alexandra
Paillon

Georgia
(b. 2017)

Alexander
Getty
(b. 1984)
m.
Tatum
Yount

Joseph Anselm
Getty
(b. 1988)
m.
Sabine
Ghanem

Anna Getty
(b. 1972)

Paul
Balthazar Getty
(b. 1975)
m.
Rosetta
Millington

Jasper
Getty
(b. 2015)

Olivia
Getty
(b. ca. 2017)

Gene
Getty
(b. 2017)

m.
Gregory
Pruss

m.
Scott
Oster

India
Pruss
(b. 2004)

Dante
Pruss
(b. 2009)

Roman
Oster
(b. 2014)

Bodhi
Oster
(b. 2016)

Cassius
Getty
(b. 2000)

Grace
Getty
(b. 2001)

Violet
Getty
(b. 2003)

June
Getty
(b. 2007)

Wolfgang
Getty
(b. 2022)

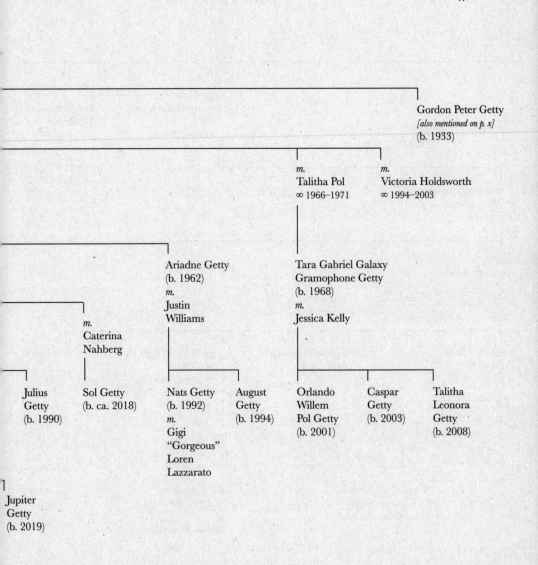

Gordon Peter Getty
[also mentioned on p. x]
(b. 1933)

m.
Talitha Pol
∞ 1966–1971

m.
Victoria Holdsworth
∞ 1994–2003

Ariadne Getty
(b. 1962)
m.
Justin
Williams

Tara Gabriel Galaxy
Gramophone Getty
(b. 1968)
m.
Jessica Kelly

m.
Caterina
Nahberg

Julius
Getty
(b. 1990)

Sol Getty
(b. ca. 2018)

Nats Getty
(b. 1992)
m.
Gigi
"Gorgeous"
Loren
Lazzarato

August
Getty
(b. 1994)

Orlando
Willem
Pol Getty
(b. 2001)

Caspar
Getty
(b. 2003)

Talitha
Leonora
Getty
(b. 2008)

Jupiter
Getty
(b. 2019)

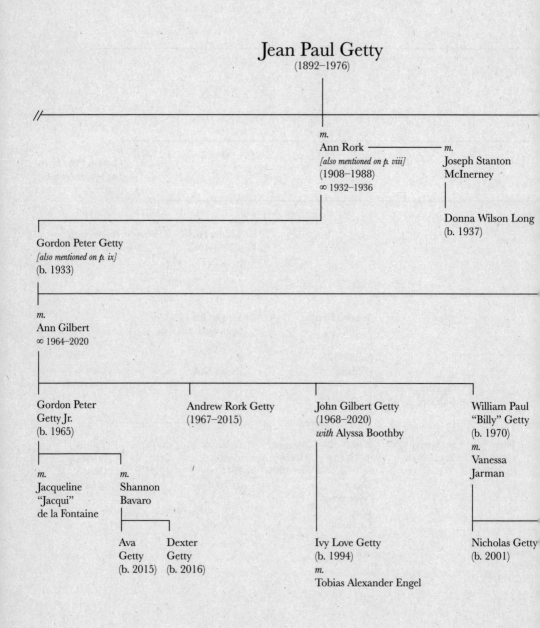

Jean Paul Getty
(1892–1976)

_m._
Ann Rork —————— _m._
[also mentioned on p. viii]   Joseph Stanton
(1908–1988)   McInerney
∞ 1932–1936

                                     Donna Wilson Long
                                     (b. 1937)

Gordon Peter Getty
[also mentioned on p. ix]
(b. 1933)

_m._
Ann Gilbert
∞ 1964–2020

Gordon Peter   Andrew Rork Getty   John Gilbert Getty   William Paul
Getty Jr.   (1967–2015)   (1968–2020)   "Billy" Getty
(b. 1965)   _with_ Alyssa Boothby   (b. 1970)
                                                                    _m._
                                                                    Vanessa
                                                                    Jarman
_m._   _m._
Jacqueline   Shannon
"Jacqui"   Bavaro
de la Fontaine

        Ava   Dexter   Ivy Love Getty   Nicholas Getty
        Getty   Getty   (b. 1994)   (b. 2001)
        (b. 2015) (b. 2016)   _m._
                                Tobias Alexander Engel

❧ THE GETTY FAMILY ❧

PART THREE

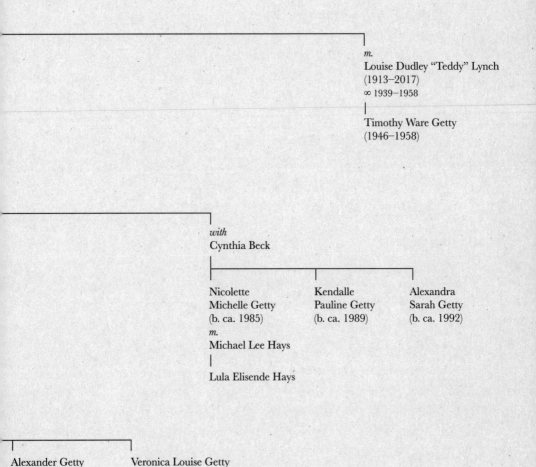

m.
Louise Dudley "Teddy" Lynch
(1913–2017)
∞ 1939–1958

Timothy Ware Getty
(1946–1958)

with
Cynthia Beck

Nicolette
Michelle Getty
(b. ca. 1985)
m.
Michael Lee Hays

Lula Elisende Hays

Kendalle
Pauline Getty
(b. ca. 1989)

Alexandra
Sarah Getty
(b. ca. 1992)

Alexander Getty
(b. 2003)

Veronica Louise Getty
(b. 2008)

Introduction

Dynasties are notoriously difficult to maintain. By a common benchmark, a family can't really be considered a dynasty until it has endured for four generations with its fortune and social rank still standing. When a family does cross that threshold, to keep them all on track at least one of the heirs generally needs to produce something original.

With its fourth generation ascendant, the Gettys tick all the boxes, though they are an unconventional dynasty. This is only fitting considering their independent-minded patriarch, J. Paul Getty. Descended from Scots-Irish stock, he was born in 1892 in Minneapolis; as a teenager, he moved with his family to Los Angeles. In 1916, he struck out as a wildcatter in Oklahoma, where he hit black gold. He built his petroleum empire stealthily, while working out of suitcases in a succession of hotel suites he occupied as he roamed around Europe for decades. Something of a one-man band, he bested many of the so-called Seven Sisters, the corporate oil oligopolies, including Standard Oil. Rich as he became, he was never an Establishment guy. To the world at large he was relatively obscure until 1957, when *Fortune* magazine named him, at age sixty-four, "the Richest American." With his estimated net worth in the range of $1 billion, he eclipsed Rockefellers, Mellons, Astors, and Du Ponts—members of dynasties that had been established several generations earlier.

Becoming "an overnight financial freak," as he later observed, he was catnip for the press, which lapped up his foibles, especially his frugality. In the beginning, the stories were comical. Everyone enjoyed the one about the World's Richest Man—as Getty was soon enough surmised to be—installing a pay phone for "the convenience" of guests at his residence, Sutton Place, the sixteenth-century mansion twenty-three miles outside of London that he bought in 1959. (After sailing from New York to London in June 1951, for what was supposed to be a few months, he never set foot again in America.)

But after the drug-related death of his firstborn child, George Franklin Getty II, in May 1973, and—just five weeks later—the kidnapping of his eldest grandson, J. Paul Getty III, the saga of the Gettys took on a decidedly darker tone.

"The Tragic Dynasty." "A Cautionary Tale." "The Getty Curse." Newspapers and magazines printed such headlines again and again, turning the Gettys into a poster family for dysfunction. They lived up to this billing in the 1970s and 1980s: JPG's third son, J. Paul Jr., battled drug addiction and depression for many years, as did some of Paul Jr.'s children, including Aileen, and Paul III, who suffered a stroke in 1981 that left him a paraplegic until his death in 2011.

Then there were the family's legal battles, most of which revolved around the source of their immense wealth, the Sarah C. Getty Trust. Begun in 1934 at the behest of J. Paul Getty's mother, for whom it is named, it was initiated with capital of $3.5 million to provide primarily for her grandchildren. Throughout his life, Getty plowed his profits back into it and, in turn, borrowed from it to grow his business empire. In the 1960s, Getty's fourth son, Gordon, challenged his father in court over the trust, resulting in a seven-year-long suit that the younger Getty lost. Following the patriarch's death in 1976 at age eighty-three, the clan was dragged into the public eye again, this time thanks to the astounding bequest he made—valued then at $750 million—to his recently opened namesake museum in Malibu. A few years later, lawsuits erupted between family members over the sale of Getty Oil. After Texaco bought it for $10.1 billion—the biggest corporate acquisition in history—the relatives litigated for another eighteen months over management of the trust, the coffers of which at that point swelled to $4 billion.

It was irresistible material for numerous journalists, biographers, and filmmakers. In his 1995 book, *Painfully Rich* (later republished under the title *All the Money in the World*), John Pearson described the Getty Trust as "probably the most destructive major fortune of our time" and pondered "why it has apparently devoured so many of its beneficiaries." Director Ridley Scott used Pearson's book as the basis for his 2017 film *All the Money in the World*, which plumbed the grisly details of the kidnapping. The five-month ordeal was an immensely traumatic event for family members, and it continues to haunt some of them. Yet in the film, the biggest villain was J. Paul Getty—not the kidnappers who brutally cut off their victim's ear and abused him before they finally released him. Overall, Getty was depicted as a monstrous figure—coldhearted, greedy, humorless, lonely, reclusive. The ultimate misanthrope.

Could J. Paul Getty have been such a thoroughly irredeemable person? Was his family so cursed?

The Getty family tree is a complicated one. During his five short-lived marriages, Getty produced four sons who lived into adulthood (his fifth and youngest boy died at age twelve); between them, they fathered nineteen children, sixteen of whom survive as of 2022. They, in turn, have produced a generation of around forty Gettys—JPG's great-grandchildren. About fifteen great-great-grandchildren have been born.

In this book, I examine the patriarch, his wives, and their descendants, reassessing some of the narratives about them that have taken root and grown—often in the fertile soil of tabloid websites. You will see that while some of the myths are based in reality—a number of Gettys have been decimated by addiction and depression—the majority of its members today are thriving. A more nuanced look at the family is thus called for.

Geographically, the descendants spread out and have lived in North America and South America, as well as Europe, Asia, and Africa. Following the lead of their international forebear, they've become a global dynasty. Some of his grandchildren might be modern-day versions of Henry James or Edith Wharton characters, having assimilated (in some cases by marriage) into European nobility. Others remain true Californians, some marrying into Hollywood royalty.

"They're weirdos, all of them, in different ways," a gentleman who has been friends with many of them told me. "In a good way," he added. "Their wealth and position in the world has allowed them to delve deeply into the things that they are interested in. So many other extremely rich people who could do whatever they want, do exactly what everybody else does. The Gettys are idiosyncratic. They all have a streak of wildness—and sometimes mental health issues."

Looking at the Gettys today, I found creative, accomplished, and philanthropic individuals. Perhaps most surprisingly—in view of what is usually written about them—a number of them indeed appear to be well-adjusted and happy. Tragedy has revisited the family on more than a few occasions, but it would be inaccurate to describe the whole of such a large clan as cursed. And a lively batch of young Gettys are starting to make their marks on the world.

The Gettys are a surprisingly tight-knit clan. Every summer, the extended family holds an annual meeting, usually in Italy; at another point in the year, typically, many of them get together in New York or take a trip elsewhere. In December, a gala party for Gordon's birthday draws many Gettys to San Francisco, where their political power is on display; in addition to family, longtime close friends and political heavyweights Nancy Pelosi, Dianne Feinstein, Kamala Harris, and Gavin Newsom are also regulars.

Though Sutton Place itself was sold long ago (at last report, it was owned by Uzbekistan-born oligarch Alisher Usmanov, the eighth-richest man in Britain), the Sutton Place name continues to figure prominently in the life of the clan, existing virtually in various of their domain names, IP addresses, and SEC filings, and terrestrially within an unmarked building on an elegant street in London's Mayfair that houses their family office, the well-staffed nerve center for all matters Getty.

"They have this sort of army of people around them," said one Londoner familiar with the family. "To an extent, then, the real world never really impinges on them. They are quite elusive and difficult to pin down. But they really care about things and want to do things properly. They don't just lend their names to a cause. At the same time, they are one state removed from the real world. When you've had that amount of money for that long, that's where you are."

Even though it has at times threatened to tear some of them apart, the legacy of the Sarah C. Getty Trust continues to bind them. In 1985, after the settlement of the family litigation in the wake of the sale of Getty Oil, $1 billion was reserved for taxes, leaving them with $3 billion, which was partitioned into four separate trusts (each worth $750 million). How rich are they today? In 2015, *Forbes* pegged the Getty family's net worth at $5.4 billion in a ranking of "America's Richest Families." But a number of Gettys hold foreign passports; at least eight of them reportedly have carried Irish passports, which have sometimes been granted in exchange for making investments in Ireland. According to several financial experts I consulted, given the extraordinary growth of the stock market over the past decades, the family's combined net worth could easily be in the neighborhood of $20 billion. (The Getty Museum's endowment, which also began around 1985 with its $750 million bequest, soared to $9.2 billion in 2021.)

"They could have done *way* better," one prominent investment manager said of the Getty family. "If they actually did smart things, and managed their taxes well, which you would expect from a respectable family trust with the resources and brainpower they'd have access to, their compound annual growth rate could have been higher than 11 percent, putting them in the $150-plus billion range."

Much of the Gettys' wealth has been shielded behind their trusts, which have provided family members with large distributions. But according to the Sarah C. Getty Trust's terms, its capital will be divided between the heirs upon the death of J. Paul Getty's last living son. So, immense windfalls await Sarah's great-grandchildren when Gordon's time comes.

Diverse as the Gettys are, they can be divided—for journalistic purposes—into two camps: the "public" ones and the "private" ones. Aside from a few flamboyant individuals, much of the family remains remarkably private. Some of them intensely so. There are many Gettys you never read about and probably have never heard of.

Some have become well-known through their achievements in business, philanthropy, and society, or have been made notorious through tragedy. Even when these "public" ones speak to the press (or, in the cases of younger Gettys, post on Instagram), they generally focus on a specific undertaking or cause. They are not inclined to cooperate with reporters attempting to pull together a big picture of the clan. You can't blame them. They don't want to read another "Tragic Dynasty" tale. A good deal of what has been written about them has been, if not inaccurate, then off the mark. And they want their achievements to be taken on their own merits.

As the new generations of the four branches of the family mature and go in different directions, a wide-angle lens is needed to look at them. One also has to debunk some of the myths that have grown around them.

I began my research into the family by delving into J. Paul Getty's personal papers, housed at the Getty Research Institute, one of the monumental travertine-clad buildings at the Getty Center in the Brentwood neighborhood of Los Angeles.

In his correspondence—including love letters to and from some of his wives—and his diaries, which span from 1938 to 1976, a figure emerges quite different from the one that has hardened in the public imagination, a man capable of humor and affection. His diaries are also a fascinating record of wealth and power in the twentieth century. Each day—in a sort of proto-Warholian fashion—he made note of business transactions great or small; the people he saw; pieces of art that caught his attention and prompted him to open his checkbook; his bodily functions and ailments.

His social life was nonstop. Well into his seventies, he was routinely out dancing at nightclubs until two in the morning, if not later. (So much for his reported reclusiveness.) One also finds note of many visits from his children, grandchildren, ex-wives, and numerous mistresses. According to accounts from the women themselves, as well as Getty, he maintained warm relations with all of his exes until the very end.

There are also details of his fervent efforts to build his art collection and his museum, shedding light on the astounding cultural and philanthropic legacy he left. His bequest to his museum was the largest donation to a cultural institution in history—which no doubt emboldened critics to mock it in its early years, particularly for its design in the form of a Roman villa, which the intelligentsia derided as "Disney-like," even as the public adored it.

When J. Paul Getty died, he left his descendants with colossal riches as well as his unconventional DNA. Wealth is often squandered; genes can split in many directions. Despite considerable tragedies, the Gettys have survived, and even thrived. Now, as its younger branches spread out, can they endure as a contemporary dynasty?

I.

THE PATRIARCH

1

Sutton Place

It was the dawn of a new decade and a new era—a day in 1960—as J. Paul Getty marched through the Tudor labyrinth of Sutton Place. Twenty-three miles southwest of London, it had been built 440 years earlier by a courtier of Henry VIII. Just now, it had been rebooted as the nerve center of Getty's worldwide petroleum empire, and his seventy-two-room home. Telex machines clattered with reports of stock market gyrations on Wall Street and the flow of oil from Arabian deserts. Bustling about were members of Getty's executive and domestic staffs, the latter headed by Francis Bullimore, his unimpeachable butler.

Getty, wearing one of his customary Kilgour, French & Stanbury dark three-piece suits, and bearing the mournful mien that made him always look, his longtime aide Claus von Bülow observed, as if he were attending his own funeral, trod through the 165-foot oak-paneled Long Gallery, draped with sixteenth-century Flemish tapestries. When Getty reached his private study, where Dutch Old Masters hung on the Honduras mahogany paneling, he shut the door.

He then unlaced his John Lobb oxfords and jumped onto a long settee.

"Come on," he beckoned to the other person in the room, his solicitor, Robina Lund, a brainy twenty-three-year-old Scotswoman employed by the starchy firm of Slaughter and May. The dealer who had just delivered the settee had vouched for its sturdiness, promising it was "strong enough to jump on," explained Getty (who stood five feet eleven and weighed 180 pounds, with a muscular build from years of weight training).

"So let's try it!" he said to Lund.

"What if it breaks?" she wondered.

"I'll send it back," he said.

Recalled Lund, "So for a good five minutes we bounced up and down, and I nearly killed myself laughing as he did an Indian warwhoop each time he went in the air."

At the sound of a knock on the door, the pair were back into their shoes in a flash. As Bullimore ushered in the next appointment, a pair of businessmen, Getty reassumed his customary countenance. "Paul gravely shook their hands," Lund remembered.

People can be so different behind closed doors. J. Paul Getty had so many doors. That day, as he settled into Sutton Place, the richest man in the world had reason to feel giddy. This was at last a permanent home—something this sixty-seven-year-old hadn't had since childhood. Over the previous decades, he'd been a virtual stranger to the households where his five wives and five sons lived. His had been a nomadic existence, unspooling in a succession of hotel suites, mostly in Europe, where his ear was glued to the phones on which he conducted business, and where he washed his own socks and underwear.

Resolutely low-profile, Getty ensured that his photo seldom appeared in print outside of the *Oil & Gas Journal* and publications of that ilk. The anonymity suited him well, allowing him to stealthily acquire stakes in companies he sought to take over, and, when he had the time, to conduct amorous meetings with an array of women.

But his cover had been blown on October 28, 1957. His first inkling came when he found the lobby of the Ritz, the hotel in

London where he was then living, swarming with journalists, all clamoring to see "the richest American." *Fortune* magazine had just published the results of a thorough and novel investigation that identified all citizens with fortunes exceeding $75 million. Getty was not only at the top of the seventy-six-person list—which was divided into five tiers—but far above the rest. His name alone appeared in the $700 million to $1 billion category. The $400 million to $700 million class included four members of the Mellon family as well as John D. Rockefeller Jr., Dallas oil magnate H. L. Hunt, and Miami real estate mogul Arthur Vining Davis.

Four Du Ponts, as well as Joseph Kennedy, Howard Hughes, Fort Worth oil wildcatter Sid Richardson, and steel heiress Mrs. Frederick Guest (the former Amy Phipps), made the $200 million to $400 million category; six Rockefellers (John D.'s kids), Vincent Astor, Doris Duke, and Mrs. Edsel Ford were bunched in with Texas oilmen Clint Murchison, John Mecom, and James Abercrombie at the $100 million to $200 million level; Henry Ford II, Mrs. Horace Dodge, Marjorie Merriweather Post, and John T. Dorrance Jr., son of the Campbell Soup formula inventor, were among those bringing up the rear, with $75 million to $100 million apiece.

The compilation, *Fortune* wrote, "only serves to emphasize the tremendous changes that American wealth has undergone in both numbers and character over the past twenty years. . . . No longer among today's Very Rich are the Morgans, the Goulds, the Guggenheims."

This rich roster was republished in newspapers worldwide. "Topping the list is Jean Paul Getty, Minnesota-born oil man and owner of the Pierre Hotel," wrote the *New York Times*, in its front-page, above-the-fold story.

For the rest of his life, Getty expressed rueful feelings over this "outing."

"I was thenceforth a curiosity only a step or two removed from the world's tallest man or the world's shortest midget. . . . I had become a sort of financial freak, overnight," he observed.

5

Yet he did invite some of those journalists who thronged the Ritz lobby up to his suite. "In a two-hour interview," wrote the *New York Times*'s reporter, "he traced the origins of his fortune, spoke lovingly of his extensive art collection, and imparted some thoughts on world affairs." Nonetheless, Getty claimed to the paper that being named the richest man in the USA was "a distinction I'm not particularly interested in. I don't think there is any glory in being known as a moneybags. I'd rather be considered an active businessman."

In 1963, he concluded that the *Fortune* piece had marked "a turning point" in his life, "in the sense that it had the effect of ending my existence as an ordinary private citizen and made me, for better or worse, a public figure, or at least a person about whom the public curiosity was whetted."

Most materially, the article prompted him to finally acquire a permanent residence. Stalkers and concerns for his security had come with fame, making hotel life problematic. Perhaps, too, he decided it was finally time to settle down. A home at last? In his own way and unique vocabulary, he envisioned it initially as "a sort of liaison base." He weighed the merits of various capitals in Western Europe (midway between the Middle East and California, twin centers of his empire, this was the place for him). Paris was his first choice. But then, one evening in June 1959, just after he'd arrived back in London, a friend drove him into Surrey to a small dinner party at Sutton Place, hosted by its owner, George Granville Sutherland-Leveson-Gower, 5th Duke of Sutherland—Geordie, to friends.

While Sutton Place and His Grace's lineage were both ancient, they hadn't, in fact, been connected so long. Geordie, one of the largest landowners in Scotland, had bought the manor in 1917 from descendants of its builder, Sir Richard Weston. (Weston's young son, Francis, had the misfortune of being beheaded by Henry VIII after the king decided that Francis had engaged in more than tennis matches with Anne Boleyn, his second queen, during royal visits to Sutton Place.)

With numerous other roofs to keep in repair, Geordie was ready to part with the twenty-seven-bedroom, redbrick pile on 700 acres. Getty made the lowball offer of £60,000, which was promptly accepted.

Although it took several months to install acres of new curtains, linens, and upholstery, Sutton Place came largely furnished—Bullimore included. A native of Norfolk, England, he had served as butler to Joseph Kennedy when he was the American ambassador to the Court of St. James's, and to Henry Ford II, before the Duke of Sutherland hired him at Sutton Place. Getty described him as "benevolently despotic."

Another indispensable employee was the footman, Frank Parkes—Bullimore's longtime companion. While guests were likely unaware of their relationship, it was evident to everyone that Parkes's floral arrangements were second to none. Some visitors even compared them favorably to the legendary florist Constance Spry's.

A rotating cast of other lively characters inhabited Sutton Place too: Getty's numerous lady friends and mistresses. Among them were Penelope Kitson, a well-bred English divorcée; Mary Teissier, a lady of Russian and French extraction with regal bearing; Rosabella Burch, a seductive Nicaraguan widow; and Lady Ursula d'Abo, née Manners, a daughter of the 9th Duke of Rutland (as well as the niece of the celebrated Lady Diana Cooper).

His protestations against the press notwithstanding, Getty warmed up to reporters. The gates of Sutton Place were opened to a variety of glossies, from *Town & Country*, with which he discussed entertaining ("The English are simply marvelous at giving a party. They're never blasé. . . .") to *Cosmopolitan*, with which he discussed, naturally, his success with women and his failure at marriage. ("You have to face facts. If you've tried to fly an airplane and crashed five times, you had better give up. It's too dangerous.")

But it was a fifty-five-minute BBC program, *The Solitary Billionaire*, aired in February 1963, that probably created the most indelible public image of J. Paul Getty. A documentary, it was also something of a precursor of reality TV. It began in the dining room, with the camera panning, and panning, down the immense seventy-foot length of the silver-plate-laden refectory table (previously owned by William Randolph Hearst), until finally coming upon the aptly named title character, who was dining in solitude. "An absolute monarch, his real wealth incalculable—remote and mysterious as someone from another planet," the announcer intoned. Trailed by Shaun, a forlorn-looking Alsatian (the four-legged kind), Getty proceeded to take the horn-rimmed host and interlocutor, Alan Whicker, on a tour of the manor, even offering him a demonstration of his fitness regimen, in which Getty, still clad in a three-piece suit, did overhand presses with a barbell, a Renoir in the background. Quizzing Getty about his already famous frugality ("There are a great many stories, Mr. Getty, of your *care* with money"), Whicker inquired about that phone booth that had been installed "to prevent guests from abusing your hospitality." "Well," Getty answered, "I think right-thinking guests would consider it a benefit. It's rather daunting if you are visiting someone, and you have to place a long-distance call and charge your host with it."

Just three weeks later, Getty made an entry into his diary verifying his celebrity status: *My name was mentioned on the Lucy show on TV tonight. Lucy was expecting a blind date.*

Throughout the sixties and seventies, Getty produced several publications of his own, through which he clearly intended to build and burnish his legend. *My Life and Fortunes*, a memoir published in 1963, struck a Horatio Alger–like note from its first sentence: "In 1914, a brawling, bare-knuckled frontier atmosphere still prevailed in Oklahoma."

Getty had a knack for coining memorable maxims. "The meek shall inherit the earth—but not its mineral rights," he declared. Then there was his advice when asked for his recipe for success: "Rise early, work hard, and strike oil."

From 1961 to 1965, he wrote monthly columns for *Playboy* in which he expounded on the themes of "men, money, and values in today's society," which were subsequently published in book form under the title *How to be Rich*. He opted not to publish these essays in any of the "staider" magazines, because they had lesser reach among his intended audience of "young executives and university students," he said. "[Whereas] Mr. Hefner's frisky and epidermal periodical attracts the nation's highest readership among men in these two categories. And it was precisely these individuals whose thinking-processes the articles were designed to prod and even jolt."

(A seventysomething Getty recalled a private chat in which he delighted in regaling a thirtysomething Hef with tales of his youthful sexual exploits, to the latter's chagrin. "Younger people," explained Getty, "are discomfited by the suggestion that members of their swinging generation are not, after all, the first to have enjoyed amorous adventures while still in their teens.")

In *The Joys of Collecting* (1965), Getty delivered a didactic art primer, with anecdotes and advice that aimed to convey to the reader "the romance and zest . . . that make art collecting one of the most exhilarating and satisfying of all endeavors."

A decade later, in the last years of his life, he wrote another memoir, *As I See It*, which appeared just after his death. Here, there's a different tone. It's not so sunny. A good deal is pessimistic and defensive. Family tragedies had taken their toll.

"The idea that people who are reputedly wealthy must be miserable seems to gladden countless hearts," he wrote. "After a time, a person who is wealthy grows a tough impervious skin. It is a protective carapace essential for survival."

During his lifetime, then, Getty cultivated his image as a rich skinflint. Following his death in 1976, it was easy to turn him into a caricature—one of the twentieth century's premiere Scrooges. But in the succession of articles, books, and films that appeared in the years to come about him—and, inevitably, his heirs—the narrative grew darker and more unsympathetic.

9

In one of the first biographies, *The House of Getty*, published in 1985, English journalist Russell Miller established a tone on his dedication page: "To my family, with heartfelt thanks that our name is not Getty."

Perhaps it was Getty's somber countenance that caused him to be depicted as such an ogre. But appearances can be deceiving.

"If he looked gloomy, it was because he had three facelifts," Gillian Wilson, the longtime curator of decorative arts at the J. Paul Getty Museum, explained to me. "So when his face lost all its plasticity, there was a great collapse and he looked rather gloomy. It took a great deal of effort to put a smile on and he didn't bother. But he was perfectly happy."

Though he was ruthless in business, people who actually knew Getty—whose eyes were described as "penetratingly blue"—liked him, his ex-wives and former mistresses included. Over time, some of them have stepped forth to offer their views.

One year after his death, Robina Lund wrote an affectionate memoir, *The Getty I Knew*. But she held back from revealing that she and Getty (forty-four years her senior) had become lovers in the early sixties, about a year after he hired her away from Slaughter and May and made her his English legal advisor and press officer. Their romance continued until his death.

Four decades later, the releases of *All the Money in the World* and the FX TV series *Trust* prompted Lund, now an octogenarian in Aberdeenshire, Scotland, to disclose the full extent of her relationship with Getty, which included two failed pregnancies, and to defend him. "Both [depictions] were gross distortions . . . complete fabrications, and obscene at that," she said in a podcast with her niece, Glenda D. Roberts, a psychotherapist. "I want people to know the truth. He's been maligned, to a disgusting extent. He was lovable and very loving . . . very caring, very gently affectionate. The only person he was mean with was himself."

More recently, she shared other fond memories of Getty with me: "What were the things I liked most about him? His kindness and empathy, especially toward people in genuine trouble; his modesty; his sense of humor and enjoyment of fun; his intellect and knowledge; his respect for women and their intellects; his willingness to debate with opposing views." Lund also recollected Getty's "very good 'party tricks.' He was, for instance, a superb, but not malicious, mimic."

In 2014, ninety-eight-year-old Lady Ursula d'Abo came forward with her own defense, in her memoir *The Girl with the Widow's Peak*. "He really was the most charming man, made into this monster by journalists," she wrote. (She was a widow in her early fifties and he was in his late seventies when she began seeing him around 1970.) "Very few people saw the kind, cozy side of Paul as more often than not he was on his guard when he mixed in society. He was clever and used to study Latin grammar at breakfast. He made you feel like you were the only person in the world when you were with him. He had a great sense of fun."

Lady Ursula, who was one of the six maids of honor at the coronation of George VI in 1937, passed away in 2017, a few days short of 101, survived by three children from her second marriage. Her eldest, John Henry Erland d'Abo—who, during his school days at Eton, spent many breaks at Sutton Place—has also stuck up for his mother's old flame. "He was absolutely not as portrayed. The movies were very inaccurate," d'Abo said. "He could be difficult. But *all* very rich people are difficult.

"You liked him," he continued. "He was funny, with a very, very dry sense of humor. He was always interested in trying to ameliorate his knowledge in matters that he didn't understand. When I see [Getty's grandson] Mark today, he is the spitting image of him."

When Jean Paul Getty was born, in Minneapolis on December 15, 1892, his parents, George and Sarah, were just beginning to rise out of the harsh circumstances that their families had endured for generations. Wealthy though they became in later life, they retained forever that particularly strict brand of Scots-Irish frugality, as did their son.

It is curious that, despite George and Sarah's Anglo-Saxon, Calvinist background, they chose the Gallic spelling for their son's first name. (He was always called by his middle name, however.)

George Franklin Getty, whose ancestors had come over from the north of Ireland at the end of the eighteenth century, was born in 1855 in Maryland. His father, John, a struggling farmer, died of diphtheria when George was six, forcing him to do what farmwork and errands he could to bring in pennies.

Rescue came from an uncle, a preacher, who brought him to Ohio for education. Resolute George worked his way through Ohio Normal University, where he met Sarah McPherson Risher—a stern-looking woman almost three years his elder. They married in 1879.

In Sarah, a fellow Methodist whose ancestors had fled Scotland for Ohio in 1746, he found his match. In fact, she may have been even more determined and ambitious than he was. He planned to become a teacher, but she steered him to law, providing $100 from her dowry to finance his studies at the University of Michigan. Their funds had to be stretched in 1880, when a daughter, Gertrude Lois, was born to the couple. Two years later, George earned his law degree, and opened his own practice.

His career was off to a promising start, but Sarah thought they could do better in Minneapolis. In 1884 they arrived in the bustling midwestern city. His legal business, which catered to the insurance industry, began to thrive. But the young family was shattered in 1890 when Gertrude perished in that winter's typhoid epidemic. Sarah was stricken too. She recovered, but her hearing declined. Though George hadn't been infected, the loss of his child shook his faith and led him to convert to Christian Science.

In 1892, when she was forty, Sarah gave birth to Jean Paul. Always to be an only child, he grew up much loved by these overprotective parents. Yet—firm, devout people that they were—they never gave him physical affection.

"My parents," Paul wrote, "knew the now apparently-lost art of showing their child great love and affection without being overly indulgent or permissive."

Paul's solitary childhood, and the Getty fortunes, were transformed in 1903, when George was called to Bartlesville, later to be part of Oklahoma but then in Indian Territory, and in the early years of its oil boom. There to settle an insurance claim for one of his clients, George lifted his sights. He invested $500 in a lease to the oil rights of "Lot 50." Within a few months, multiple wells to which he had rights were gushing.

By 1905 the Gettys were wealthy people, and they relocated, at Sarah's behest once more—this time to Los Angeles. At 651 South Kingsley Drive, adjacent to a still-unpaved section of Wilshire Boulevard, George constructed a fine two-story stucco house. The architectural style: Tudor.

Paul was a voracious reader, but his academic record was hardly stellar. Structured environments like schools didn't bring out the best in him. He did well enough at Harvard Military Academy and then at the University of Southern California, where he studied economics and political science, but his more stimulating and formative experiences came through his summer jobs, working for his father's company, Minnehoma Oil (the name being an elision of Minnesota and Oklahoma). Later, Getty senior bought or established other companies, including George F. Getty Inc.

After earning his stripes as a roustabout (a laborer who performs the heaviest and dirtiest work on a drilling site), Paul rose up to become a tool dresser (an assistant to a driller). A "toolie" was required to be a crack technician and skilled blacksmith in order to do his tasks of sharpening drilling bits and tools and keeping them in optimal order.

To master this craft, Paul convinced a leathery veteran known as Grizzle to take him under his wing. "Such was his reputation in the fields that when he pronounced that he considered me a qualified toolie, it carried more weight than any dozen university diplomas," Getty wrote.

But the strongest influence in Paul's life, and, to an extent, his parents' too, lay a continent and an ocean away. Early on, the Gettys developed a profound reverence for Europe. Its art and refined culture were beacons to them. As a family, they undertook three grand tours, each one lasting at least a few months. The first, in 1909, when Paul was sixteen, took them to England, France, Germany, Switzerland, Monte Carlo, and Holland.

In 1912, Paul convinced his parents to send him to Oxford to continue his education. The US, he said, was "insular, isolationist . . . it largely ignored what transpired outside its borders." Before reporting to Magdalen College in Oxford, he spent two months traveling through Japan and China. A year later, upon finishing his exams, he embarked on a yearlong solo trip that took him across Scandinavia, Russia, Greece, Turkey, and Western Europe. When he reached Paris in June 1914, his parents were waiting; another family grand tour had been organized. But their itinerary was altered by the assassination of Archduke Ferdinand in Sarajevo later that month, by which time they had reached London, where they awoke to learn that Austria had declared war on Serbia. Arranging passage back to the States was difficult, as most ocean liners were being pressed into service as troop transports.

George eventually prevailed upon the Cunard Line, and on September 12 the Gettys set sail back to America on the *Lusitania*. Several months later, the ship sank to the bottom of the Atlantic after being hit by German torpedoes.

Prior to World War I, it was uncommon for West Coast families, even wealthy ones, to undertake such extensive European travel. Certainly, few of Getty's fellow wildcatters harbored such worldly curiosity. It's interesting to compare Getty to his peers on that *Fortune* rich list, such as Sid Richardson. Born one year apart, they were exact contemporaries. But Richardson rarely strayed far from Fort Worth. "I don't want to go nowhere outside the US," he declared.

Getty was also a whiz at languages. He became fluent in German, French, and Spanish; he got along commendably in Italian, Russian, Greek, and Arabic—which he taught himself so he could negotiate better terms in the Middle East. He could also read Latin and ancient Greek.

Once back in California, Paul expressed his desire to become a diplomat or a writer. To entice Paul into the oil business, his father advanced him $10,000. Paul could invest it in whatever oil fields he chose, but most of the profits would go back to Minnehoma—save 30 percent, which Paul could keep. Within a year, oil was flowing from wells he had taken leases on. At twenty-three, he had made his first million.

In the ensuing decade, J. Paul Getty also devoted a good deal of his energy to another vocation: marriage. Unlike his business career, which he pursued till almost his dying breath, this one had a compressed and finite time frame, though his strong interest in women endured till the very end.

By 1958, he had five failed marriages behind him—each to a woman about half his age. The first four marital unions were particularly short-lived: his maiden trip to the altar came in 1923 and his fourth divorce decree was issued in 1936.

In *My Life and Fortunes*, he shoehorned in a speedy summary of weddings. His opening sentence: "Then, in October 1923, two months before my thirty-first birthday, I took my first plunge into the troubled seas of matrimony."

Jeannette DeMont, a nineteen-year-old beauty of Polish extraction, had just graduated from high school in Los Angeles. He described her as having "a vibrant and magnetic personality and remarkable degree of intelligence." They eloped to Ventura, then returned to Los Angeles and surprised his parents with news of the wedding. In a house he rented not far from George and Sarah, marital life began well enough.

Jeannette was soon pregnant. But after the birth on July 9, 1924, of his first son, George Franklin Getty II, named after his father, "jarring notes of dissension and discord crept into the relationship." Two months after George was born, Jeannette filed for divorce.

Getty accepted the blame, and pinpointed the problem, in his inimitable fashion: "No wife wants to feel she is being neglected for an oil rig." In fact, Jeannette had diagnosed the same problem. "I married you, not your oil rigs," she pouted.

That conflict—between the demands of business and the responsibilities of marriage—was the crux of all his subsequent divorces, he maintained.

After their separation, Getty admitted to feeling "stunned and dismayed." There are discrepancies, however, regarding the date the divorce decree became final. In his memoirs, Getty says it was February 15, 1925; other sources have said it arrived September 22, 1927.

In any event, Paul soon enough resumed a warm rapport with his ex-wife, the start of a pattern. "Once the acrimony that accompanies any divorce was dispelled, Jeannette and I re-established a friendly relationship, and have remained friends ever since," he wrote in 1963.

In the aftermath of the divorce, Paul had little time for reflection. It was a banner year for Minnehoma Oil. Several wells were gushing.

By the spring of 1926, with his fortunes flush, he took a break. Driving in his Duesenberg to Mexico, he enrolled in Spanish language and history courses at the National University of Mexico City, where he met Allene Ashby, seventeen, the tall, slender daughter of a Texas rancher, who was there with her elder sister, Belene. Getty recalled being "enchanted" by the "vivacious, attractive, and brilliant" Allene when they took romantic horseback rides together. Within weeks, they drove to Cuernavaca and, impetuously, were wed. If some sources are correct about the date of his divorce decree from Jeannette, the marriage was bigamist.

At the same time, Paul became very close to Belene. There is some conjecture as to how close—we will return to that a bit later.

For now, suffice it to say it was a splendid summer. But when it drew to a close, he and Allene realized they had little in common, that they'd made a mistake rushing into marriage. In September, they parted amicably, though they kept in touch; apparently they also kept the marriage—Getty's only one that did not produce a child—a secret from some family members. "Somewhat later," according to Paul, "Allene got around to suing for divorce." *That* decree came finally late in 1928—in the nick of time for his third wedding.

After Paul steered the Duesenberg back to LA, the thirty-four-year-old millionaire resumed his established patterns, another of which was bunking again on South Kingsley Drive. "I always went back and lived at my parents' home between marriages," he told *Cosmopolitan*. "I had a great love and respect for them both. They had a marriage any two people could be proud of. . . . I could never achieve that, I'm sorry to say."

When the spring of 1927 wheeled around, these septuagenarians and their son embarked upon another grand tour. Accompanied by George's devoted Japanese valet, Frank Komai, they crossed the continent by rail, then sailed on June 7 from New York aboard the SS *Resolute*. By all accounts the next months were idyllic, their itinerary encompassing London, Paris, Strasbourg, Baden-Baden, Venice, Rome, Naples, Augsburg, Munich, Innsbruck, and Cortina d'Ampezzo.

As summer came to an end, Paul waved the trio off as they boarded the SS *Olympic*. In no rush to return to America, he rented a *petit meublé* in Paris for six weeks. It was during this time that Getty made a decision to thenceforth spend five months a year in Europe, a vow he broke only when it was made impossible by war in 1939.

Tearing himself away from Paris in October 1927 wasn't easy, but his father was ailing (George had a stroke in 1923 from which he never fully recovered), so Paul's attention was needed more than ever at the Getty businesses. An agreement was reached for the son to buy 30 percent of the stock in his father's company for $1 million, "which would give me a considerable voice in the management of the company." It was another demonstration of the Gettys' capacity to simultaneously negotiate contracts and familial relations.

With business on an even keel, Paul returned to Europe in the summer of 1928. One of his first stops was Vienna. Dining at the Grand Hotel, he became infatuated with a flaxen-haired, blue-eyed beauty at a nearby table. The future third Mrs. J. Paul Getty was Adolphine "Fini" Helmle. Seventeen, she was seated with her parents. "Romance blossomed despite the strictly chaperoned climate in which it was nurtured," Paul recounted.

Herr Dr. Otto Helmle—a wealthy engineer who headed the Badenwerk industrial complex in Karlsruhe, Germany—was not amused by a twice-married thirty-six-year-old American courting his teenage daughter. But Getty's charms won out. Young Fini, convent girl that she was, was determined enough to override her father's diktat.

In December, Paul arranged for her and her mother to sail to Havana, where he and Fini were married (the ink on his divorce decree from Allene perhaps barely dry). Once wed, the pair enjoyed a two-month honeymoon in Miami and Palm Beach, and then a leisurely cross-country drive back to Los Angeles, where Fini was introduced to Paul's parents, surprised again.

George and Sarah took an immediate liking to Fini, which was fortunate, since Paul, too busy with work to find a new house, deposited his new bride with them on South Kingsley Drive. Fini, who spoke little English, became pregnant in the spring. Lonely, she sailed that summer back to Germany for the birth of their child. Paul promised to follow as soon as he could. In October 1929, just as he was ready to embark from New York, the stock market crashed. He reached Berlin just in time to be beside Fini for the birth, on December 19, of his second son, Jean Ronald, whom he would call Ronny.

Getty's happiness over becoming a father again was tempered by his new father-in-law's opposition toward him. Helmle issued an ultimatum that Paul would have to live permanently in Germany with his wife and child, or he would insist Fini get a divorce. Paul remained in Europe for several months, trying to work things out. But in April a cable reached him with the dire news that George had had another stroke and his condition was serious. Getty departed immediately for California.

Amidst the drama surrounding the death of George F. Getty at age seventy-five on May 31, 1930, and the early months of the Depression, Helmle pressed the divorce case forcefully. By the time the decree was finally issued in August 1932, Getty had to agree to a large financial settlement, which left him bitter at Dr. Helmle, though not at his daughter. "I was forced to admit ruefully to myself that, in Dr. Helmle, I had encountered a businessman who was most certainly my equal," Getty wrote. (Grief and loneliness may well have propelled Helmle's actions: his wife, Fini's mother, had died unexpectedly in the early 1930s during what was supposed to be a routine operation.)

As war clouds gathered in Germany, Fini and Ronald moved to Switzerland for safety. Dr. Helmle, a Catholic and a staunch opponent of Hitler, was imprisoned. Eventually he was released, but his fortune was seized by the Nazis. In 1939, Fini and Ronald fled to Los Angeles.

Back in Los Angeles, even as Paul faced the enormous financial repercussions of his father's death and the divorce negotiations, he began his next romance. Things being as complicated as they were, it would take some time to get to the altar for this wedding.

In 1930, Ann Rork was twenty-two. In fact, Ann and Paul had first met at a restaurant in Hollywood when she was a spirited fourteen-year-old. Some electricity between them was evident, but her parents forbade them to see each other.

Her father was producer Samuel Edwin Rork, who made movies with Douglas Fairbanks Jr., Rudolph Valentino, Will Rogers (Ann's godfather), and silent picture "It girl" Clara Bow—who was also reputed to be his lover, which was perhaps what prompted Ann's mother, onetime starlet Helen Welch Rork, to relocate with Ann to Boston.

Eventually Ann found her way back to Hollywood, where she got parts in a few early "talkies," and somehow reconnected with still-legally-wed Paul in 1930. Gossip that they were dating began to circulate around Hollywood, prompting Paul to transfer their romance out of town. In early 1931 he took her to Berlin, where he dealt with continuing divorce drama; in August he brought her to New York, where he established her in a series of hotels and apartments, while he continued to live in Los Angeles.

They took two more trips together to Europe, including a summer holiday to Italy during which, on September 7, 1932, she gave birth to Getty's third son, at sea. They were en route from Naples to Genoa.

Owing to miscommunication with the notary in the port of La Spezia, where Paul and Ann disembarked with their precious little bundle, confusion over this son's name has persisted. His father asked for him to be named Jean Paul Getty Jr. But the Italian clerk wrote down "Eugenio Paul" on his birth certificate. Once in America, that turned into Eugene. When he returned to Italy as an adult, he officially changed his name to J. Paul Getty Jr. To make things more befuddling, he adopted the anglicized spelling of his first name: his obituaries referred to him as John Paul Getty Jr. In any event, his first name was never used—during his lifetime he was just Paul, or Sir Paul, to pretty much everybody.

Once the divorce from Fini was at last sealed, wedding number four took place on December 2, 1932, in Cuernavaca, Mexico (just like marriage number two). "I embarked upon yet another marital venture," the groom recorded. Now legally wed, Ann and Paul moved into a beach house he bought in Malibu, though Paul continued to keep his clothes at his mother's house. Sarah, for her part, was frosty to poor Ann. As usual, business pulled Paul away. By the birth on December 20, 1933, of Gordon Peter, the marriage was on the rocks, and the couple separated. She continued to live in Malibu and later sued for divorce, as he decamped to New York. Their divorce decree came in 1936.

Ann, described by contemporaries as "madcap," went on to compile a colorful and impressive marital résumé of her own. In the club car of the train bound for Reno, Nevada, where she was heading to obtain her divorce from Paul, she met Herbert Douglas Wilson, an Ohio-born stockbroker. Their marriage lasted less than a year, but before it ended in divorce it produced a half sister for Paul and Gordon, Donna Wilson Long. (A resident of Palm Beach, she is an equestrian and an artist with an active social life.) The records vary, but 1941 appears to be the likely year of Ann's wartime marriage to Jay Ruppert Ross, an aviator who volunteered for the British Royal Air Force. Four years later, she married Joseph Stanton McInerney, an attorney, with whom she settled in San Francisco. Though this marriage was not to endure either, she remained in the Bay Area, where she brought up the children.

During their childhoods, Paul Jr. and Gordon could enjoy the camaraderie that came with being the only pair of full siblings born to J. Paul Getty. Like all the Getty sons, they seldom saw their father, or their half brothers. "Oh, this is your brother Ronald. Do you know him?" Paul Jr. was asked by his father during a rare get-together at the Getty Oil offices in Los Angeles, when the boys were on the verge of puberty. In fact, they hadn't yet met.

In the autumn of 1931, Ann Rork, temporarily domiciled in Manhattan, pined for her lover a continent away.

"Darling," she addressed J. Paul Getty in a letter postmarked September 18, 1931, from 38 E. Fifty-Ninth Street in New York City and mailed to him at the Subway Terminal Building in Los

Angeles. "The letter I wrote yesterday is now void and I am again on top of the world. . . . There is now hope of my being able to become pregnant. . . . You have no idea sweetheart how badly I want a family. . . . I'm so happy that you're phoning tonight."

Over the next months, she wrote him a series of poignant letters. His replies are not in the archives of the Getty Research Institute. But, if one can judge only by the ardor of Ann's missives, it is hard to believe that the recipient was the cruel, coldhearted misanthrope some have accused him of being.

The letters do, however, confirm one stereotype: Getty was cheap. He was putting her up in far from royal style, in the depths of the Depression. Cans of sardines were sometimes all she could afford for dinner in her room, unless a friend treated her to a meal out.

A letter of October 8 indicates she wasn't in it, as it were, for the money:

"In spite of the fact that you are a very wealthy man I live as would become the sweetheart of a striving young poet, but, my love has not flown nor will it ever," she assured him.

Yet in the same letter, she chided her beau. She has caught wind that he has been veritably bragging to her friends and family— including her mother—how parsimonious he has been with her: ". . . by much propaganda I had them ready to love you for being so good to me. Then you turn around and admit that you kept me without bus fare for months! . . . So please stop that conversation. . . . Remember I'm one of the few people in the world that have gone to the pain of trying to understand you and that you make things very difficult for me by alienating people whose high opinion of you is necessary to my happiness."

Not to say it is all penury. She wrote excitedly of shopping for pretty hats, coats, and shoes—but on sale, or at wholesale. But then, on October 2, she wrote, "Sweetheart Angel—I learned something last night. It's no fun to look beautiful when the man you love isn't there to see you."

On occasion, she partook of glamorous Manhattan society. "Expect tonight will be gala. Condé Nast is having a party after the concert at his penthouse and Mrs. Stotesbury is having one at the Casino. Mrs. Hearst also wanted to entertain. . . ."

She also curled up with some good new books: "I'm reading Ernest Hemingway's *The Sun Also Rises* and it fills me with the most terrific nostalgia for Europe. When can we sail?"

Mostly, however, she pines for her "Angel Mine," as she often addresses him.

"Oh darling, I love you so, miss you so."

"I love you, only you, ever you."

"I'm so frightened. Oh why aren't you here? I need you so badly. . . . Oh please dear come to me."

"It's raining cats and dogs—very depressing. But your wire makes me believe I'll never be unhappy again."

On October 31, it was all blue sky and sunshine ahead, when Getty phoned her to say they would be departing the following week on a round-the-world voyage: "I'm simply breathless over the itinerary. . . . I'm practically packed—will finish Sunday. . . . Oh blessed to be with you again Thursday—I'm afraid I'll burst!"

Two years and two babies later, it didn't end happily ever after for the couple. But in her letters to Getty in the years after their breakup, it is clear that they remained mutually affectionate.

By May 2, 1934 they had traded coasts—she in Santa Monica and he in New York, at the Hotel Biltmore. She wrote, "Try to eat regularly and if you get too tired go away for a few days."

"Dearest Paul," she wrote on February 25, 1941 (five years after their divorce decree). "Such fun to speak to you yesterday, and such a temptation to accept your suggestion of Acapulco." Before signing off, she asked him: "Do you suppose I'll ever get over missing you? . . . hoping you are happy—Always, A."

On July 7, 1941, she sent a letter from the Lake Placid Club in the Adirondacks, where she was participating in the summer ice-dancing competitions that were all the rage. "The boys seem to be having a wonderful time at camp," she opened, before reeling off her plans for the remainder of the summer, which included Newport and East Hampton. In closing, she said, "I do miss you darling. Be a little careful about a girl that works at Saks. All the saleswomen are pointing her out to their customers as a girl that won't be working there much longer because of Mr. Getty. Love—A."

There is another touching, and illuminating, file of correspondence in the Getty archives: letters written by J. Paul Getty to Allene and Belene. They were discovered by Belene's granddaughter, Christine Banks, a Carlsbad, California, cosmetologist, after the death in 1984 of her grandfather Orell "Frank" Smoot. Belene Ashby Smoot predeceased him by four years, at the age of seventy-six; they'd had one child together. Allene died in 1970 at age sixty-one, never having remarried or had children.

While rummaging through her late grandfather's desk, Banks found stacks of uncashed checks made out to Belene, stock certificates, and notes, all with the name Getty on them—a name she'd never heard of. After a good deal of research, including visits to staff members at the Getty Center, she learned who J. Paul Getty was, and that in his will he'd left Belene $183,281 of Getty Oil common stock, and $300 a month for the remainder of her life. Over the previous forty years, he had also been sending her regular checks, letters, and a dozen roses on her birthday every year.

Christine Banks nonetheless concluded that her grandmother and Getty had not been lovers, though others have drawn that conclusion. In any event, he maintained great fondness for both sisters his entire life, as his letters attest. (Unfortunately for Christine, none of Getty's beneficence reached her. While Belene "never spent one penny of it," she recalled, her daughter—Christine's mother, Donna—blew through it on "spur of the moment" spending that included several time-share condominiums. Donna died "virtually broke.")

Paul's first letter to Allene was postmarked from Los Angeles on November 20, 1926—a few months after they parted in Mexico. "I was indeed glad to hear from you. You broke a long silence. Of course, I am not mad at you," he wrote. "I have too many trials and tribulations in my business ventures to relish silly anger. . . . Trusting to see you very soon."

"Hello Infant," began a sunny letter he composed to her on June 26, 1927, from "Le Beau, Paris," where he and his parents, on one of their grand tours, had very much enjoyed the Grand Prix that day. "But I would like it much better if you were here," he told her. "Do take care of yourself and Beanie and don't see too much of your friend . . . Did you get the cable and allowance all right? I will send you the other fifty a little later," he finished the letter, signing off "With loads of kisses."

A short Western Union cable sent to her two months later indicates he sought to resume their romantic relationship: "Dearest Precious, Expect your first letters in New York. Love you, please leave now."

There is no record of the two ever seeing each other again. In a letter sent June 24, 1928, from the Grand Hotel Wien, Paul mentioned meeting someone he doesn't name, but doubtless he was referring to Fini: "I found the girl I wanted to see, in Vienna." Yet he maintained his warm tone toward Allene: "I have certainly missed you. . . . The 28th is your birthday—just think how smart you will be—nineteen—it doesn't seem possible . . . Please write me."

Three months later, a letter from Paris is full of shock:

"I just received your letter. . . . Are you really in a sanitarium? . . . I got such a nice letter from you in early June. I have always been very proud of you and liked the way you do things and then, like a bolt from the blue, came the letter you wrote June 15th. It was so terrible. I'll never get over it. . . . But if you have really been ill I am terribly sorry. . . . I had expected to come home about July 4th, but when I got your letter in Vienna, I decided that I didn't want to come back at all. This summer I just figured you out of the picture. Can you blame me? Once such letter, and then not a line for six weeks, from you or Beanie?"

The Ashby-Getty correspondence continued for decades, but henceforth all the notes were addressed to Belene, who, like her sister, lived in the Los Angeles area. "Dearest Beanie," he wrote on August 9, 1950, from the Grand Hotel Victoria-Jungfrau, Interlaken: "Your letter just came. I am glad Allene is feeling better . . . use your discretion about the gift, tell her it was from me, if you want to. I hope to be back in October."

In a February 1969 letter from Sutton Place, Paul thanked Belene for her "very welcome Valentine" as well as for some photos from that distant summer. "The Mexico City pictures brough back vivid remembrance of our sojourn in Mexico 1926. What a wonderful time we had and how jealous Van turned out to be!"

One year later, he reached out to her following Allene's death: "I have been trying to phone you. . . . It is tragic to think that poor Allene has gone. She had so much to cope with in her life. I know that nothing I can say will be helpful. We both know what a sweet person she was."

He wrote again in October 1971: "Dear Beanie, it has certainly been much too long since we have seen each other and I am planning to be back some time next spring. I wish you were here to go on a long walk with me and the dogs. I think often of you and the many years of unbroken friendship." Over the forty-three years since Paul's divorce from Allene, and his three subsequent marriages, his fondness for the Ashby sisters had persisted.

Before getting to the story of J. Paul Getty's fifth and final wife, let's rewind to 1920, and go back to the subject of business.

Getty began his career as a wildcatter—an independent operator—

and he kept that mentality all his life. He usually went against the grain of prevailing trends, fashion—and big corporations. In the twenties, while many were feverishly buying stocks as values soared, Getty sank his money into buying leases on lots, betting that he would strike oil.

On the question of where to drill, Getty certainly had good instincts, but he put his faith in science—petroleum geology, to be specific. It was a field of study then in its infancy. Many old-time oilmen sneered at the notion that "some damned bookworm" could help them find oil. While Getty didn't consider this branch of study an infallible science, he realized its potential. "I felt that, as with all things in nature, there must be some logical order to the manner in which petroleum was distributed within the earth's surface," he noted. "I was convinced that geology provided the oil prospector with certain generally fairly reliable guides and indicators to aid him in the search for oil."

When the Depression came, Getty, not freighted with collapsed stocks, was in an advantageous position. He went from strength to strength, now snapping up stocks at a fraction of the value of the oil in the ground.

He began assembling holdings in a number of companies, then sought to gain controlling interests in them. Among the first was Pacific Western, one of the largest oil producers in California, which he acquired in 1931. The ultimate prize would be Tide Water Associated Oil, then America's ninth-largest oil company, with over 1,200 service stations as well as refineries, storage, and marketing arms. It would provide the centerpiece of his master plan to become a fully integrated oil company. But in the first decades of the twentieth century, the idea of Getty acquiring Tide Water was akin to David slaying Goliath.

He began circling it covertly, his great white whale, buying up Tide Water stock quietly so as not to alert its management to a takeover threat or drive up the share price.

Concurrently, he had to deal with his mother. To Getty's shock, his father had left virtually his entire $15 million estate in her hands. Ironically, while Paul became a world-famous tightwad, his father felt he was a spendthrift; he also disapproved of his son's multiple divorces. Thus Paul had to contend with Sarah as well as with the board of George Getty Inc. At Christmas 1933, she offered to hand over her shares to him. A letter from mother to son illustrates the businesslike way in which Gettys communicated amongst themselves:

> *This offer shall remain open to and until 12 o'clock noon, December 30, 1933, and if not accepted by you in writing on or before that date and hour shall be considered as withdrawn by the undersigned and shall be wholly terminated and at an end.*
>
> *Very truly yours,*
> *Sarah C. Getty.*

Soon after, he succeeded in easing her out of the company and gaining full control. In return, she insisted that they establish a family trust. "I want to be certain that you and your sons are financially secure and protected against the possible catastrophe which may result from speculation," she reasoned. The paperwork was drawn up in December 1934; she contributed $2.5 million and he put in about $1 million. The Sarah C. Getty Trust commenced its work.

While the trust was meant to provide for all her descendants, there was one glaring inequity: Ronald was virtually excluded from it (he would receive just $3,000 a year—though his children would eventually share in the trust) because Paul, bitter at his former father-in-law for his role in the divorce from Fini, felt that the wealthy Helmle could shoulder the financial care of Ronald. But the loss of the Helmle fortune during World War II put Ronald at a great financial disadvantage compared to his brothers.

By the terms of the trust, Paul, its sole trustee, could borrow from its funds for purposes that would grow his business, such as buying stocks. In turn, he plowed his profits back into the trust. The capital grew and grew.

Days after signing the trust's documents, Getty boarded a train traveling up the California coast, bound for America's Valhalla, San Simeon, where press baron William Randolph Hearst and his mistress, Marion Davies, had invited him to a house party to ring in the New Year. On January 1, 1935, Getty received a long-distance call from New York that gave him the most momentous stock tip of his life. Though at first it sounded like a disaster.

A friend, Jay Hopkins (later the founder of General Dynamics Corporation), broke the news that the Rockefeller-family-dominated Standard Oil of New Jersey was transferring its large block of Tide Water shares to a new holding company, Mission Corporation, through which shares would be distributed to its own stockholders. Effectively, that would put gaining control of Tide Water out of Getty's reach forever.

But Hopkins had an inside track: he knew that John D. Rockefeller Jr. was somehow unaware of the reasons behind Standard's transfer, and that he was willing to sell his Mission shares. Having committed a fortune to building Rockefeller Center in Manhattan just as the economy collapsed, the Rockefeller family was then stretched a bit thin—for them.

Getty was only too eager to buy John D.'s shares, but he assumed that Standard's management would quickly talk Rockefeller out of selling.

"Not a chance," Hopkins told him. "He's aboard a train bound for Arizona. They can't reach him, and I have his authorization to sell."

Getty closed the transaction on the spot, which gave him his breakthrough leap forward in his quest for Tidewater (now one word), though he would not gain clear-cut control until 1951.

(In the 1970s, Getty slyly recalled what happened after Rockefeller debarked from the train and Standard Oil managers got hold of him: "They said, 'Oh, Mr. Rockefeller, we were very anxious to get in touch with you. We wanted to tell you to be sure not to sell your stock in Mission Corporation because we're in a big proxy fight.'" Informed that he had, they pressed him for the identity of the buyer. "'I understand he's a very nice young man, but I can't remember his name,' said Rockefeller. And they all said: 'His name wasn't Getty, was it?' He replied: 'Yes, I think it was.' They answered: 'Oh my God.'")

Fresh from his triumph at San Simeon, Getty had yet to work out the details of his divorce from Ann. Amicable as she might have been, her lawyers were less accommodating. Legal proceedings, which Paul described as "noisome," dragged on in Los Angeles. It must have seemed a good idea to get out of town. So, breaking one of his old habits, instead of moving back in with his mother postdivorce, he opened a new chapter of his life in New York.

Flush as he was, he opted for once to splurge, taking a sublease on one of Manhattan's most palatial apartments. Its address was prophetic: 1 Sutton Place South.

The furnished penthouse he rented there would become a pivotal influence in his life, for it belonged to a great connoisseur, Mrs. Frederick Guest. One of Getty's fellow *Fortune* listees some decades later, the former Amy Phipps was the daughter of industrialist Henry Phipps, Andrew Carnegie's partner, and the wife of English aristocrat Freddie Guest, a cousin of Winston Churchill. In 1947, Amy and Freddie's son married Lucy "Sissy" Cochrane—C. Z. Guest, who became a celebrated style icon.

The 6,400-square-foot aerie atop Sutton Place—the building itself had been commissioned around 1920 by Amy's father—featured wraparound terraces and seventeen rooms, including a pair of boiserie-lined forty-foot drawing rooms. But it was the contents of the apartment— Amy Guest's magnificent collection of eighteenth-century French and English furniture—that so inspired Getty.

"This, I suppose, more than anything, motivated me to begin . . .

my own collection," Getty explained. "I suddenly became aware that fine furniture was no less fine art than a painting or a piece of sculpture. . . . It wasn't that a spark was struck. It was rather like a blazing torch was applied, and my collector's urge flared high."

It was a propitious time to embark upon a collecting career. In the depths of the Depression, there were great bargains to be had. Getty became well-acquainted with the leading art dealers and auction houses in New York and Europe and methodically studied art history and the art market. He began to acquire museum-quality pieces of fine and decorative art, items that propelled him on the road to the museum he founded decades later.

During this New York interlude, he picked up another trophy, the Pierre Hotel. A forty-two-story tower at Fifth Avenue and Fifty-Ninth Street, it had been lavishly erected in 1930 at a cost of $6 million. In the distress of 1938, Getty snapped it up for a relative song, paying only $2.35 million.

Romance returned to his life one night in May 1935, when friends brought him to the New Yorker, a smart supper club on East Fifty-First. They'd just been ushered to a ringside table when a raven-haired chanteuse appeared in the smoky spotlight and hit it with "Night and Day." It was the future fifth Mrs. J. Paul Getty, Louise Dudley Lynch, age twenty-two. "I was hopelessly smitten," he said.

Teddy, as everyone called her, was no nightclub vamp. Born in Chicago to a prosperous merchant family, she'd been raised in Greenwich, Connecticut, and her name was listed in the *Social Register.* Financier Bernard Baruch was an uncle. Unbeknownst to the patrons at the New Yorker and most anyone, she harbored serious ambitions to become an opera singer.

As soon as she finished her set and the applause died down, she found herself looking into "the bluest eyes of an immensely charming man," she recalled.

"This is Paul, my friend from California," said her friend Betzi Beaton, who happened to be one of Getty's tablemates.

Dispensing with further chat, he swept Teddy into his arms. "Let's dance," he said.

"I closed my eyes and let my body follow his. We moved as one," she remembered. "He was a fabulous dancer."

"You're very beautiful, Teddy, and your voice is too," he said when the music ended, in the semidark. "You know, you should study opera. You'd be a great Carmen, or Tosca."

Transfixed by this mysterious stranger, she caught her breath and asked, "And what do you do, Paul?"

"He's in oil," Betzi cut in.

"*Oil?* What show is that?" Teddy asked.

Within months, they were engaged. In January 1937, when he brought her to meet Sarah in Los Angeles, she passed muster.

This time, it was his fiancée's schedule as much as his that delayed the wedding. At his encouragement, she threw herself into serious vocal study, which he paid for in exchange for a promise of 10 percent of her future earnings—her idea, she maintained. She also began traveling to give concerts and recitals. At last they sailed to Italy and were married in November 1939, in the Palazzo Senatorio, Rome's palatial city hall in the Campidoglio overlooking the Forum.

But there was no honeymoon. She wanted to stay on in Italy to continue her studies, and he had business in California. So, after a postwedding lunch at the Ambassador Hotel, he rushed for the train to Naples, where he boarded the *Conte di Savoia* to New York.

Although World War II had begun, Italy was then still neutral. After Italy joined the Axis, Teddy extended her visa by signing on as a correspondent for the *New York Herald Tribune*—which the National Fascist Party cited as the grounds for her arrest in December 1941. Suspected of being a spy, she was interned in Siena. In June 1942, she was released and repatriated aboard the Swedish boat *Gripsholm*, along with a group of American diplomats.

In her absence, Paul and his eldest son had joined the war effort. Paul moved to Tulsa, Oklahoma, where he revved up production at the Spartan Aircraft Corporation, an asset of one of the many companies he had bought. George enlisted in the army. Commissioned as an infantry second lieutenant, he served in the Pacific theater.

The year 1941 ended on a sad note. At Christmastime, Sarah died, age eighty-nine. *How I miss her! No one ever had a better mother*, Paul wailed in his diary. Decades later, he observed, *The years have done little to lessen my sense of loss.*

Following Teddy's arrival on the *Gripsholm*, she reunited with Paul in Tulsa, moving into his stucco bungalow near the Spartan factory. Her first morning, she woke to find a note in a familiar scrawl: "Darling . . . I'm at the factory. . . . Have a good breakfast. Love."

But he was a tiger in bed: "He was as demanding and passionate as I. Strong and well-built from years of weight-lifting. . . . But it was also his mind, his sensitivity, that aroused me. I could never say no to this man . . . who so perfectly satisfied me sexually," she recalled in her memoir, *Alone Together: My Life with J. Paul Getty*, published in September 2013, days before her one hundredth birthday.

· After the war ended, she set up housekeeping in a beach house in Santa Monica that Paul acquired. "Paul was always leaving, for somewhere," she recalled. But when he was home it was lovely. Sometimes they went over for dinner with their next-door neighbors, Marion Davies and William Randolph Hearst. Just the four of them, and "WR" would run pictures too—often Marion's old films.

About this time, another great bargain came to Getty's attention: 64 oceanfront acres in Malibu (now Pacific Palisades), part of an old Spanish land-grant ranch. Snapping up the property, he drafted plans to rebuild the two-story cottage standing on the grounds, which came to be known as the Ranch House. While he never lived there (he stayed only a few nights), it was where his increasingly large shipments of art and antiques were sent. In the 1970s, the J. Paul Getty Museum rose on the site.

In June 1946, Teddy gave birth to Timothy. Two months premature, Timmy, as he was known, weighed five pounds and suffered from anemia. "I rejoiced at his arrival," wrote Paul in his first memoir. At fifty-three, he had his fifth son.

"But this pleasant, peaceful interval did not last long, for in 1948 I was on the threshold of seizing the greatest opportunity and taking the biggest gamble of my entire career," he later reminisced. Getty was not being hyperbolic. For he was about to enter . . . the Neutral Zone.

To almost everyone else in the world, the Neutral Zone was nothing but a barren wasteland—a 1,500-square-mile tract of desert between Saudi Arabia and Kuwait. No evidence existed that oil lay underneath it. Once again Getty relied on his instincts and science. He commissioned the finest geologist he knew, Dr. Paul Walton, to make an aerial survey over the territory. After landing, Walton sent Getty a terse cable: STRUCTURES INDICATE OIL. In 1949, Getty offered the king of Saudi Arabia unheard-of terms for a sixty-year concession on the Saudi side. In addition to $9.5 million in cash, Getty agreed to pay $1 million per year for the entire term, whether or not oil was struck, plus the hefty royalty of 55 cents a barrel. Most of the oil industry laughed, predicting that the expenditure would be Getty's ruin.

Four nerve-racking years passed before he saw a drop of oil. During that time, to facilitate the drilling operation, he had to invest another $18 million building infrastructure where absolutely none existed. The longed-for first strike came in 1953, and with it the stunning realization that vast deposits were waiting to be tapped. Still, before a dime could be made, Getty had to solve the massive challenges of how to transport and refine all this petroleum. He spent $600 million building an entire fleet of supertankers and state-of-the-art refineries. As the Neutral Zone assets began to be exploited, Getty's fortune doubled.

Back in Santa Monica, Teddy made a reluctant choice. "I'm the kind of woman who needs a husband," she told Paul. "But, Teddy, you *do* have a husband. It's just that I can't always be home," he responded.

She asked for an end to the marriage in January 1951. That June, when he sailed to Europe for his annual European stay, did he have any idea he would never see America again?

The couple attempted a reconciliation in 1955, in Paris, but it didn't take; their divorce decree was issued in 1958. Later that year, she married a long-standing friend, William Gaston, with whom she had a daughter, Louise "Gigi" Gaston, before the marriage ended in divorce in 1966.

For the remainder of the 1950s Getty was a true nomad, operating out of one hotel suite after another, from which he oversaw his empire, and occasionally his children. Number-one son George, who had been summoned in 1949 to the Neutral Zone, was sent back to America, where he became president of Tidewater and seemed destined to one day ascend his father's throne. (Tidewater finally merged with Getty Oil in 1967.) In 1951, George married Gloria Gordon, a pretty brunette debutante from Denver, the granddaughter of a Colorado senator. The following year, their daughter Anne Catherine was born—Paul's first grandchild. Her sisters Claire Eugenia and Caroline Marie followed in 1954 and 1957.

Ronald graduated in 1951 from the University of Southern California, where he studied business, then became Tidewater's vice president of marketing before being sent to Hamburg, where he utilized his German skills running Veedol, Tidewater's motor fuel operation.

Paul Jr. and Gordon both graduated from St. Ignatius High School in San Francisco, then enrolled at the University of San Francisco, another Jesuit-run school. Life in their mother's house on Clay Street was relaxed. But the "madcap" Ann was not always the most stable parent. The brothers spent a good deal of time on nearby Jefferson Street at the home of William "Bill" Newsom III, their St. Ignatius classmate. It was the start of an intimate family friendship, spanning generations, between the Gettys and the Newsoms, including Bill's son, Gavin, who became the fortieth governor of California in 2019.

During the Korean War, Paul Jr. served in the army, stationed in Seoul. In the wake of the conflict, Gordon was called up for active duty at Fort Lee, Virginia. Both sons subsequently entered the family business, at the bottom. They pumped gas at Tidewater stations before entering the Tidewater training program. In January of 1956, Paul Jr. married his childhood sweetheart, Abigail "Gail" Harris, a swimming champion and the adored only child of a prominent federal judge, George B. Harris.

During their younger years, none of J. Paul Getty's sons had grown up in luxury in their respective maternal households; their absent father had paid just reasonable alimony and child support. So when the October '57 issue of *Fortune* appeared with its list, the brothers were as stunned as anyone, if not more. *"Holy mackerel!"* said Gordon. "Paul and I were surprised. We didn't have any idea." The following year, their father planned to send Paul Jr. to the Neutral Zone; but after meeting Gail and one-year-old Paul III, he reconsidered sending the new father off to that harsh clime. So Gordon got shipped there instead, while Paul Jr. was dispatched to Getty Oil Italiana.

Timmy had been enduring a long series of painful operations after the diagnosis of a brain tumor. After some six years, the cancer was cured, but he was left with severe facial scars. Doctors suggested cosmetic surgery. In August 1958, the twelve-year-old underwent an operation in New York, which was supposed to be routine. Instead, it was fatal. Teddy flew home to Los Angeles with his body. Getty was in Lugano, Switzerland, at the villa of his good friend and fellow art collector Baron Heinrich "Heini" Thyssen-Bornemisza.

Getty has been widely castigated for not returning to America to see his son during his illness, or to attend his funeral. Getty never again boarded a plane after 1942, when a harrowing trip from St. Louis to Tulsa instilled in him a morbid fear of flying. (In later life, boarding an ocean liner became almost as daunting to him.)

Eventually, in the 1970s, Timmy's body was moved to a grave site on a bluff overlooking the Pacific Ocean, on the grounds of the Getty Museum, where he was interred next to his father and eldest brother. Not a mausoleum, it is a simple, low slab of marble engraved only with their names and dates. In the first paragraph of his book, Russell Miller described the burial plot as "forlornly unvisited."

Yet a number of Getty grandchildren and great-grandchildren have described it as an especially meaningful place, which they visit regularly. Getty Museum employees have considered it a very special spot too. "It's a small space at the end of a quiet, tree-lined path," said one curator. "It is so modest—there is no structure, no religious symbols. But with its view to the ocean, the feeling of tranquility and peacefulness is utterly magical. I used to take people there because it was so beautiful, and we had so much to thank [J. Paul Getty] for. When I worked there, many of the staff had known him and bore him in mind."

However, as the image of J. Paul Getty as Scrooge solidified, the narrative of his family as a little-loved "cursed dynasty" took root. To what extent were these depictions anchored in fact? For some insight, it is enlightening to read Getty's diaries from the last sixteen years of his life—the Sutton Place years. When he moved in in 1960, his sons ranged in age from twenty-seven to thirty-six. Six of his grandchildren had already been born. According to the journals, all of his progeny visited Sutton Place regularly in these formative years. Getty wrote about them with affection.

The journals also provide entertaining snapshots of daily life for the richest man in the world. Typically, Getty stayed up until three or four in the morning, strategizing and placing calls to the Middle East. Rising around 10 a.m., he worked through the day, breaking only for lunch and for a walk or a weight-lifting session in the late afternoon. Evenings were social. He hosted dinners at Sutton Place, or frequently drove into London. An average evening—a Tuesday in March 1963—began with drinks at the Ritz, followed by dinner at the fashionable Mirabelle, dancing at the groovy new Garrison Room, and nightcaps back at the Ritz at 2:30 a.m. The cast included Aristotle Onassis, Drue Heinz (wife of condiment magnate H. J. Heinz II), the Marquess of Blandford (the future Duke of Marlborough), Bindy Lambton (the future Countess of Durham), and a member of the Livanos shipping dynasty. *Wonderful music. We did the Twist and enjoyed it. Live bands are out. Records are better,* JPG noted. (Once back to Sutton Place, his nocturnal phone calls to the Middle East would begin.)

In the mid-sixties, his preferred hangouts included the 400 Club in Leicester Square and Trader Vic's, the Polynesian-themed tiki bar in the basement of the Hilton on Park Lane, where he was partial to the mai tais. On October 26, 1967, he noted a new favorite: *I like Annabel's. It is the best nightclub in London.*

His close companions included the Duke of Bedford and members of such dynasties as the Guinnesses, the Rothschilds, and the aforementioned Lambtons and Mannerses. Today, Getty's heirs socialize with many of theirs. "Our families are part of the same landscape. So we're sort of wrapped up with each other," said fashion icon Daphne Guinness of her family and the Gettys.

Snobbish as English aristocrats can be, they're practical. So Getty's reception in England contrasted with his initiation in Italy earlier in the decade. A number of Italian blue bloods had been welcoming enough, prompting Getty in 1965 to purchase La Posta Vecchia, a palatial sixteenth-century seaside villa at Palo Laziale, close to the Italian capital. He launched an extensive renovation, but his ardor for Italy cooled the following year, when he hit a Roman roadblock.

Charming as those Italian princes and counts could be—with their ancient titles but often-depleted bank accounts—they had limits on how far foreigners could get, even the richest (*especially* the richest, perhaps). Getty had been a guest at the inner sanctum of Italian nobility, the Circolo della Caccia, housed in the Palazzo Borghese in Rome, but when he made a bid for membership in 1966, he was blackballed. The rejection stung.

In England, the Queen Mother and other members of the royal family and the aristocracy congregated at Sutton Place. Getty also enjoyed the full spectrum of London's social and cultural offerings. An avid movie buff, he attended seemingly every gala premiere, including *Cleopatra* (he noted: *I thought Elizabeth Taylor good, Harrison, excellent as Caesar*), *Dr. Strangelove*, *The Night of the Iguana*, *My Fair Lady*, *Doctor Dolittle*, and *Funny Girl* (*Barbra Streisand is terrific*).

An animal lover, he never missed a Crufts show, the premiere international dog competition. The subjects of some of his most loving diary entries are his fearsome canines—Shaun, above all. He also doted on his lions, Nero and Teresa, who were kept in large cages on the grounds of his estate. Scratches and bites from these animals often sent guests and staff running to the local hospital, where the attendants automatically asked, "Sutton Place?" when the wounded turned up.

In the course of each year, Getty unfailingly noted the anniversaries of the births and deaths of family members: *Walk and think of Timmy. Timmy! Papa was born 116 years ago. Mama was born 112 years ago. How I still miss her!* In another tribute, he named one of his supertankers after her. The 80,000-ton *Sarah C. Getty* was christened in Dunkirk in 1963. Shaun's passing was dolefully acknowledged as well. *I pick two roses and put them on Shaun's grave. I was devoted to him. Gone 3 years.*

His ex-wives and girlfriends pop up frequently—on the phone, in the mail, at the door.

Dear Belene ph at 8am.

Sent red roses to Jeannette.

Fini and Marion arrive. Both look well. To Annabel's for dinner, but I never saw it look so empty.

Ann Light ph from Palm Beach, inviting me for Xmas.

SP [Sutton Place], *to lunch, Ann looking well and is chic. Her last husband left her 30 million.*

Teddy, her 8 year old daughter, Gigi, her sister Nancy and Nancy's daughter for lunch. Teddy looks as well as she did in 1955.

Getty's sons and their growing families appear often. Although he was surely an absentee dad when his boys were young, he established relationships with them as they reached adulthood. And he became a doting grandfather.

George and Gloria's brood beguiled him on their visits. *Charming girls*, he notes of Anne, Claire, and Caroline. He is *very glad to see them*, and always regretting when it's time for them to leave. *My 3 girls leave for Los Angeles at 11:05. Sad.*

Following George's 1967 divorce from Gloria and his subsequent 1971 marriage to Jacqueline "Jackie" Riordan, a wealthy widow with two sons and a daughter, the new blended family was welcomed into Sutton Place. *Geo and his bride arr. I like her*, he wrote in the fall of 1971. The next spring, there's a visit from *Jackie and the Riordans.* By this point, George's girls are reaching their teenage years and moving with the times: *Geo's daughters dress in hippy style and are pretty.*

In October 1964, Ronald, then thirty-four, married Karin Seibel, the blond, twenty-one-year-old daughter of a businessman from Lübeck, Germany. Fini was a witness in the civil ceremony at that Baltic seaport, which was followed the next day by a wedding mass at the Maria Grün Roman Catholic church outside Hamburg. The honeymoon couple began paying visits to SP, including one during which Mr. and Mrs. John D. Rockefeller Jr. joined them for lunch. The diary notation of a visit with Ronald and Karin's firstborn, Christopher, who came into the world in 1965, is classic Getty: *Ronny, Karin, and Baby Chris here . . . a fine little fellow. . . . Chris plays with the puppies, Sugar and Spice. Valuation of Getty Oil is 2 billion, 7 million dollars net. I have 79% of it.*

News of the couple's first daughter, Stephanie, was also noted enthusiastically, in 1967: *Ronny and Karin have a baby girl!* Cecilia and Christina followed in, respectively, 1970 and 1975.

Meanwhile, Paul Jr. and Gail embraced parenthood too. Following the birth of Jean Paul III in 1956, Aileen, Mark, and Ariadne were born over the next six years.

Diary, December 27, 1963: *Father Albion baptizes Ariadne Joanne Noel Getty, 18 months old . . . Mary* [Teissier] *and I were godparents. Touching ceremony. The little girl is very good and pretty.*

Her parents' marriage did not last, however. *To SP. My dear son Paul here. He flew from NY. Gail has left him,* Getty writes sadly on June 6, 1964.

Getty became fond of his son's second wife, Talitha Pol, a stunning Dutch beauty whom Paul Jr. married in 1966. They paid visits to SP, along with their son. Born in 1968, he was christened with three middle names: Tara Gabriel Galaxy Gramophone. *Paul, Talitha, and Tara my 15 month grandson here. He is a fine platinum blond.*

But as Paul Jr. and Talitha succumbed to heroin addiction, a particularly common scourge at the time among members of their class, their marriage unraveled—beginning the cycle of tragedies that would befall the family.

Mckno [Getty's right-hand man] *here. He tells me Paul Jr has a dope problem.*

Gordon ph I tell him about Paul's weakness.

Papa's birthday. . . . Talitha arrives. . . . Dinner at SP. Talitha complains that Paul is idle and always about the house.

Ph that the lovely Talitha is no more. [She died of a heroin overdose in Rome.] *Shocked and sad. Ph McKno. Paul phs and I try to comfort him.*

Paul ph from Palo [Getty's Italian villa] *and lost his temper. I didn't know this side of his character. I ph back and Gail replied. I think Paul is mentally ill.*

Shortly after, Paul Jr. fled to a house in London that he had acquired, where he became a virtual recluse. Through this stormy time, the valiant Gail watched over the children, including Tara, whom she took into their apartment in Rome. Gail and the children continued to pay visits to SP. In April 1972, Getty's eldest grandson, Paul III, arrived for a stay on his own. They watched a Spencer Tracy and Kate Hepburn movie (*a great pair*, Grandpa noted). But a concerning note was registered: *Dinner and supper with Paul III. I don't approve of his smoking cigarettes.*

Gordon, Getty's youngest son, was the last to marry and begin a family. Before he did, he gave his father a run for his money—literally.

Disgusted with Gordon, the old man veritably spat into his diary, uncharacteristically, on February 13, 1963. *He cables he will sue for declaration of his rights to the 1934 trust.*

Gordon, considered the most absent-minded son, with the worst head for business, was the one who challenged his father by requesting an increase in the then relatively meager income he was receiving from the trust. The trust had always paid its dividends in stock, thereby sheltering its funds from taxation. Gordon wanted cash. If he succeeded in changing the terms of the trust, severe penalties could be levied on the Getty fortune.

While Gordon's lawsuit against his father dragged on for seven years, normal family relations carried on, per the Getty way.

Talked NZ [Neutral Zone] *with Gordon.*

Cable from Gordon in Squaw Valley that he married Ann Gilbert [the daughter of a Sacramento Valley rancher]. *She is unknown to me. I hope they will be happy. Jeannette ph last night.*

With Paul and Gordon to National Gallery to see my Raphael and Veronese. Robina joined us.

Ann, Gordon's bride arr. She seems a nice girl. Gordon and she seem happy and devoted to each other. Wish them a happy marriage.

Snow still covers the ground. Talk business with Gordon, Claus. . . . Walked a mile with Shaun.

Read business reports. Played tennis for 25 minutes with Gordon.

Gordon Getty Jr. born today. Ph. Gordon in NY to congratulate. [After the birth in 1965 of Gordon Jr., known as Peter, came three more boys: Andrew Rork, born 1967; John Gilbert, 1968; and William Paul "Billy," 1970.]

Usual mail. . . . Gordon files trust suit. Ph Hayes, Maltby.

To London, excellent dinner at Wilton. . . . Then went to Annabel's. Gordon, Ann, Papamarkou [Alexander "Alecko" Papamarkou, a Greek-born stockbroker, who figured prominently in the later life of the clan].

Then to SP. Watch the men on the moon. Dinner with caviar, gift of the stunning wife of Gordon.

Ann ph that Gordon might drop his suit.

Gordon Ann and 2 children arr.

Ann Getty and Mr. and Mrs. Pelosi here.

Gordon and Ann ph yesterday. He said he is dropping his claim re stock dividends and he thought it best to do so.

That December, some two hundred guests gathered at the Dorchester Hotel in London to celebrate J. Paul Getty's eightieth birthday. The gala was hosted by his close friend Margaret, Duchess of Argyll. The daughter of a wealthy Scottish industrialist, "Marg of Arg," as she became widely known, was one of the most fascinating and alluring women of her time. The 1930 Debutante of the Year, she was wed first to golfer Charles Sweeny; soon after, Cole Porter immortalized her in his most famous song, "You're the Top."

> *You're Mussolini,*
> *You're Mrs. Sweeny,*
> *You're Camembert.*

In her 1975 memoir, *Forget Not*, Margaret reflected on Getty. "Paul has been my very dear and staunch friend for many years . . . and has been unwavering in his loyalty," she wrote, alluding no doubt to the many people—including her own child, Frances—who shunned her following her scandalous 1963 divorce from the 11th Duke of

Argyll, wherein the judge excoriated Margaret for being "a highly sexed woman." (Frances, who Margaret had with Sweeny, became a duchess herself upon her marriage to Charles Manners, the 10th Duke of Rutland—a brother of Lady Ursula d'Abo. Though Margaret and Frances held sway as one of Britain's rare sets of mother-and-daughter duchesses, the ladies remained permanently estranged.)

When Paul's milestone approached, "I felt that he deserved the best possible birthday," Margaret recalled. Although her friend was "essentially gentle and shy" and "fundamentally a modest man," she nonetheless pulled out all the stops for a splendid evening.

It began when Richard Nixon phoned from the White House to extend his congratulations. His daughter Tricia came to the Dorchester in his stead. Other attendees included Umberto, the former king of Italy, Ambassador Walter Annenberg, and Getty's fellow oilman Nelson Bunker Hunt, as well as Ann and Gordon.

At midnight, as a giant birthday cake was wheeled into the ballroom, bandleader Joe Loss launched into a custom rendition of Porter's classic:

> *You're the top, you are J. Paul Getty*
> *You're the top, and your cash ain't petty*
> *You're a Franklin Fellow with a Paris medal as well,*
> *Got your own museum, let's sing a Te Deum to such a swell*
>
> *You're the top, you are like Jack Benny,*
> *You're the top, wouldn't waste a penny. . . .*

The evening was the pinnacle of a life of extraordinary accomplishment. From here, it was downhill for J. Paul Getty—not financially, but emotionally and physically. His *annus horribilis* was about to begin.

2

The Tragic Years

New Year's Day 1973 began on a fresh note. J. Paul Getty ventured into London for a haircut and manicure at the Ritz. But dense fog made the drive back to Sutton Place uneasy, and then there was a worrisome portent. *Had increased tremor in hands and jaw today*, he recorded.

It began to be reported around this time that Getty had Parkinson's disease, but he persistently denied it, even to himself. *To dentist. . . . While waiting read Time and read that I've Parkinson's!* he scoffed.

His handwriting deteriorates around now. His shaky hand renders the pages of his diary increasingly difficult to decipher (until October 29, 1974—from which point secretaries wrote them from Getty's dictation).

The pace of his social life lessened. However, he and Ursula had an enjoyable visit in late April to the County Durham estate of his good friends the Lambtons, where the grounds held surprises: *U and I to Biddick. Bindy and the children welcome us, also a black Labrador, a greyhound and 3 or 4 others. . . . Bindy drives us through the Safari Park in a Land Rover. An ape nearly got inside.* But not long after, Getty received a phone call that must have been serious from Lord Lambton on May 21—

the day he wrote Prime Minister Edward Heath a letter tendering his resignation from the Cabinet. A few days later, the sex scandal that precipitated his departure exploded in the press and rocked Great Britain. (Norma Levy, the sought-after dominatrix with whom Lambton had been caught in bed, later told the *Daily Mail* that her gilt-edged client list had also included the Shah of Iran, Greek shipping tycoon Stavros Niarchos, the 11th Duke of Devonshire, and J. Paul Getty. For the septuagenarian Getty, she would don a white robe, then lie down in an open coffin for about an hour, playing dead. "Jean Paul would just stand over me in his underpants, just looking at me," she recounted.)

From Getty's journal, it appears that he offered Lambton the use of Posta Vecchia as a refuge from the storm: *Tony Lambton ph re Palo. He will be there May 31.* (Lord Lambton soon acquired a glorious seventeenth-century Italian villa of his own called Cetinale—located just a few miles from Orgia, the refuge of Gail Getty—where he enjoyed a splendid exile, and the younger members of the families became neighbors. Recently, producers of *Succession* rented Cetinale from Lambton's son, Ned, to serve as the location for the Roy family's epic season-three finale.)

Pleasures aside, the pressure was rising at Sutton Place. Getty Oil was risking huge sums of money to explore in difficult new territory, so far without success. *North Sea well news is bad,* JPG wrote on April 16. That winter and spring, there was a high volume of communication with number-one son. The diary is peppered with *ph Geo, Geo ph, Geo arr, Geo lv,* and the like. In February, George arrived from Los Angeles for a two-week stay at SP.

Since the merger with Tidewater, George F. Getty II had served as executive vice president and chief operating officer of the Getty Oil Company. (Paul was president.) In the view of many, George modernized the combined company and made it a success. And outside the company, he was a respected civic leader (the Los Angeles Philharmonic's chief fund raiser), and he enjoyed his real passion—

thoroughbred horses, which he bred and raced. "He got more joy and happiness from seeing his horse win a race than from anything else money could buy," a friend recalled. (The winners in his stable included Gentle Thoughts, Injunction, and Natashka.)

But he always had trouble measuring up to his father, whom he habitually referred to as "Mr. Getty." "He's president in charge of success and I'm vice president in charge of failure," George said glibly.

Following his split from Gloria in 1967, he stayed in LA and she relocated with the girls to the San Francisco Bay Area. Like her father-in-law's ex-wives, she felt her husband had put business ahead of their marriage. After his 1971 remarriage to Jacqueline Riordan, George moved into her mansion in Bel-Air. He was under increasing pressure, which sometimes led to drinking binges, which probably contributed to his weight gain, for which, in turn, he was prescribed medications. He developed a masochistic tic of stabbing his hands with a letter opener.

Various accounts of what happened the night of June 5, 1973, have been told. At dinner, George drank a few glasses of wine. Later he ran to the kitchen, grabbed a barbecue knife, and inflicted a superficial wound across his upper abdomen. Blood was drawn, but his vital organs weren't punctured.

Jacqueline placed three calls: to Dr. Kendrick Smith, Getty Oil's in-house doctor; to Stuart Evey, the Getty Oil vice president who was George's most loyal right-hand man; and to the Bel-Air Patrol, the wealthy community's private police force. Just after midnight, the patrolmen arrived first, which panicked George. He ran to his bedroom and locked the door. Evey and Smith got there soon after. After about an hour of trying to communicate with George, they broke down the door and found him on the floor. He was snoring, blood dripping down his stomach.

Evey then asked Dr. Smith not to send George to the nearby UCLA Medical Center. Reporters monitored admittances of celebrity patients there; the incident would likely hit the news. So George was taken on a longer ambulance ride to the smaller and quieter Queen of Angels Hospital downtown. After being admitted there under an assumed name, again at Evey's insistence, George seemed to be stabilized and merely in need of recovery from an alcoholic stupor.

About 2 a.m., Evey went to sleep on the floor beside George's bed. A few hours later he was woken by the staff swarming over George, who had fallen into a coma. Shortly after, Jacqueline arrived. She showed Evey two empty pill bottles that had contained barbiturates. She had discovered them in the bathroom when the doctor and Evey were with George in the bedroom, but her fear of scandal had prompted her to withhold them at that moment.

To control George's appetite, his doctor had prescribed amphetamines, which revved him up in the day but made sleep difficult. The same doctor prescribed barbiturates to help him sleep. Uppers combined with downers and then even a small amount of alcohol can be fatal. George died a few hours after Jackie arrived at the hospital.

"Mr. Getty's death was the result of a slowly increasing personal stress which was triggered into an acute reaction by alcoholic intoxification and which manifested itself in violent and self-destructive behavior," the coroner concluded. "We believe Mr. Getty took the pills in the brief time he was in the bathroom, that the pills were ingested on impulse. . . ."

In 2004, Evey published a memoir, *Creating an Empire*, in which he explained his fateful choices that night. He didn't view his actions as a "coverup." Loyalty and deep affection guided him: "Everything I did was to protect the image of the one person in the world to whom I owed everything in my adult life," who had been "like a brother to me—not just my boss, not just my mentor."

George's death sent Evey into a deep depression. "For five long years, I simply went through the motions of showing up for work and being alive. I drank. I disappointed myself." (In late 1978, however, Evey, who was then in charge of Getty Oil's nonpetroleum businesses, turned his life around after a former minor-league hockey announcer walked into his office and pitched "a crazy idea" for a twenty-four-hour all-sports cable network. In those pre-CNN days, the idea had been turned down by eight other companies. Evey persuaded the Getty board to invest $10 million for an 80 percent stake in this "crazy idea"—ESPN. Evey later explained that memories of outings with his old friend at the racetrack guided his decision to back ESPN, which was launched in 1979. "I did this primarily because I thought George Getty would like it," he said before he died in 2017.)

It fell to Evey to phone J. Paul Getty to tell him his son was dead. He reached Paul at the home of the Duchess of Argyll, where she was giving a dinner for the Turkish ambassador. Getty took the call in the duchess's library. After he hung up, "he beckoned me in . . . to say, 'George is dead,'" she recalled in *Forget Not*. She stayed up with him until about 3 a.m. He could do little but stare blankly into space and say repeatedly, "George has gone. He is with God."

Tragic! Shattered, he inscribed in his journal. *I walked to church and said a prayer for my dearest son. . . . George was a splendid son.*

Family visits provided intervals of comfort: six days after George's death, Ronald and Karin arrived with their children. *We walk about and watch the lions.* Two weeks later, Gordon and Ann and their boys came to stay. Paul Jr.'s son Mark was there too. *A fine boy.* They watched TV: Wimbledon and Watergate.

On July 10—just thirty-five days after George's death—came the next catastrophic event. The scrawl in the diary is almost impossible to read: *Message for Paul . . . that Paul . . . is kidnapped.*

A group of Calabrian mafiosi had snatched sixteen-year-old Paul III, Getty's eldest grandson, as he was walking home about 3 a.m. on a dimly lit street in Rome.

Along with the ear that Little Paul eventually lost, the most indelible element of the narrative was J. Paul Getty's initial refusal to pay the $17 million ransom demanded by the kidnappers, which he announced in his statement: "I have fourteen other grandchildren, and if I pay a penny of ransom, I'll have fourteen kidnapped grandchildren." From then on, it was more or less cemented in the public imagination that J. Paul Getty didn't care about his progeny, that he was heartless.

Entries in his diary over the next five months contradict that narrative. *I hope that he is not kidnapped and that he is OK,* Getty wrote when news of the abduction reached him. There were numerous strategy meetings and conversations with advisors and family members, including Gordon: *Indoors all day. Long discussion of Rome. . . . Crisis in Rome.*

I shudder at the boy's peril, Getty wrote after a newspaper in Rome received an envelope with Paul III's right ear.

Monitoring the press coverage, he took issue with some reports: *Rome TV news . . . castigating me for heartless refusal to . . . Actually I am putting up all the money. Ph Robina.*

On December 16, a day after Paul III was released, amidst frenzied global media coverage, he spoke to the young man on the phone. *Talk to her* [Gail] *and then to Paul,* he wrote in his diary. Most published accounts have said that the grandfather refused to talk to his grandson.

Excruciating as the five-month-long ordeal was, the Gettys have had to endure having it "told" again and again, in the forty years since, with creative license.

One of the few people still alive who was actually there at Sutton Place was Robina Lund. She agreed to share her views with me in writing, from her home in Aberdeenshire.

J. Paul Getty was far from heartless, she wrote. But he deliberately crafted the *perception* that he was heartless:

"Paul III was his eldest and favourite grandson. He loved all of his children and grandchildren but was also well aware of the frailties of some of them although he never publicly criticized them. His public refusal to pay any ransom was deliberately made to save ALL the other family members from immediately becoming potential hostages. There were many people and journalists who understood and agreed with the approach and so publicized, on JPG's behalf, his 'disinterest' and refusal to pay. The public fell for it and so did the kidnappers."

(No other Gettys were kidnapped, but seven weeks after Paul III's release, publishing heiress Patricia Hearst, nineteen, was abducted in Berkeley, California. The following year, Samuel Bronfman II, a twenty-one-year-old heir to the Seagram liquor fortune, was taken and held for ransom in New York. Throughout the 1970s, Italy suffered an epidemic of kidnappings—hundreds of individuals from wealthy families were abducted by organized gangs.)

Lund also described how misperceptions surrounding Getty—"the gross distortion of facts and characters"—have been perpetuated:

"Many [journalists] and, later, authors who could not get an interview with him (especially after his death when he couldn't answer them back or, more importantly, sue them for defamation!), built their works of fiction based on previous publications and news-clippings or interviews with grudge-holders, their aim, of course, being to make money. Scandals sell; hagiographies bore. . . . Many, particularly the later authors and film-makers, none of whom had ever met JPG, did not want to know the truth about him. 'Never let the truth get in the way of a good story.'"

She even deflated the other Getty Ur-myth. The infamous pay phone was *her* idea, she says. During the gala housewarming party that Getty threw at Sutton Place, AP and UPI reporters had kept a phone line open to Los Angeles for six hours. Costly as transatlantic calls were then, the bill amounted to over $40,000 in today's money. On another occasion, when Sutton Place was open for a charity function, a visitor phoned Tokyo for three hours. At the next directors' meeting of the Sutton Place Property Company, the holding company that she had formed to run the estate, Lund called for the removal of the phone extensions in the public rooms and installation of a pay phone. "NOT, please note, a red telephone box!" she wrote. Located in the downstairs cloakroom, for use by the press and the public who were not JPG's personally invited guests or company employees, it was removed after eighteen months, she added.

Four days after the kidnapping drama concluded, Gloria and her daughters—the Georgettes, as they are sometimes called—arrived at Sutton Place for the holidays. (Gail soon took Little Paul and his siblings away to the Austrian Alps for two months, to help them recover from the ordeal.) On the verge of their twenties, George's offspring were making their own decisions, which Grandpa wasn't always of one mind with. *Claire wants to go to school in Rome. I don't agree.* But it appears they had a happy visit, opening Christmas presents, having dinners, and watching TV. *Upstairs, Downstairs* was his current favorite. *Hudson, the Butler, hopes to marry a young girl.*

Walk 40 minutes. Nero roaring, he wrote in the last log of that tumultuous year. *U and Gloria, Claire and Caroline watch 1974 come in. We are in 1974. We drink a glass of champagne.*

In these early years of the 1970s, despite his declining health and family traumas, Getty remained laser-focused on the plans for his namesake museum, which was rising out of its building site on the Malibu coast. He micromanaged its construction remotely, via drawings, models, photos, and films that were sent the six thousand miles to him.

At the same time, his newly hired curators made regular trips from Malibu to Sutton Place, bringing with them photographs of treasures they hoped to convince him to buy. Among the frequent visitors was Gillian Wilson. Born into a middle-class family in England, she moved to Los Angeles in 1971 at age thirty to begin her job as the J. Paul Getty Museum's first curator of decorative arts. Essentially self-taught, and anything but prim (she had a fling with the Rolling Stones drummer Charlie Watts), she assembled an unrivaled collection of eighteenth-century European furniture and decorative arts for the Getty, building on the holdings J. Paul Getty acquired personally.

"It was big and freezing cold. He always saw you at the most peculiar hours," Wilson recalled of her visits to Sutton Place. "He would stay up until very late ringing Saudi Arabia and places like that. At three in the morning—and you were jet-lagged—Bullimore would fetch you: 'Mr. Getty will see you now.' Every so often [Getty] wanted to show you his oriental carpets in the Long Gallery. He would get on his hands and knees. So I had to as well. I remember thinking, *This is rather peculiar—here I am crawling along with the richest man in the Western Hemisphere in the middle of the night.*"

On January 16, 1974, just weeks after Paul III's release, the J. Paul Getty Museum opened at last. It was the culmination of Getty's life as a collector, the legacy he wanted to leave to the world. The cultural elite greeted it with scorn.

The complaints from the critics focused not on the art but on the building. In the late sixties, when he settled on the design, Getty went against the grain of prevailing fashion and trends, as usual. At the high noon of modernism, he chose to build a replica of an ancient Roman villa, and a colorful one at that. "I refuse to pay for one of those concrete-bunker-type structures that are the fad . . . nor for some tinted-glass-and-stainless-steel monstrosity," he said.

Ten days before its doors opened, the *Los Angeles Times*'s art critic weighed in with a preview: "L.A. intelligentsia . . . will find that the Getty outstrips any existing monument to expensive, aggressive bad taste, cultural pretension, and self-aggrandizement, south of Hearst Castle."

Other critics piled on, ridiculing it as "Pompeii on the Pacific" and "an intellectual Disneyland."

"For the majority of the architectural establishment who still at least give lip service to the canons of the Modern Movement [it] is not only disgusting but it is downright outrageous," another author summed up.

Getty tried to downplay the drubbing ("certain critics sniffed at the new museum," he wrote), but, according to biographer John Pearson, the poor reviews "genuinely shook him." Soon enough, however, the public vindicated him. By March, 100,000 visitors had besieged its gates, backing up traffic on the Pacific Coast Highway for miles. Ever since, it has been one of California's most popular destinations. (In 1997, the J. Paul Getty Trust expanded its operations substantially, with the opening of its acropolis-like campus in Brentwood, designed by Richard Meier at a cost of approximately $1 billion. The two sites, which charge no admission fee, typically draw two million visitors a year.)

In time, even the intelligentsia came around—some of them, anyway. One fan of the villa was Joan Didion, who described it as "mysteriously and rather giddily splendid" in a 1977 *Esquire* piece (subsequently published in her collection *The White Album*) in which she pondered how differently elite and popular audiences had responded to it.

"The villa . . . manages to strike a peculiar nerve in almost everyone who sees it. From the beginning, the Getty was said to be 'vulgar,'" she wrote. "To mention the museum in the more enlightened of those dining rooms . . . is to invite a kind of nervous derision, as if the place were a local hoax, a perverse and deliberate affront to the understated good taste and general class of everyone at the table.

"The Getty is a monument to 'fine art,' in the old-fashioned didactic sense. . . . The place resists contemporary notions," she continued. "As a matter of fact large numbers of people who do not ordinarily visit museums like the Getty a great deal, just as its founder knew they would. There is one of those peculiar social secrets at work here. On the whole 'the critics' distrust great wealth, but 'the public' does not."

Another positive but more concise assessment appeared in *The Andy Warhol Diaries*. "Went to Getty Museum. . . . It was thrilling. Bought a book on painting ($17)," the artist wrote on September 21, 1978.

Despite the harsh reviews, his physical decline, and lingering traumas, 1974 and 1975 were mellow for the old man. His final two full years were filled with visits from his progeny and various ex-wives.

Teddy continued to make her customary visits to Sutton Place, with her daughter, Gigi. "We came every summer," recalled Gigi, who became an equestrian and a filmmaker in Los Angeles. "Paul was more of a father to me than my own father. He played toys with me and, when I turned thirteen, he taught me how to mix a rum and coke. I have only very fond memories of him." (Gigi had watched him enjoy his beverage of choice in previous years and asked for the lesson; she didn't imbibe, except for a sip.)

The Georgettes and their mother, Gloria, were guests at Sutton Place numerous times. Claire delayed college and traveled around the world. Between countries, she returned to Sutton Place for long stretches, and she sometimes brought foreign friends back with her. *Claire and a nice Italian man friend of hers were here for a swim and dinner*, JPG noted in July of 1975. She also joined lunches and dinners Getty hosted for his wide variety of friends, ranging from Jacques Cousteau and Zsa Zsa Gabor to Charles Wrightsman, Getty's fellow oilman and art collector, who came with his wife, the divine Jayne.

Getty also took Claire to meet the head of the Mitsubishi Oil Corporation, a strategic partner of Getty Oil. (A couple decades on, Claire's sister Anne, an environmentalist, went to battle against Mitsubishi.)

Gloria, on her own, sometimes overnighted at Sutton Place en route to France, Scotland, or some other holiday destination. Other times, George's second wife, Jacqueline, arrived with her son, Mike. At a loss after George's death, Jackie, a slim blonde, had taken up

George's equestrian hobby, and found great satisfaction in it. In June 1975, one of her three-year-olds pulled off a sensational victory at Royal Ascot, running in one of the week's most prestigious races, which Paul was delighted to attend: *Her horse Blood Royal won the Queen's Vase in a thrilling fashion. I had five pounds on it.*

Mike, a graduate of USC, also got hooked on the sport of kings. Over the years, he had great success with his horses, including Are You Kidding Me, Dunbeath, and Bates Motel (Mike's also a film buff).

Getty's second son, Ronald, and his family came to visit from their home in South Africa. Summer afternoons, they enjoyed the lovely weather by the pool. *They are very nice looking children and well behaved*, the old man noted in June '74, of Cecilia, Stephanie, and Christopher, who ranged in age from four to ten. By their next visit, in January, the brood had expanded. *The special attraction is a young lady aged 4½ months*, he wrote delightedly of Christina, his sixteenth grandchild.

Karin and the children usually arrived and departed by air, while Ronald always voyaged by sea. Like his father, he had developed a fear of flying.

Getty biographers have portrayed Ronald as being bitter at his father over his exclusion from the Sarah C. Getty Trust (caused by Paul's anger toward Ronald's rich maternal grandfather). But the diaries indicate Ronald had certainly some warm feelings for his father. In these final years, Ronald made efforts to coax him into returning to America at last. With their shared terror of airplanes, the son was empathetic. *Ronny wants me to go with him on the* [ocean liner] *France and I would like to. But business!* Getty wrote in August 1974. And in early 1976: *Talked to Ronny. He would like me to come with them on the boat which goes to Miami via Lisbon and Nassau. It is 24,000 tons. I would like to but I have a Government Participation meeting January 21st.*

Ronny's mother—Paul's third wife—also arrived, with a girlfriend, for a weekend: *Fini and Marian arr at 8 last night after a stormy Channel crossing. . . . Both look well.*

Paul Jr. was not allowed at Sutton Place. Big Paul refused to see him until he kicked drugs. Paul III, then eighteen, married his German girlfriend, Martine Zacher (who later became known as Gisela), and the couple moved to Los Angeles. The patriarch was delighted to hear about the birth of their son, Paul Balthazar, in January 1975, from Paul III's maternal grandparents: *I received a cable from Judge Harris: 'Boy born to Martine and Paul, Congratulations, George and Aileen.' This makes me a great-grandfather.*

The rest of the brood visited frequently: *Gail and the 3 children to tea. We all remark how nice Mark, Aileen, and Ariadne are.* They were in their teenage years—or, in the case of the baby of the family, just beginning them. *Had a birthday lunch with a cake with candles for Ariadne*, he wrote on July 23, 1975. *She is 13 today. I gave her ten pounds in cash and a wooly bear, which she liked. She found another ten pounds in the bear. She is a nice child. She said, 'Now I am a teenager.'*

There were lovely afternoons with them on the grounds: by the pool (*they all swim like porpoises*), the garden (*we walked and admired its beauty. The Rhododendrons are out in all their glory*), or farther afield (*Went Blackberrying . . . there is a good crop this year*).

Their eight-year-old half brother visited with his maternal grandmother: *Tara and Mrs. Pol to lunch. . . . Tara is a handsome boy and has good manners.*

Gordon and Ann were back and forth from San Francisco, together and separately. Gordon was at Sutton Place for his father's final weeks, in the spring of '76. *He looks good*, Paul observed of him that April. The couple's four boys, home in California, ranged from age five to ten.

Getty's last wife kept tabs remotely: *Teddy phoned from the Algonquin Hotel in New York just for old time's sake. I remember the Algonquin back in 1935.*

With his face looking more funereal than ever, Paul got a chance to see himself in a way that only a few have experienced. *Miss Simpkins and Miss Fraser here from Madame Tussaud's to make a wax replica of me*, he reported in late '74. A few months later, he was pleased, at least with his placement and apparent popularity. *Saw my image in wax. It is next to Katharine Hepburn. There are big crowds.*

By the beginning of 1976, his body was in considerable pain, especially in his neck, leaving him challenged. *Bullimore helped me put on my socks and shoes and fasten the neck button on my shirt.* Parkes, the under-butler, suffered a stroke at the same time. Getty noted: *We were told it would be a long time before he is ready to work again.*

That spring, Getty was informed he had prostate cancer. He never acknowledged this in the journal; he just described his pains, which made sleeping in his bed difficult. He began spending nights in an armchair in his study.

In his final weeks, he rallied to have several conversations with Gail. The trial of Paul III's kidnappers was finally about to start in southern Italy. She and Little Paul were determined to attend and face the perpetrators. Security was a big concern. JPG made arrangements for them to stay at Posta Vecchia and in another villa he owned on Gaiola, an island off Naples.

Gail called to say they are leaving tonight for PV and then on the 11th will go to Gaiola, he wrote May 7.

The trial was a grim ordeal for Paul III and Gail. It lasted ten weeks. Finally, a three-judge court convicted only two of the nine defendants.

J. Paul Getty never learned the verdict. He slipped away quietly on June 6, 1976—three years to the day after George's death—in the chair in his study, next to the settee upon which he had once jumped so boisterously.

Upon his death, J. Paul Getty was no longer the richest man in the world. But he was up there.

There were two vast piles of wealth to sort out—Getty's personal fortune and the Sarah C. Getty Trust. In theory they were separate, but they were very much intertwined, because the value of both lay in Getty Oil Company stock.

His personal fortune consisted of 12 percent of the company's stock, valued then at $750 million. Three days after his death, it was revealed that virtually all of this (save for some bequests to his lady friends) was bequeathed to the J. Paul Getty Museum. In Malibu, the staff nearly fainted collectively. Getty had never let on that he would leave them anything approaching this. The rest of the art world was equally staggered. Overnight, this eccentric little museum became the best-endowed cultural institution on earth. (While George, Ronald, and Gordon served on its board for periods over the years, the family has never been involved in the management of the museum.)

The Sarah C. Getty Trust held a 40 percent stake in Getty Oil, worth about $2 billion. In theory, the trust's path was preordained: the vast distributions it would provide to the heirs in the coming decades, until the death of J. Paul Getty's last surviving son, at which time the principal would be divided up among the heirs.

Within a few years, disagreements in the family led to titanic battles over the fate of Getty Oil and the trust. Once again, the Gettys were exhibited as a poster family for dysfunction. As the media painted it, the Gettys were at each other's throats. It was brothers against brothers, nieces and nephews against uncles, cousins against cousins. Pure rancor. Those headlines kept coming—"the Tragic Dynasty," "the Getty Curse," "the War between the Gettys"—which, in turn, provided many Gettys with ample reason for never wanting to speak to the press.

When there are this many zeros involved, however, it's rare when there isn't litigation. Some of Getty's contemporaries left far messier estates. Howard Hugues, who died one month before Getty, didn't leave a legitimate will, a situation that led to years of bizarre courtroom battles among his many would-be heirs. More than thirty-five years after the death of H. L. Hunt, a bigamist who produced fifteen children from three overlapping relationships (a clan that makes the Gettys seem like the Brady Bunch), some of his heirs were still litigating over their trusts. It would take nearly a decade to settle all the complicated financial issues for Jean Paul Getty's heirs, his company, and his museum.

II.

BRANCHING OUT

3

The Georgettes

While the demands that came with being J. Paul Getty's firstborn son ultimately took their toll on George F. Getty II, his early years were placid. Born in 1924, he grew up in the verdant community of San Marino outside Pasadena, where his mother, Jeannette, settled with her second husband, stockbroker William H. Jones, who was a kind stepfather to George.

After attending the Webb School in nearby Claremont, George enrolled at Princeton University, though the war interrupted his studies. He enlisted in the army in 1942 and received a second lieutenant's commission in the infantry in 1944. He spent sixteen months in the Pacific.

Thenceforth he was under his father's command, and dispatched to a variety of harsh locales, including the Neutral Zone and West Texas. On a break home in California, he got engaged as the second half of the twentieth century dawned.

"Vivacious" was a word used to describe Gloria Alice Gordon. In March 1951, the *Los Angeles Times*'s society page buzzed with the news ("Betrothal Announced") that this dimpled, Denver-born debutante, now a senior at Marymount College, was "the summer bride-elect of George Franklin Getty II."

The couple's June wedding at the Church of the Good Shepherd in Beverly Hills was also avidly covered: "The bride's radiant brunette beauty was accented by her period gown fashioned with a fitted bodice and portrait neckline. . . . The full skirt of pleated ruffles of taffeta and tulle completed the bridal gown. On her dark curls was a tiny crown of Chantilly lace delicately frosted with pearls from which floated a veil of illusion." After the ceremony, the guests, including her maid of honor and five bridesmaids, continued to the reception in the Crystal Ballroom of the Beverly Hills Hotel, before the newlyweds departed for their honeymoon cruise on the Mediterranean.

Being the wife of a rising young oil executive (especially the first-born son of J. Paul Getty) entailed a considerable number of moves over the next decade, as her daughters were born. A November 1952 issue of the *Princeton Alumni Weekly* carried this news from the Class of '46: "A young Texas miss arrived in Midland on Thursday, Oct. 9. The young lady's name is Anne Catherine Getty. . . . Her father is a Texan-for-Ike, manager of the Mid-Continental Division of the Pacific Western Oil Company."

Two years later, around the time Claire Eugenia was born, the family moved to Tulsa, and later to New York. In 1957, when Caroline Marie arrived, they relocated to San Francisco, where, according to the *Oil & Gas Journal*, "George F. Getty II is making the family name synonymous with the oil business." By the fall of 1958, they were Southern Californians. "The attractive honorees, George and Gloria, have moved to Our Town from New York (via a short stop-over in San Francisco) and will make their home here," the *Los Angeles Times* wrote.

All those moves must have been taxing for Gloria. She and George separated in 1965; their divorce decree came a few years later. She relocated with the girls to Hillsborough, the mannerly community south of San Francisco on the Peninsula, while George remained in Los Angeles. By the time he remarried—to Jacqueline Riordan in 1971—Gloria had moved to the livelier shores of Newport Beach in Orange County. Gloria joined "the new sea set" and bought a little motorboat, which she christened *Titanic*. It blew up on its maiden voyage. "She went ahead and called its replacement, a whippy little motor launch with a bright blue-and-white fringed canopy, the *Titanic Too*," it was reported.

On June 9, 1973, three days after George's shocking death at age forty-eight, he was buried on a bluff overlooking the Pacific Ocean on the Getty Ranch in Malibu, where the J. Paul Getty Museum would rise. Caroline was fifteen, Claire eighteen, and Anne twenty.

After the girls finished school, Gloria returned to the San Francisco Bay Area. At Trader Vic's, she was accorded her own table in the Captain's Cabin, "the most sacred region where only the best-known are seated," the *San Francisco Chronicle* noted.

She traveled in Europe. In the summer of 1984 she attended a starry gala, a benefit for United World Colleges, at Sutton Place, which had been purchased by Milwaukee-born timber heir Stanley J. Seeger. Familiar as the surroundings were, the art and the crowd were different. Under the ownership of Seeger, a reclusive gay collector of modern art, a Francis Bacon hung where a Gainsborough had been; instead of the Queen Mother, Prince Charles and Princess Diana were on hand. (Two years later, Sutton Place was bought by yet another rich, eccentric, gay American—Koch Industries heir Frederick Koch, who also rivaled Getty in extreme frugality.)

In the aughts, Gloria could be found at the Balboa Cafe, now under the management of young up-and-comers Billy Getty, her nephew, and Gavin Newsom; in 2002, she was seen encouraging fellow patrons like Will Hearst to sign a petition for homeless reform that fledgling mayoral candidate Newsom hoped to get on the ballot. In 2013, she and her offspring attended her former brother-in-law Gordon Getty's gala eightieth birthday party. Her daughters had grown up to become exemplary citizens—and very private ones.

On an afternoon in November 2019, as a nor'easter lashed Manhattan with forty-mile-per-hour gusts and torrents of rain, the recipients of the Carnegie Medal of Philanthropy climbed the marble steps of the ornate New York Public Library.

In the world of philanthropy, a Carnegie Medal is the equivalent of an Academy Award. Like some of J. Paul Getty's forebears, Andrew Carnegie had arrived in America from Scotland penniless. In 1889, when Carnegie had amassed a fortune from steel that put him on par with robber barons such as John Jacob Astor, Cornelius Vanderbilt, and Jay Gould—whose excesses spawned the Gilded Age—he published a manifesto, "The Gospel of Wealth." Influenced by his strict Scottish heritage, he urged his fellow millionaires to embrace social responsibility and to donate their money to organizations that would address the root causes of poverty and social ills. He gave away $350 million, the bulk of his fortune, to such efforts. It was the birth of modern philanthropy.

Biennially, the international network of institutions that Carnegie endowed recognizes philanthropists who embody his spirit of giving. Medals have gone to some of America's most recognizable names, including Brooke Astor and Michael Bloomberg, as well as the Mellon, Rockefeller, and Gates families.

The 2019 class of medalists included financier Henry Kravis and George Lucas, who in his acceptance speech quoted "my friend Yoda," to make the point that "everyone has the Force inside them—the light and the dark . . . and hopefully we're able to move it a little more toward the bright side."

Next up to the podium was a petite sixty-seven-year-old brunette whom few Americans would be able to identify—Anne G. Earhart. According to her citation that night, her efforts over the decades to protect the environment place her "prominently within the ranks of today's great conservationists."

Many in the audience probably had no idea what the G. stood for. (Her biography in the program didn't mention it.) In her acceptance speech, J. Paul Getty's eldest grandchild said simply, "I knew that when I inherited a large sum of money, that some good should come of it." (There was also a certain triumph for a Getty grandchild to be accepting an award named after Carnegie, who is credited with coining the adage "Shirtsleeves to shirtsleeves in three generations"— a warning that wealth gained in one generation will likely be lost by the third.)

"I joke that it was the Catholic nuns who gave me my perhaps overdeveloped sense of responsibility," Anne also stated that afternoon. According to her biography, her schooling was at the hands of the Sisters of the Immaculate Heart.

The few times that Earhart's name has appeared in the press, the words "intensely private" invariably have run alongside it. The same goes for her sisters. While almost all the members of the extended Getty family could be described as private, the descendants of Gloria and George F. Getty II have the strongest aversion to being in the public eye, even as they've been models of social responsibility.

As Anne continued her remarks, she made one more personal reference. "I want to ensure that my grandson and all of his generation will get to see the wondrous sights that I have been privileged to see," she said, referring to four-year-old Finn, who was in the audience with his mother, Sara Earhart Lowell, then thirty-eight, and her brother, Nicholas Earhart, thirty-four.

One of those wondrous sights, she recalled, was a baby gray whale with which she came eye to eye four decades before. She had been on a boat when a pod of whales broke the surface and a pair of enormous orbs the size of baseballs focused on her. "To be with an animal that has chosen to come up and look at you in the eye is a transcendental experience. . . . It is magic," she recalled in *A Force for Nature: The Story of the NRDC and Its Fight to Save Our Planet*, by John H. Adams, founder of the National Resources Defense Council.

That encounter took place in Laguna San Ignacio in Baja California. Some 450 miles south of the Mexican border, it is a narrow 16-mile inlet of sparkling jade-green waters, surrounded by a 6 million-acre desert reserve teeming with pronghorn antelope, bighorn sheep, and mountain lions. One of the most pristine places on earth, it is here, every winter, that thousands of gray whales conclude their epic journey from their summer feeding grounds in the Arctic Circle. Despite having been hunted nearly to extinction along this route in the nineteenth and twentieth centuries, these forty-ton, forty-five-foot-long marvels continue to undertake the 10,000-mile migration (the longest-known of any mammal in the world) to Laguna San Ignacio, where they mate and calve in the warm, salty waters, and are renowned for their friendliness. They often nuzzle up to boats; a mother will sometimes even nudge her curious offspring forward, to afford them a look at the strange creatures aboard the vessels.

After her trip to San Ignacio, Anne left California for several years, as a rare newspaper item about her, published in the *Los Angeles Times* on June 6, 1980, reported: "Anne Catherine Getty, daughter of Mrs. Gloria Getty of Newport Beach and the late Mr. George F. Getty II, married John Edwin Earhart in Corona del Mar. The newlyweds are living in Paraguay, where he is with the Peace Corps. He is the son of Mr. and Mrs. Edwin Earhart of Rogue River, Ore."

While living in South America, Anne gave birth to Sara in 1981; she also became an environmental advocate. After seeing devastating destruction of land in Paraguay and Brazil, she studied environmental issues and began engaging with leaders in the conservation movement.

In 1983 the family relocated to Connecticut, where John earned a master's degree in forestry from the Yale School of Forestry and Environmental Studies. By 1985, when Nicholas arrived, they were back on the West Coast, in Seattle and finally Laguna Beach, where they settled. (She and John divorced in the 1990s.)

By then, Anne and her sisters were young women of great means, being the beneficiaries of their father's income from the Sarah C. Getty Trust. (Because of his early death, the girls came into substantial wealth two decades before some of their cousins.) Though the value of the trust doubled after the sale of Getty Oil, the trio had initially opposed the deal. After they did acquiesce to the sale, they continued to press a lawsuit against their uncle Gordon, the sole trustee, over his management of the trust (his brother, Paul Jr., joined them in this action). Reserved and youthful as the women were, they were no pushovers.

The upheaval began in 1982, six years after J. Paul Getty's death. Until then, Getty Oil had continued to be run by its management, headed by chairman and chief executive Sidney R. Petersen, a company veteran. All along, however, there had been a power behind the throne: the iron-willed C. Lansing Hays, Paul's longtime attorney, and a trustee of the Sarah C. Getty Trust. Gordon was cotrustee, but habitually deferred to him in the running of the trust as well as Getty Oil, where the management largely deferred to Hays too.

Hays's death in May 1982 set off the extraordinary drama. In essence, Gordon now became sole trustee, which gave him increased power over Getty Oil and the trust.

For the first time, Gordon developed a serious interest in the management of the company. After studying it, he wasn't happy with what he saw. The value of its stock had declined significantly. He wondered why it was underperforming. Getty Oil's management and board, which had long considered Gordon a docile, rather eccentric character—an absent-minded professor type, the member of the family least cut out for business—were taken aback.

At the height of the merger mania then sweeping Wall Street, Gordon began to chat with bankers and other oil companies, which put Getty Oil in play. In late 1983, Pennzoil was on the verge of consummating a deal for the company when Texaco swept in, setting off one of the most sensational takeover battles ever. Texaco ended up buying Getty for $10.1 billion, the biggest corporate acquisition in history. (Pennzoil then launched a colossal and ultimately successful multibillion-dollar lawsuit against its rival that bankrupted Texaco. *That's* a whole other story: the Getty family wasn't a party to that suit, their billions from Texaco having already been banked.)

During the run-up to the sale of the company, Getty Oil management schemed to neutralize Gordon. They sought to enlist other family members to challenge Gordon's position as sole trustee in order to block the sale, eventually drafting Paul Getty Jr.'s youngest son, Tara, then fifteen years old, for the role.

But the strongest challenge to Gordon came from the Georgettes. Loyal to the memory of their grandfather and their late father, they didn't want to see the family legacy dismantled. Nonmaterialistic, too, they thought they were rich enough. "Why, Uncle Gordon, since the trust has so much money already, are we trying to get more?" they asked him during a meeting. "A very interesting philosophical question," he replied. "But it is my duty to maximize the wealth and income from the trust and to prevent it from falling into a weak minority position." (These conversations were drawn from depositions Gordon had to give when the young women later brought legal action against him.)

In January 1984, the sale went through, because Gordon got the museum, with its 12 percent of the stock, to vote with him. The fortunes of both the museum and the family doubled. With the trust now worth $4 billion, some heirs questioned how it was being managed by Gordon, the sole trustee. For the next eighteen months, branches of the family litigated. Finally, in 1985, a judge agreed to a plan to partition the Sarah C. Getty Trust into four separate trusts, so each branch could oversee its own. But the matter was still far from settled. A major legal hurdle had to be cleared, which was accomplished when the California State Legislature enacted a new law that allowed family trusts to be split upon agreement of all the beneficiaries. Bill Newsom helped steer it through in Sacramento, from the statehouse to the desk of Governor George Deukmejian, where it was signed. But getting all twenty-six living Getty heirs to sign the eighty-nine-page agreement to divide their Trust took another three years, largely due to disagreements over tax issues.

"Were my nieces and Paul mad at me? Believe it," Gordon wrote in a preface to *Logic and Economics: Free Growth and Other Surprises,* an economics primer he self-published in 2018. He placed the blame for the family friction on the attorneys, however. "Lawsuits get that way. Lawyers on both sides say nasty things," he wrote. But amicable family relations continued, according to his account: "Problem solved. The Trust was split into four in 1988, and an unhappy chapter ended. My nieces and I are as close as ever. So were Paul and I until his death."

While cordial relations between nieces and uncle did resume, this distaff branch of the Gettys—George's daughters and their children— veered in its own direction, largely going its own way. To use a whale metaphor, they stay in their own pod, while the other three branches of the family swim together, more or less.

In 1986, Anne established the Homeland Foundation, which initially focused on helping disadvantaged women. When environmental causes became her primary focus, she renamed it the Marisla Foundation. (The Marisla Seamount is a group of three underwater peaks rising from the sea floor eight miles off the coast of Baja California; Marisla is also Anne's daughter's middle name.)

The Marisla Foundation emerged as a particularly effective leader in marine conservation, working to mitigate habitat destruction, pollution, and overfishing. While her efforts have made Anne a hero to conservationists, the public knows little of her philanthropy, by her choice. In the early nineties, for example, she provided about $400,000 to the NRDC so it could lead the opposition to a proposed billion-dollar toll road that would plow through the idyllic San Joaquin Hills near Laguna Niguel south of Los Angeles. The battle lasted years. Area residents who also opposed the highway were surprised when the *Los Angeles Times* revealed that the Earharts had been footing the bills for the resistance.

It was also reported that funding from Anne's foundation typically came with a request that the recipients never talk about the couple or the foundation. It was a deal that grassroots activists in California were happy to keep. "I'd say we'd be in deep trouble without them," said one of them. (Despite Earhart's efforts, the road was ultimately built.)

As Anne's children grew up, Laguna San Ignacio became a favorite family destination. They camped in the desert and voyaged out to see the whales. "I love this land of high winds, desert, and mangrove and water alive with whales, porpoises, and pelicans," she also recalled in *A Force for Nature*.

In 1994, Anne learned that this paradise was coming under attack. The Mexican government planned to build the biggest salt-production plant in the world here, in partnership with the Mitsubishi Corporation. Their joint venture, Exportadora de Sal SA (ESSA), had already built a sizable saltworks in Laguna Guerrero Negro, a hundred miles away.

Anne's grandfather and the Japanese firm had a long history, going back to 1924, when the fuel department of the Mitsubishi Trading Company secured exclusive rights to sell in the Far East the petroleum products made by the Getty-owned Associate Oil Company of California. In 1928, Mitsubishi entered into a broader joint venture with Tide Water. There was an interruption after Pearl Harbor, but by 1950 the companies resumed their partnership. By the 1970s, Getty Oil owned 49.7 percent of Mitsubishi Oil; the affiliate was a significant part of Getty business. But disaster struck on Christmas Eve 1974, when the rupture of a storage tank at Mitsubishi's Mizushima refinery resulted in the largest oil spill in Japan's history—an event that was environmentally devastating and financially costly. Some eleven million gallons poured into the scenic Inland Sea, creating a huge slick.

In the wake of this calamity, Mitsubishi's top executives paid a visit to Sutton Place in April 1975, when Anne's middle sister, Claire, happened to be in residence. Getty was concerned about the damage. *This is an anxious time,* he wrote. *Mr. Watanabe, Mr. Nimura arrived at noon. Long discussion about Mitsubishi and the catastrophe. They say it might cost a hundred million dollars. I recommend a dyke to be built around the 3 Mitsubishi refineries.*

The troubles notwithstanding, *Mr. Watanabe is very charming*, he noted. *Claire was with me. Mr. Watanabe was very fond of George. George liked Japan very much and so do I.*

Anne—who since the 1984 sale of Getty Oil had no financial interest in Mitsubishi—got wind of plans for the San Ignacio plant, which would cover 130,000 acres and include a mile-long pier, in a roundabout way. A local fisherman, Don Pachico Mayoral, had somehow gotten his hands on a set of blueprints. A guru-like figure in the small community, Pachico lived on the edge of the lagoon in a wooden shack with a sand floor and no telephone. He showed the blueprints to an American PhD candidate, Serge Dedina, who was at the lagoon carrying out research for his dissertation on gray whales; Dedina in turn alerted Anne. She sprang into action. She enlisted the NRDC to spearhead the largest coordinated global environmental campaign to date. During the ferocious five-year-long battle, her support went unreported.

In early 1995, the *Los Angeles Times* broke the story of the impending peril; it punched holes in the environmental impact statement that had been prepared, which had concluded that the proposed project's impact on the whales would be "insignificant," discounting the likelihood of toxic chemicals contaminating the lagoon and not contemplating how the pumping of 462 million gallons of seawater out of the lagoon a year might reduce the salinity of the water. Its high salt content is thought to make the whales more buoyant, and account for why females with calves gather there.

The Mexican government, eager for the plant's projected $100 million in annual revenue, blasted the "disinformation." Mitsubishi wouldn't return reporters' calls or respond to the frightened population who lived near the lagoon—a small community of fishermen and people who work in the ecotourism business.

The NRDC gathered an international coalition to raise awareness of the situation: environmentalists, fishermen, artists, intellectuals, writers, and dozens of world-renowned scientists, including nine Nobel laureates. They focused on getting consumers around the world to care about this remote spot that most had never heard of. Editorials appeared in newspapers worldwide. In the *Los Angeles Times*, Robert F. Kennedy Jr. and NRDC senior attorney Joel Reynolds raised the cry for "the one place on earth where the last of the gray whale species can breed and calve undisturbed by human intrusion." A campaign of boycotts, disinvestment initiatives, petition signings, and letter and postcard writing was orchestrated. Some 700,000 postcards were mailed to Mitsubishi car dealerships worldwide.

Mitsubishi's public relations offensive included full-page newspaper ads touting the plant as "a partnership with nature." Then, in December 1997, Baja fishermen made a gruesome discovery: ninety-four highly endangered giant black sea turtles floating dead downstream from Laguna Guerrero Negro. An investigation found that they had been poisoned by a spill of toxic salt brine wastes from the ESSA plant there.

In March 2000, Mexican president Ernesto Zedillo helicoptered to the site with his family and a group of friends. They boated on the lagoon to view the whales, then camped onshore for a night. A week later, he announced the cancellation of the project. "This is a place that has had minimal interference by humans—one of the few places like that left on the planet," he reasoned.

"We came to appreciate a number of arguments by people that this is an area that should be left as is for ecotourism," a Mitsubishi spokesman commented.

It was a watershed victory that broke new ground in environmental activism, and was soon viewed as a case study in how to conduct a grassroots campaign—developed with multilayered sophistication—in the era of globalization.

A decade later, NRDC president John H. Adams reflected on the battle in his memoir. "Multifaceted campaigns like this are hugely expensive, and this one cost millions of dollars," he wrote. "It could

J. Paul Getty with Teresa, one of his pet lions, at Sutton Place in the 1960s

Getty Research Institute, Los Angeles

THE FIVE WIVES OF J. PAUL GETTY

Jeannette DeMont
Getty Images

Allene Ashby
*Institutional Archives,
Getty Research Institute, Los Angeles*

Adolphine "Fini" Helmle
Getty Images

Ann Rork
*Los Angeles Times Photographic Archive
Department of Special Collections/
Charles E. Young Research Library/UCLA*

Louise Dudley "Teddy" Lynch
Getty Images

J. Paul Getty with Robina Lund
Dezo Hoffman/Shutterstock

Sutton Place, southwest of London, was built in the early 1500s
and acquired by J. Paul Getty in 1959.
Print Collector/Getty Images

J. Paul Getty with Margaret, Duchess of Argyll, en route to his eightieth birthday party in London, December 1972

Pierre Manevy Express/Hulton Archive/ Getty Images

ABOVE: George Franklin Getty II

Express/Hulton Archive/Getty Images

LEFT: J. Paul Getty with John Skinner at Goodwood, England, 1962

Keystone-France/Gamma-Keystone/Getty Images

Christopher Getty and Pia Miller at their wedding in Bali, 1992

Collection of Christopher Getty

Isabel Getty at Royal Ascot, June 2019

David M. Benett/Getty Images/Ascot Racecourse

MOROCCAN WAKE-UP

MR. AND MRS. PAUL GETTY, JUNIOR, HAVE SHAKEN TO LIFE
A DESERTED HOUSE IN MARRAKECH,
MADE IT IMAGINATIVE, RARE –
WITH A LITTLE MYSTERY

"This house is really a stage," Talitha Getty said of the nineteenth-century ramble of rooms,
courtyards, and terraces that she and her husband came upon on their honeymoon about four years
ago and bought: "Things happen here spontaneously." The spontaneity of this holiday house for
the Gettys, who live most of the year in Rome and London, depends on their care as they gradually,
joyfully restore its old graces, its harems and friezes, and add treasures of their travels.
Above: On the terrace overlooking the souks, the towering Koutoubia, and the
snowy Atlas Mountains, Paul and Talitha Getty, wearing Moroccan caftans.
Left: The Riad, or main courtyard, its fountain floating flowers, its paths glistening with tiles
specially made for the Gettys, and with the flare of lanterns; "We light the house with a hundred
candles and lanterns," said Mrs. Getty, who lights this house, too, with a continuum of friends.

PATRICK LICHFIELD

Paul Jr. and Talitha at Palais de la Zahia, Marrakech,
as seen in the January 1970 issue of *Vogue*

Patrick Lichfield/Vogue/© Condé Nast

Wormsley Manor in Buckinghamshire, England was acquired by Paul Jr. in 1985.

Christopher Simon Sykes © Condé Nast Shutterstock

Sabine Getty and the *Talitha*

Jason Schmidt/Trunk Archive

Paul III on a forty-foot ketch, embarking for Catalina Island, 1977, photographed by Jonathan Becker

© *Jonathan Becker*

Tara and Jessica Getty at Wormsley, 2011

© *Dafydd Jones*

Balthazar, at right, with (from left) wife, Rosetta, and children Grace, Violet, June, and Cassius at the CORE Gala, Los Angeles, January 2020

© *Kevin Mazur/Getty Images*

Paul III and his wife, Gisela, at home in Los Angeles with their children
Balthazar and Anna, 1977, photographed by Jonathan Becker

© *Jonathan Becker*

LEFT: Julius Getty and his father, Mark, at the opening of the Julius Getty Gallery, London, 2019
Jeff Spicer/Getty Images

RIGHT: Alexander and Tatum Getty, San Francisco, 2012
© *Drew Altizer*

BELOW: Sabine and Joseph Getty with daughter, Gene, at home in London, 2019, photographed by Simon Watson
© *Simon Watson*

Aileen Getty and Christopher Wilding,
photographed by Firooz Zahedi

© *Firooz Zahedi*

Aileen at a Fire Drill Friday,
Washington, DC, December 2019

Collection of Aileen Getty

Honoree Aileen at the
amfAR Inspiration Gala,
Los Angeles, 2013, with
her sons Caleb Wilding
(at left) and Andrew
Wilding with his wife,
Alexandra

Jason Kempin/Getty Images/amfAR

Ariadne Getty with her children Nats and August
at home in Beverly Hills, 2018

Emily Berl/The New York Times/Redux

Gigi Gorgeous and Nats Getty at their wedding
in Montecito, July 12, 2019

Alex Welsh/The New York Times/Redux

Gordon and Ann Getty at the memorial service for his father
in San Francisco, 1976, with their sons Peter, Andrew, John, and Billy

Steve Fontanini/Los Angeles Times Photographic Archive/Department of Special Collections,
Charles E. Young Research Library, UCLA

Ann Getty departing her mansion in San Francisco,
aided by footman Frank Parkes (right) and butler Francis Bullimore,
photographed by Horst for *Vogue*, 1977

Horst P. Horst/Vogue/© Condé Nast

ABOVE: Gordon and Ann in their Pacific Heights drawing room, 1988, photographed by Jonathan Becker

© Jonathan Becker

RIGHT: Billy and Vanessa Getty, Davis Symphony Hall, San Francisco, 2007

© Drew Altizer

Ivy Getty at the amfAR Cannes Gala, 2019

David Fisher/Shutterstock

never have happened without the support of Anne Earhart, the president of the Marisla Foundation. Anne's philanthropic strategy was to look for people with passion and give them whatever they needed to get the job done."

When Anne received her Carnegie Medal, Serge Dedina—now the mayor of California's southernmost city, Imperial Beach, and the director of his own nonprofit, Wildcoast—recalled her support. "Anne has this really quiet presence. Not everybody knows the work she does. But she's out there, kind of like a coach, pushing everybody forward. She's like that surfer on the beach that watches the gnarliest waves on the biggest day of the year, and instead of watching it from the beach, she decides to paddle out."

She inspires others to paddle out too, he added, because they know she has their backs: "She is always there for you when you are an activist in a heavy situation."

As she concluded her remarks that night at the New York Public Library, Anne explained how her meeting with the gray whales had set the direction of her philanthropy: Initially she focused on marine mammals because they were her passion. Soon enough she realized that these animals were "the canaries in the coal mine, as they filled up with the toxins that were dumped into the oceans, the plastics that were becoming ubiquitous in the sea, and the specter of climate change."

Some progess has been made, she allowed—gray whales are still swimming the 10,000 miles to Laguna San Ignacio to mate. But with warming water in the Arctic endangering their feeding grounds, this is "an all-hands-on-deck moment," she declared: "We are not separate from these sentient beings. . . . We need to understand we are one community and now is the time for service to that community in any and every way that we can."

With annual giving of around $50 million, Marisla has in recent years provided funding to more than six hundred nonprofits that work to address global environmental challenges. According to a Carnegie release, Earhart-funded philanthropy has helped preserve 4.5 million square miles "and counting" of ocean.

A board member of another conservation foundation described Marisla as "absolutely top-notch. . . . They really do their homework and pick the most worthy grantees to support. They go the extra mile and do things no other foundation does, like providing enhanced security to environmental defenders. In many parts of the world, these people are in real danger.

"They are caring, thoughtful people," he added. "Anne is quite soft-spoken. She doesn't speak often [she prefers to remain in the background, leaving most of the public work to Marisla's executive director Herbert M. Bedolfe III]. But when she does, she speaks forcefully, and is very well-informed."

Sara Earhart Lowell shares her mother's interests. After graduating from Laguna Beach High School and the University of California, Santa Cruz, where she double-majored in environmental studies and Latin American history, she worked as a tour guide in Laguna San Ignacio. For her master's degree in marine affairs, which she earned in 2008 from the University of Washington, her thesis examined the impact of ecotourism on the Laguna population. An Orange County resident, she has served as the Marisla Foundation's marine program director since 2016. She oversees efforts to create protected marine areas, advance sustainable fisheries, and protect coastal lands in California, Hawaii, Baja California, Chile, and the broader Pacific.

Another thing mother and daughter have in common is an aversion to the press. "We prefer to keep a low profile," Sara said, turning down a request for an interview. Her brother, Nicholas, expressed reticence as well. "I'm just not comfortable appearing in a book about my family [or] talking about my kinfolk," he wrote in a polite email. Furthermore, he felt that people "would take no pleasure in reading about the pallid and humdrum events of my daily life. It mostly consists of writing, fly-fishing, and golfing."

"Nico" Earhart is a writer and adventurer. He has posted a number of his pieces on his website and blog, the Wind-Blown Golfer. Since graduating in 2008 from the University of Denver, where he majored in international/global studies, he has made Colorado (his maternal grandmother's birthplace) his home. From there he travels to the Australian outback, the Alaskan Great North, and other far-flung locations to write about his sporting pursuits, including fly-fishing and surfing but primarily golfing. "There are no limits to where my golf bag and I will go," the bio on his site says.

A foodie too, he apprenticed at a restaurant in Italy, then returned home to the Rocky Mountains to continue his culinary progress, which he described in his piece "Coming to Fruition."

During his six months in Northern Italy, he had worked eighteen-hour days without compensation, mostly in a damp, chilly basement—peeling potatoes, hand-rolling gnocchi, "and dispatching and butchering every woodland creature under the canopy." It was all worth it: the twenty-four-year-old chef upstairs was that good.

"And now, here I was back in the U.S., ready to grab the Denver culinary scene by the throat," Nicholas continued. His foray into a Colorado kitchen, under the thumb of a sadistic chef, was short-lived, but it made for an engaging piece.

"Claire Getty, daughter of Mrs. Gloria Getty of Hillsborough, was feted at a family dinner marking her election as senior class president at Castilleja School in Palo Alto," the *Times* of San Mateo, California, reported in 1972, in one of the rare newspaper items about George II and Gloria's middle daughter. "Claire plans to attend the University of Salzburg in the fall, where she will study music and languages and will be accompanied on a pre-college trip to Europe by her sisters. . . . En route, the three girls will stop in Denver to visit their maternal grandparents. . . . They will also plan a stop in London with their paternal grandfather, J. Paul Getty."

Like other Gettys before her, Claire was captivated by European art; given her interests, her grandfather's masterpiece-laden house alone provided much to study. She spent a few years in Europe during the mid-1970s, during which she gave birth to her first son, Beau. According to John Pearson's book, Beau was born "as a result of a love affair with an Italian she met at Perugia University."

In 1980, she was living in Washington, DC, and enrolled at Georgetown University's School of Foreign Service. As she pursued her degree in international economics, which she received in 1983, complicated issues surrounding Getty Oil and the management of the Sarah C. Getty Trust were demanding her attention too. She was the first of the sisters to contact their father's younger brother to question the control he was beginning to assert. "Dear Uncle Gordon," read a handwritten letter she composed to him. "I do not mean to be critical of you, but I think you would admit that your business management background is limited."

Nevertheless, she, like her sisters, wanted to stay out of the papers. "If you want a story, try my uncle Gordon. He enjoys publicity. We don't," she said to a reporter who managed to get her on the phone around that time.

While an undergraduate, she also helped found a major new museum in Washington.

Art collector and patron Wilhelmina Cole Holladay had long harbored a dream to open a museum of works by female artists, which would be run by women. Throughout the 1970s, she organized countless meetings, trying to drum up enthusiasm as well as financial backing for her pie-in-the-sky idea. Thus far, it hadn't crystallized. But it was about to.

"An experience with a new neighbor brought it to a head," Holladay wrote in her 2008 memoir, *A Museum of Their Own*. "A young woman who had come to study at Georgetown University moved in the house next door to ours on R Street NW. Claire, who turned out to be an attractive girl; her fiancé, a former member of the Peace

Corps; a darling three-year-old boy; and their Great Dane brought to our quiet street a lively household." (Claire's future husband, Noel Perry, a Rhode Island native, had served for two years as a Peace Corps volunteer in Yemen.)

Holladay first met the couple after their dog left a mess on her driveway, which Holladay's husband stepped into.

"That evening the doorbell rang, and there on the threshold stood two sweet young things, almost in tears. 'We're so sorry,' Claire blurted out. 'We just want to be good neighbors.'" A few weeks later, Claire was at her front door again, this time in a panic. Beau had fallen and cut his head. Wilhelmina called her grandchildren's pediatrician, and all was soon fine. A grateful Claire asked Wilhelmina what she was involved in. Informed about the museum idea, Claire perked up. "I find that fascinating," she said, as Holladay elaborated in an oral history she conducted with the Smithsonian Institution's Archives of American Art.

As it happened, a meeting was on the calendar for the next Tuesday with a group of young women, a junior committee; Holladay invited her neighbor to drop in:

"Claire attended, became excited, and declared, 'A building is needed.' I replied, 'Someday, my dear.' She said, 'You know, Mrs. Holladay, I really want to help.' And I said, 'Well, tell me what committee you want to be on and we'll do something about that.' And she said, 'No, I mean I really want to help.' And I said, 'Well, that's wonderful, my dear . . . we'll talk about it.'"

With that, Claire had to rush out to a class, at which point one of the other girls piped up, "Is that Claire *Getty*? As in J. Paul?"

"It had never occurred to me," Holladay recalled.

Soon enough, after a discussion Claire had with her financial advisor, she pledged $1 million to start a building fund; she got her sister Caroline to come across with the same amount. (Gloria became involved in fund-raising events too.) The gifts were instrumental in finally making the museum a reality. In 1983, a 70,000-square-foot former Masonic Temple was purchased for $5 million. After extensive renovations of the 1908 building, a few blocks from the White House, the National Museum of Women in the Arts opened in 1987. It is still the only major museum in the world dedicated exclusively to recognizing the achievements of women artists.

In 1995, Claire earned a PhD in art history from Stanford University, after working on it for a decade. Along the way she and Noel had been raising Beau and the four boys they had together in the 1980s. Byron was born just three months before she began graduate school at Stanford. Twins Somerset and Sebastian arrived next, and finally Winslow, the baby of the family.

When the family settled into their home in the community of Woodside, near Stanford, they spearheaded a drive to plant three hundred little oak trees along a forlorn stretch of Cañada Road, at the entrance to the town.

The university embarked on a major project to rebuild its art museum. When it opened in 1894, the neoclassical Leland Stanford Jr. Museum was the largest privately owned museum in America. It was built by Jane and Leland Stanford as a memorial to their only child, a lover of European art who died of typhoid at age fifteen.

The museum had bad luck. The 1906 earthquake wrecked much of it. During World War II it was closed altogether. Portions were rebuilt in the 1960s; then the 1989 Loma Prieta earthquake decimated it again. When it finally reopened in January 1999—renamed the Iris & B. Gerald Cantor Center for Visual Arts at Stanford University—Dr. Claire Perry was its curator of American art. She curated its inaugural exhibition, *Pacific Arcadia: Images of California, 1600–1915*, which was based on the dissertation she wrote for her doctorate. (Oxford University Press published the accompanying 256-page catalog, the first of several books she has written.)

Pacific Arcadia illustrated how, over five centuries, the idea of the

"California dream" came to be. The notion of abundance, the promised plenty of the Golden State, was at the heart of the show. To mount the show, Claire sifted through masses of images—paintings, drawings, maps, photographs, newspaper and book illustrations, printed ephemera—before ultimately selecting the works to display. Perhaps not unlike the way her grandfather prospected for oil, digging through layers and layers of sand and shale before finally striking black gold, she mined for ideas. She focused on how, beginning in the seventeenth century, with the creation of elaborate maps and depictions of fertile valleys and other natural wonders, the concept of the Golden State had been marketed and promoted by merchants, railroad owners, financiers, and real estate speculators in order to lure settlers. They presented the state as the ultimate fulfillment of the American dream and established it as a land of infinite possibilities in the mind of the American public.

Claire investigated American culture in other exhibitions and books. *American ABC,* which opened in 2006 at the Smithsonian American Art Museum in Washington, DC, scrutinized childhood in nineteenth-century America. In 2011, *The Great American Hall of Wonders,* also at the Smithsonian, examined nineteenth-century America through the lens of its technological innovations and native ingenuity. *California: The Art of Water,* a 2016 show at the Cantor Center, where Claire is now a guest curator, examined the state's complicated water story through works by a diverse roster of artists, including Albert Bierstadt, David Hockney, and Ansel Adams. For the exhibition, she successfully lobbied to have the walls of the galleries painted swimming-pool turquoise.

Like others in her family, Claire supports environmental causes, and in doing so she has tangled with powerful interests. In the fall of 2010, a ballot initiative that would have suspended California's greenhouse gas law, Proposition 23, was gaining steam. Big money from oil-related interests—including $1 million from Koch Industries—was pouring in to stoke the Yes campaign for the measure. It seemed like a David vs. Goliath situation, in which the environmentalists would be crushed. Claire stepped up to help fund the No campaign with two $250,000 contributions over the next weeks. The tide turned, and the measure failed in the November voting.

Since his days building water projects in rural Yemeni villages with the Peace Corps, Noel Perry has been a green advocate too. He established Baccharis Capital, one of the early "socially responsible" venture capital funds, which has invested in education and health-oriented consumer products, including organic foods. An amateur painter and sculptor, he founded several nonprofits, including 100 Families Oakland. Dozens of multigenerational families from across the city were brought together in workshops over ten weeks, where they were taught to paint, quilt, and sculpt. "Possibilities happen when you get around a block of clay: people learn about themselves and others—how to work together. . . . It's mind-expanding," Perry told a community newspaper, which described him as "intensely private."

Both Claire and Anne married men who shared their aversion to publicity. "We are private people and trying to remain that way. People hate rich people," one of the husbands once explained.

The oak trees that the Perrys helped plant on Cañada Road grew into a veritable forest. When Beau, their eldest, grew up, he planted something of a forest of his own, underwater. A mariculturist, he is the largest grower of seaweed on the Pacific Coast of North America.

"I have loved seaweed all my life. As a surfer I've spent an eternity bobbing up and down amidst California's kelp forests—often getting it tangled around my legs, fins, or leash. Sometimes I'll even chew on a nice-looking frond while waiting for the next set of waves," he wrote on Instagram.

"Travelling the coast you can find surf spots with a variety of kelp beds—giant kelp, bull kelp, sea palm, the list goes on and on—and they feel as different to me as beech, redwood, or oak forests. When the water is clear you can see them waving in the current under the board, parting occasionally to reveal the vibrant life beneath the canopy—fish, crab, lobster, urchins, anemones, octopi. . . ."

Following in his mother's footsteps, Beau earned his undergraduate degree in 1999 at Georgetown, where he majored in foreign service and international relations and affairs. At the Presidio Graduate School, he got an MBA in sustainable business. Like his aunt Anne, he traveled to Baja California. Instead of the plights of whales, it was the effects of overfishing and destructive seafood farming practices that alarmed him.

Blue Evolution, the company he founded in 2013 in Los Altos, another San Francisco Peninsula town, began propagating seaweed in onshore tanks in Baja. In 2014, he expanded and went north, heading to Alaska's Kodiak Island, in perhaps the same pioneering spirit with which his great-grandfather arrived in Bartlesville. Perry was among the first entrepreneurs who saw the potential to cultivate seaweed in these waters.

His company contracts with local fishermen, transforming them into sea farmers in winter—the growing season for seaweed and the off-season for fishing. Blue Evolution provides them with the seed stock, which it makes by extracting spores from wild kelp; the seedlings are grown on pieces of string known as seed pipes, then given to the farmers, who wind the string along long ropes that are suspended from a floating frame in the ocean. After the "planting" is done in late November, the ribbons of kelp grow up to a foot a day. Weaving and protecting the lines is arduous. Beau has also involved members of the Indigenous population: the seaweed, once harvested, is processed at a facility in Kodiak owned by the Sun'aq Tribe.

Now the largest commercial seaweed hatchery in the US, Blue Evolution is at the forefront of sustainable marine aquaculture. Some of its seaweed is blanched and frozen and sold to restaurants and food service operations throughout the country. The company also sells a line of seaweed-infused products, including pastas and pop-corns, under its own label. "Blue crops" have the potential to change the climate equation. Seaweed requires only sunlight and seawater to grow—no expenditures of energy, fresh water, fertilizer, or pesticides. And seaweeds naturally detox the ocean through photosynthesis, helping to combat marine acidification and global warming.

In May, Beau and his cohorts haul up the fruits of their labors—tons and tons of slimy green bunches. "Harvesting dawn to dusk. I'm really proud of the crop this year and the hard work put in by all. Major increase and improvement over last year," read a 2019 tweet from @beaugperry ("Dad, sea farmer, surfer, Founder and CEO of Blue Evolution"). Two years later, *Vegworld* magazine reported that his eight-year-old animal rights activist son was already supporting his plant-powered endeavors.

In a family so press averse, Byron is something of an outlier. In 2011, when he was twenty-seven, he founded an unconventional media enterprise out of his apartment in Bangkok.

His trajectory began when he was an undergraduate at George-town. English was his major, but he took a journalism class his senior year. "Something clicked," he said.

After graduation, he worked as a fact-checker for *San Francisco* magazine, then as a copy editor and writer in Los Angeles at *Variety*, where his responsibilities included coming up with the pun-laden headlines for which the publication is known.

When he got laid off during the crash of 2009, he embarked on a trip to South America and Asia. Southeast Asia appealed to him, so he looked for a job there, and landed one with the *Phnom Penh Post*, Cambodia's leading English-language newspaper. He wasn't stationed in the capital city, but in sleepier Siem Reap (home of the historic Buddhist temple Angkor Wat), where he found his stories riding around on his bike.

He moved on to Bangkok, Thailand, where the city's brashness and quirkiness fascinated him. "I saw there was an opportunity. Nobody was covering all the really weird, crazy stuff happening, in English," said Byron, a burly, bearded fellow with an easygoing manner.

He started a local-news website, which he called Coconuts Bangkok. ("Brands named after fruits have done pretty well," he reasoned.)

Launching it on a shoestring, he wrote and produced everything himself the first year. He got traction through posts he shared on Facebook. Thanks to a couple of small, successful angel-investor rounds, he was able to expand operations. Coconut Media is now an English-language news and video network that reaches up to 26 million people per month in eight cities across Southeast Asia, with a staff of about twenty-five. Coconuts TV, its video production arm, makes documentaries and films that have appeared on networks such as Discovery and streaming platforms including Netflix.

Coconuts takes an irreverent approach to most of its coverage, but has also produced insightful coverage of democracy protests in Hong Kong, the catastrophic floods in Bangkok, and Covid-19's impact across Asia, among other stories.

Byron's brother Sebastian has been a creative collaborator. He produced and hosted several films. *Highland*, a docuseries about Thailand's cannabis legalization movement, was acquired by Netflix, while *Hijab Riders*, a look at a group of women shaking up the male-dominated world of motorbike racing in Malaysia, received an award for Excellence in Video Reporting from the Society of Publishers in Asia. In *Nagaland: Twilight of the Headhunters*, Sebastian took viewers on a journey through Nagaland, an isolated corner of India sandwiched between Myanmar and the Himalayas, where he tracked down some of the last living Naga headhunters, as well as the new generation of Naga.

The other Perry brothers live in the Bay Area. Somerset, another Georgetown graduate, received his JD from the University of California, Berkeley School of Law in 2013. Since 2015, he has been deputy attorney general in the Environmental Section of the California Department of Justice. Winslow, the baby of the family, an intern at UCSF Medical Center, directed *The Edge of Purpose*, a forty-one-minute documentary, in 2019, which focused on nine people from different backgrounds who followed their passions as they built unique routes to success.

In this very discreet branch of the Gettys, the most private one of all has been Caroline, George and Gloria's youngest daughter. Though she's now in her early sixties, her name has appeared in the press only a handful of times.

In 1976, she was mentioned in a society column covering a wedding in Walla Walla, Washington: "Flying in for the party are Gloria Getty and her daughter Caroline (a student at Reed College)."

Academically rigorous Reed College, founded in 1908 in Portland, Oregon, was a haven for antiwar activists, hippies, and nonconformists of all stripes during the 1960s and '70s. Sweatshirts worn by many students during that era bore their unofficial motto: "Communism, Atheism, Free Love."

In 1989, Caroline was accorded a distinction she probably didn't like—being the youngest person on the Forbes 400 list; at age thirty-two, she ranked as the 322nd-richest American, with $330 million. (Her sisters, ranked alongside her, possessed equal fortunes.)

The anonymity she has enjoyed since was broken only around 2002, when a series of headlines began appearing in California papers about a "mystery donor" who had contributed $1 million to an advocacy group, the Nature Conservancy, enabling it to campaign on behalf of three state ballot propositions, all intended to protect clean water, open spaces, and farmland, among other wholesome things.

Self-appointed "watchdog groups" began digging around for the identity of this secret donor, whose contributions were made under the names of mysterious-sounding LLCs, one of which was named, yes, Rosebud.

Caroline was eventually outed as the donor, and identified as a resident of Corona del Mar in Orange County. After she gave the Nature Conservancy permission to confirm that she had written the checks, her troubles were hardly over. The California Fair Political Practices Commission filed a thirteen-page lawsuit against her, seeking $520,000 in penalties and asserting that she had used the LLCs (another was named Wild Rose) as conduits to disguise that the money was coming from her personal trust account. "Panel Accuses Getty Heiress of 'Campaign Money Laundering,'" blared a headline in the *Los Angeles Times*.

She refused to admit any wrongdoing, but in March 2004, a settlement was reached. Getty agreed to pay a $135,000 penalty. Her lawyer issued a statement saying that she and her company settled the case to resolve the matter and "recommit their full attention to California's critical conservation needs." The attorney also called on the state to clarify its vague campaign reporting requirements "so that other civic-minded and well-intentioned individuals won't be discouraged from supporting the environment or other worthy causes."

One can understand, then, why Caroline and her sisters prefer to remain anonymous.

4

The Ronald Line

Of J. Paul Getty's five sons, Jean Ronald, the second, was the only one born and reared on European soil. (His younger half brother Paul Jr. came into the world on European waters, off the coast of Italy, but he was quickly bundled up and brought back to Los Angeles.)

In the wake of the stock market crash, Paul barely made it to the Berlin hospital before Fini, his third wife, went into labor on December 19, 1929. Four months later, when his father was stricken, Paul raced back to Los Angeles alone. As war clouds gathered, Fini and Ronald remained in Germany as long as they could, then took refuge in Switzerland. In 1939, after the Nazis arrested her anti-Hitler, staunchly Catholic father, they fled to California.

Ten-year-old, German-speaking Ronald was a European at heart, and remained so all his life. He established the most predominantly international branch of the family. It is also the only one that has no public record of tragedies or substance addictions. Ronald's progeny appear to possess, overall, the sunniest dispositions in the extended family.

Their oceanic crossings sometimes went in surprising directions. Homesick Fini had broken up with Paul (their divorce decree came in 1932) in order to raise Ronald in Germany. The war forced them to return to California for safety—but, after peace was restored, she didn't repatriate. She remained a Los Angeleno until her death in 2009 at age ninety-nine.

Living in Beverly Hills, she never remarried, but she was no loner. "I think she had lots of boyfriends," recalled her grandson Christopher. "She kept herself very trim and fit. In her mid-eighties, she had better legs than many girls I was dating."

Ronald, by most accounts the quietest of the brothers, graduated in 1951 from USC, where he studied business. Capitalizing on his German-language fluency, Paul sent him to Hamburg to run Veedol, Tidewater Oil's German subsidiary.

In 1964, in a church near Hamburg, thirty-four-year-old Ronald— six feet four, dark-haired, with a pencil mustache—said "Ja" when he married Karin Seibel, twenty-one, the blond daughter of a Lübeck businessman. They had met three years earlier at a ball in Hamburg— where the couple remained for a year following their wedding, and had Christopher, the first of their four children. English was Ronald's third language. After German, he learned French when the family relocated to Paris. Over the next decade, as the family moved back and forth between Europe, California, and South Africa, Karin gave birth to Stephanie, Cecilia, and Christina in, respectively, 1967, 1970, and 1975.

Thanks to his parents' acrimonious divorce and the wealth of his maternal grandfather, Ronald was virtually excluded from the Sarah C. Getty Trust (though his children are beneficiaries of it). The unforeseen loss of the Helmle fortune during the war put him on a considerably lower financial footing than his half brothers. But he was still a multimillionaire, thanks to gifts from his paternal grandmother, Sarah.

In the late 1960s and early 1970s, he executive-produced and financed a few movies, including *Flareup*, a thriller starring Raquel Welch, which was released by MGM, and Warner Bros.' *Zeppelin*, a World War I aerial spectacle starring Michael York and Elke Sommer. The films had respectable runs and generated a fair amount of buzz, thanks to their high-profile stars and the last name of the producer. But it was the pursuit of profit, not glamour, that motivated him to invest in movies, as the normally press-shy Ronald said in a few interviews he gave ahead of the October 1971 premiere of *Zeppelin*. He revealed little else. "I've been an avid moviegoer for many years. . . . I don't believe in following the crowd," he said in a sit-down with the *Los Angeles Times*, in which he was described as "unostentatious in manner."

In the early 1980s, he invested tens of millions into a large hotel development near Los Angeles International Airport. It was ill-timed, coinciding with the onset of a deep recession and a glut of newly built properties on the market. In order to keep the development afloat, Ronald personally guaranteed its debts. Nevertheless, the project went bust, after which creditors pursued him over the next decade, eventually leading him to file for bankruptcy in 1992 in San Juan, Puerto Rico, where he and Karin had moved. After they resolved their financial difficulties, the couple settled in Munich, Germany, where Ronald died at age eighty-one in 2010.

As a widow, Karin took up residency in America again, moving to Miami Beach, where her youngest daughter, Christina, resides. Meanwhile, Stephanie and Cecilia (who is called Cecily by family and friends) straddle the hemispheres: each divides her time between South Africa and various locations in Europe (England, Germany, Austria).

During his young adult years, Christopher lived in California, New York, Brazil, Russia, and England, among other places. A few years ago, he settled in Rome.

So, while some Gettys remain elusive due to their penchant for privacy, with others perhaps it's a factor of their peripatetic natures.

While they crisscross the globe, groupings of Gettys alight in certain places at certain times, such as the London "Season." Commencing in May with the opening of the Chelsea Flower Show, the Season's a succession of splendid events, including the Royal Ascot races and Wimbledon, that draws the beau monde to London.

The V&A Summer Party, held in the Victoria and Albert Museum's courtyard garden, is perhaps the Season's smartest invitation. The June 2019 edition, hosted by Nicholas Coleridge, head of Condé Nast Britain, drew a microcosm of England's elite, including former prime minister David Cameron, three dukes, four Windsors, Dame Joan Collins, Lord Andrew Lloyd Webber, singer Kylie Minogue, artist Grayson Perry, and actress Cressida Bonas (an ex of Prince Harry's). Among the Gettys in attendance: San Francisco–born Ivy Getty, twenty-four, Gordon's granddaughter (dashing around with American paper heir Peter Brant Jr.); Mark's middle son, Joseph, and his fashion-plate wife, Sabine (*Vogue* pronounced her elegant cream three-piece Yves Saint Laurent suit "ravishing"); and a Getty relation by marriage, Princess Marie-Chantal of Greece.

As readers of glossy magazines in the 1990s will recall, Marie-Chantal and her sisters, Pia and Alexandra—daughters of "duty-free" billionaire Robert Miller and his wife, Chantal—made the most brilliant marriages since the Cushing sisters some fifty years earlier.

Pia, the eldest, got to the altar first, with Christopher Getty. In 1992, they tied the knot on a mountaintop in Bali. Native attendants dressed the bride and groom in brightly colored sarongs and elaborate golden headpieces; Balinese tribesmen transported them on ornate litters up to the temple. Scores of children showered them with rose petals. One of the hundred friends and family members who attended the ceremony described it as a "fantasy production worthy of Cecil B. DeMille." (A minister from Boston conducted a quiet Christian-faith service beforehand.)

Three years hence, nearly every crowned head in Europe gathered in London for the wedding of Marie-Chantal to Crown Prince Pavlos of Greece—a critical mass of royals hardly seen since the wedding of Queen Elizabeth and Prince Philip, who were among the guests. The monumental festivities celebrating the union included a ball featuring a re-creation of the Parthenon.

Within a few months, Alexandra marched down the aisle with Prince Alexander Egon von Fürstenberg, scion of a thousand-year-old dynasty begun during the Holy Roman Empire, at Manhattan's St. Ignatius Loyola Church, where the pews were crammed with a good portion of the *Almanach de Gotha*.

As the 1990s unfolded, the young couples enlivened Manhattan society significantly. After Marie-Chantal threw a rollicking Roaring Twenties–themed party at the Cotton Club in Harlem to celebrate Pavlos's thirtieth, Pia one-upped her with a cross-dressing party for Christopher's next birthday, at their house in Southampton. The sisters, like most of the female guests, wore tuxedos and top hats, while the brothers-in-law transformed themselves into *la dolce vita* icons— Pavlos was Gina Lollobrigida and Christopher Anita Ekberg.

The elder two Miller sisters did not meet their Prince Charmings by chance. They were carefully matched up by longtime Getty family consigliere Alecko Papamarkou.

J. Paul Getty met him in the 1960s at Woburn Abbey, where both were guests of the Duke of Bedford. Papamarkou, then a young BBC Radio journalist, became a stockbroker, as well as a frequent visitor to Sutton Place, where he and Ann Getty hit it off on her visits from San Francisco. The Princeton-educated son of a Greek government minister, he became a close friend and investment advisor to the family. With his gregarious personality, he amassed an unrivaled list of friends in high places, becoming, in the words of writer and bon vivant Taki Theodoracopulos, a fellow Greek, "the Sir Edmund Hillary of social mountaineering." As Papamarkou invested his clients' money, he also enriched their social and personal lives. What good is having all the money in the world if you don't know how to spend it, or, worse, if nobody knows who you are? As lore has it, it was a teen-age Marie-Chantal who, having heard about Papamarkou, lobbied her father to hire him, which he did. He subsequently stood as her godfather when she converted from Catholicism to the Greek Ortho-dox religion before her marriage.

"Alecko was the ultimate connector—whether it was people's business or romantic lives," said Marie-Chantal. "He was great with the guys, he was great with the women, and he mixed together their children. He made sure people were connected."

According to Marc Leland, a financial advisor to Gordon Getty (who spoke before Papamarkou's death), "He manages to balance an enormous amount on the head of a pin. He is one of the few people who can talk everyone's language: money managers, major investors, socialites. . . ."

Christopher and Pia Getty—amicably divorced since 2005—were unable to make it to the V&A that evening in 2019 as they were making their way back from day two of Royal Ascot with the eldest of their four children, Isabel, an artist and musician who was born in 1993. The proud parents had viewed an artwork Royal Ascot com-missioned Isabel to create, or remake, as it were. She was asked to paint one of the benches along the track in the Royal Enclosure. Just above it sat the Queen, Prince Charles and the Duchess of Cornwall, and other members of the royal family. Isabel transformed the bench with crosshatching inspired by the forms and colors of Viennese Secessionists Egon Schiele and Gustav Klimt.

Per the strict rules for visitors to the Royal Enclosure, the Gettys were in regulation attire—top hat and morning coat for him; dresses "of modest length . . . with straps of one inch or greater" and fanci-ful hats for the ladies. A mass of violet-hued feathers extended from Isabel's bonnet.

The same week, Christopher attended a cocktail party in honor of

American supporters of Prince Charles's charities at Clarence House, official residence of the Prince of Wales and the Duchess of Cornwall. Square-jawed and wearing horn-rimmed glasses, he was handsome and affable, chatting about his new apartment in Rome.

That weekend, an exhibition of photographs by Nick Knight opened at Albion Barn in Oxfordshire. Afterward gallerist Michael Hue-Williams hosted a lively lunch on the bucolic grounds for a fashionable group. Isabel was among them, now clad in a fringed suede jacket, jeans, and biker boots.

Born in New York City, where she spent her early childhood in her parents' six-story townhouse on the Upper East Side, she's a picture of transatlantic poise. "To my English friends, I'm a foreign friend. To my American friends, I'm English," she said. At age eight, around the time her parents separated, Isabel moved with her mother to London; enrolled first at Harrodian, she later boarded in Switzerland at Le Rosey, Pia's alma mater, where she was a member of the choir and the school band. For college it was back to the States. Isabel arrived at New York University thinking she should study law or business, but music, she decided, made her happiest. She transferred to NYU's Clive Davis Institute of Recorded Music. But despite her boarding-school vocalizing, the idea of performing solo frightened her. Of all people, it was Diana Ross who helped her get over her stage fright. It was May 2013, at Farmington Lodge, Marie-Chantal and Pavlos's eighteenth-century manor house in England's Cotswolds, where four hundred guests had gathered to celebrate her maternal grandfather's eightieth birthday. At one point, Ross, the gala's entertainer, pulled Isabel onstage. *It's Diana Ross passing you the mike—you better bloody sing*, she remembers thinking to herself in panic. Isabel deftly belted some classic Supremes lines. "It was pretty epic," she recalled.

After graduating from NYU in 2016, she moved back to London, celebrating with a *Midsummer Night's Dream* theme party for three hundred friends at One Marylebone (she went as a fairy in a gold Oscar de la Renta gown), and temporarily reclaiming her room in her mother's Knightsbridge mansion. Pia, who is regarded as the bohemian one among her sisters, had just launched a film production company, Pia Pressure, which aims to support emerging talent—particularly female—from underrepresented backgrounds. Toward that goal, Pia (who has directed multiple documentaries) created the Pia Pressure Award. That year, it was bestowed on two young British filmmakers—Johnny Kenton and Debs Paterson—who each received a $35,000 grant.

That fall, Isabel landed on the cover of *Tatler*, wearing a silk-velvet coat by Etro ("The Heiress: Glamour, Talent, Two Fortunes . . . Yes, Isabel Getty Has It All," read the cover lines), and then on Dolce & Gabbana's runway in Milan, where she walked in the designers' Fall/Winter 2017 show.

With two friends—Ali on guitar and James on keys—she formed a band, Jean Marlow. (Its first name was a nod to actress Jean Harlow, the last to sixteenth-century English poet Christopher Marlowe.) Isabel identified herself—the group's singer-songwriter—as Izzy Getty. "I still had terrible stage fright. It's easier—there is more freedom—in going by another name. I liked the concept of creating this other persona when I go onstage." Getty's voice is soft, slightly raspy; the band has a soulful, grunge, soft-rock sound. "We're die-hard acoustic musicians," said Isabel. On Spotify and iTunes, they have released several EPs, with titles including "Spin" and "Run Leon," for which she drew the album art. In 2020, following a stay in Los Angeles, where Isabel had retreated during the lockdown months, the group released "Santana Winds," a hypnotic ballad inspired by Southern California's fierce and sometimes evil autumn winds.

"There was so much destruction going on," she recalled a year later, by phone from Gstaad, Switzerland. By this time, things were considerably brighter. Working remotely, she had been helping her father manage real estate investments, primarily in Germany and Portugal. She had just returned from Mykonos in Greece, where she and her South African–reared cousin Vanessa Waibel staged a high-spirited bachelorette weekend for their San Francisco relation Ivy Getty. Photos of the girls—at one point in matching pink hot pants, dancing stageside at Jackie O', the fashionable beach club—splashed across Instagram and the *Daily Mail*. (Ivy's elaborate wedding that November would draw much coverage too.)

"They are like sisters—we grew up together," Isabel said of Vanessa and Ivy. (Living thousands of miles apart is no hindrance in this family.) "I'm very close to a lot of my cousins. . . . I feel very fortunate—a lot of people don't get along with their families."

Isabel acknowledged that her family has had its troubles. But she puts them in perspective. "Everyone has tragedies in their families. It's just that ours have been more public. There has been a lot of suffering, but that's why it's important to stay grounded and together."

That September, Isabel moved back to New York to study for her MBA at Columbia Business School, while simultaneously pursuing her musical career. "I've always followed my own path. I don't like to be dependent on anyone," she said. "I want to make my own way."

Christopher is not the first Getty to reside in Rome. "This is where my grandfather would spend the winters. He felt very happy here," he said. It was during those stays that J. Paul Getty visited the Capitoline Museums and became inspired to found his museum in Malibu. "This classical civilization, this humanist tradition, is what they aspired to," Christopher said, referencing also his paternal great-grandparents. "They were austere Scottish peasants who hooked into this worldview."

The city continues to cast its spell on their descendants. Aside from the obvious charm of Roman life, Christopher said he also enjoyed the disorder endemic to it. "They give you just the right amount of grit," he said.

He was eleven when his grandfather passed away, but memories endure. "Sutton Place was the most fun place in the world," he recalled. Every night before dinner, they would watch the lions being fed. Family meals were punctuated by amusing banter about which truants might be thrown to the beasts. There was a golf buggy he could sneak off with, to tear around the grounds. But once, as he was plowing through the prized rose garden, he looked up at the house and saw his grandfather staring down from a window. That night at dinner, not a word was said about it, surprisingly. But the next morning, when Christopher jumped into the buggy for another spin, the battery had been removed.

"That was him," he said. "I remember him as a very calm man. He was not a shouter. He was very easy—easier than many grandfathers I've come across. That was my view as a child, and sometimes a child has the best view."

The world's richest man was "almost a bit of a hippie," he added. "He could have been a beachcomber . . . he was never part of the Establishment . . . he was not a mainstream character."

The tougher one was Grandmother Fini, who, he noted, remained true to her Germanic stock till the end: "She didn't have any sense of humor!"

Christopher's middle son, Conrad, a graduate of Harrow in England, was attending Berkeley, where he was excelling in math—a first for a Getty, Christopher claimed—as well as physics, which was a subject Conrad's great-uncle Gordon enjoyed discussing with him during their weekly dinners at Gordon's mansion in Pacific Heights.

While his youngest, Max (short for Maximus), is an undergraduate at NYU, the eldest son, Robert ("Bob"), is a budding filmmaker. He has directed several short movies, including a horror flick, *Unbaptism*, in which two priests find themselves trapped by evil when they arrive at a remote house to investigate paranormal activity, and *Untitled Chat Show*, a comedy about a failed talk show pilot in 1978 (which carries a credit for Pia Miller in the role of "hippie").

"They're all coming along nicely," Christopher observed of his offspring. He expressed the same sentiment about the close-knit cousinage to which they belong. (Marie-Chantal and Pavlos have five children; Alexandra and Alexander, who were divorced in 2002, have three.) "They're all good kids . . . they run in a pack," he said. All of them attended the lavish ball that Marie-Chantal and Pavlos threw in 2017 for the twenty-first birthday of Princess Olympia, their eldest. Held at Farmington Lodge, it drew a stunning assortment of the royal, the rich, the young, and the beautiful. It was "the party that had everything," the *Daily Mail* reported.

Even as perceptions persist that the clan is riven with strife and factions, the reality, according to Christopher, is different. "Everyone is interested in what other people are doing, and wishing them well," he said.

Members communicate over joint investments too. Christopher was among the founding investors in some of the family's marquee ventures, including Conservation Corporation Africa, Getty Images, and PlumpJack, which began with a small wine store in San Francisco and now produces some of the best Cabernet Sauvignon in the world. "I was the first investor," he said, as he ordered a bottle of excellent Amarone.

A talent for viniculture runs in the family. Christopher's middle sisters, Stephanie Getty-Waibel and Cecilia Getty-du Preez, produce some of South Africa's most internationally lauded bottles, alongside their respective husbands, Alexander Waibel and Pierre du Preez.

Considering their avocation, it's not surprising that a friend of the women used wine vocabulary to describe them—as well as their youngest sibling, Christina: "The girls are all very bubbly and attractive. At first blush, they might seem like dizzy blondes, but they all have depth."

Both the Getty-Waibels and the Getty-du Preezes divide their time between Europe and South Africa's Constantia Valley, where they own adjacent wine-growing estates located on the mountainous slopes overlooking Cape Town and its breathtaking bay.

Alexander Waibel's family history in South Africa goes back to 1950, when his maternal grandfather, Dr. Manfred Thurnher, relocated operations of BMD, the enormous textile business begun by his wife's family, from their native Austria. The reins of the company eventually passed to Manfred's son-in-law, Dieter Waibel, who had five children with Manfred's daughter Rosemarie. Alexander was the firstborn.

In the 1960s, the Cape Town region became a second home for the family when they purchased their 150-acre estate in the valley, where they built country houses and enjoyed rustic life. In fact, the land had been farmed for grapes by Dutch settlers beginning in 1680. Then the acreage was left to lie fallow for centuries.

In the late 1990s, after a mountain fire devastated much of the landscape, Dieter, a lover of Bordeaux wines, hatched the idea to bring the land back to its earlier function. Alexander and Stephanie joined the venture.

It was a mammoth undertaking to clear the ravaged land and plant their vineyards on the steep slopes. Their inaugural Sauvignon Blanc was released in 2007; sales of reds began three years later. When Alexander took over the operation, he and Stephanie stuck faithfully to his late father's vision of creating world-class Bordeaux-style wines. Under their label, Constantia Glen, four premium wines are produced: two reds (Constantia Glen Three and Constantia Glen Five) and two whites (Constantia Glen Sauvignon Blanc and Constantia Glen Two). The numerals reflect the number of Bordeaux varieties in each blend.

With their three daughters—Marietheres, Sigourney, and Vanessa—the Waibels could be a wine dynasty in the making (there is a strong tradition of matrilineal succession in this branch of the family). "They . . . will be the true beneficiaries of what we were doing," said

Alexander, referring to his offspring as well as future generations. "Perhaps they will nod and remark that we knew what we were doing."

Mousy, as their eldest is called, started stomping grapes and pitching in on the farm at the age of ten. Now, on the verge of thirty, she's Constantia Glen's export manager. "I watched Constantia Glen grow from an idea to something bigger," she wrote in a Facebook post. "The fact that I could be part of that process makes me so proud and happy to still be involved in the farm today." Sigourney, meanwhile, is studying for her doctorate in neurotechnology at Imperial College London.

In 2000, another devastating fire swept through the area, and from its ashes sprang Beau Constantia, a vineyard created by Stephanie's sister and brother-in-law.

Coming from a Sunday lunch at Stephanie and Alexander's, Cecilia and Pierre, a South African–born investment banker, noticed a FOR SALE sign on a burnt-out goat farm—a property on even steeper slopes.

They planted vineyards over the 55 acres they acquired, on which they built a modern glass and concrete home, for themselves and their daughter, Lucca, and son, Aidan, born in the first years of the new millennium. They have literally produced a family of wines: Cecily, their Viognier, debuted in 2010 (it received a very respectable 92 points from wine authority Robert Parker). The portfolio grew to include Pierre, a Sauvignon Blanc; Lucca, a Merlot/Cabernet Franc blend; and Aidan, a spicy red blend of 35 percent Shiraz, 23 percent Malbec, 23 percent Petit Verdot, and 19 percent Merlot. In memory of Pierre's mother, there is also Stella, a Shiraz, while Karin, a Blanc de Noir, celebrates Cecilia's German-born Floridian mother.

After the death of her husband, Ronald, in 2010, Karin moved to Miami Beach, where her youngest, Christina, has lived since her wedding in 2002 to investor Arin Maercks, with whom she had three children before their divorce around 2013. An attentive grandmother, Karin has taken well to the South Beach lifestyle, according to one Miamian, who described her as "a live wire." The apple hasn't fallen far from the tree. "She's the life of the party," said another local of Christina. "She has a big personality. But she's down-to-earth too. She doesn't have the airs of someone who grew up in Europe. She's not stuffy."

Given her outgoing character, Miami is an appropriate place for her. "Her impact here is being 'the Miami Getty.' San Francisco is full of Gettys, but she's our only one. Though ninety-nine percent of Miami doesn't know what a Getty is," said a resident.

Along with her fiancé, Juan Pablo Cappello, a Chilean-born lawyer and tech entrepreneur who is the father of three girls, Christina is a cofounder and investor in NUE Life Health, a business start-up that will use psychedelic drugs such as ketamine to treat mental illness. "With one in five women in the United States relying on an antidepressant to get through the day, and with our losing twenty-two veterans a day to suicide, we felt compelled to launch a different kind of mental wellness company," Christina said.

A supporter of worthy institutions such as the Bass Museum of Art and Nicklaus Children's Hospital, Christina is a regular at charity events. She also sends out, biennially, one of South Florida's most coveted invitations—to her "Bad Santa" party, which she usually throws at her house on Sunset Island (where neighbors have included Enrique Iglesias and Lenny Kravitz). In 2018, it outgrew the premises; Christina and Juan Pablo transferred the party to Soho Beach House Miami. Traditionally, the party has been a good-natured exercise in flouting the boundaries of taste, with strippers, dancers, Playboy Bunnies, and bawdy Christmas tree ornaments—"pornaments," as one guest called them.

"It's something we all look forward to," said one prominent Miamian. "It's all in good fun. She just wants her friends to enjoy themselves. She could care less if anybody thinks it's in bad taste. She doesn't care about impressing people."

That outlook, according to someone who knows a variety of Gettys, is a hallmark of the family: "They don't give a fuck about what other people think of them. They're not snobs and they don't think in terms of something being 'correct' or 'incorrect.' In a weird way, they are liberated from that paradigm."

III.

THE PAULS

5

Paul Jr.

Born at sea in 1932, J. Paul Getty Jr. was brought up first in Los Angeles. Around 1945, as he entered his teenage years, he moved to San Francisco. His mother, the madcap Ann, and her fourth husband, attorney Joseph Stanton McInerney, settled Paul and his brother Gordon—fifteen months Paul's junior—into a rambling house on Clay Street. But perhaps *settled* is a word that never applied to the young Gettys. Within a few years, McInerney was gone, and sometimes their gregarious, artistically inclined mother was absent as well, leaving the boys—the only full siblings born to J. Paul Getty— to their own devices. "They were raised by a mother who wasn't always available," recalled Bill Newsom III, their St. Ignatius High School classmate and lifelong best friend.

Paul Jr. was considered the best-looking and most charming of all the Getty brothers. Tall and thin, wearing horn-rimmed glasses, he liked music and literature, which he studied at the University of San Francisco before his army service in Seoul during the Korean War. Abigail Harris, whom he married in January 1956 in a modest ceremony at Our Lady of the Wayside Church on the San Francisco Peninsula, was the outgoing one. Pretty and athletic, Gail was the adored only child of a federal judge. The pair had known each other since childhood, when she attended the Convent of the Sacred Heart; they were sweethearts during her years at Dominican College in Marin County. From the start of their marriage, she tried to curb her husband's drinking. "Paul had been grounded by Gail in the cause of temperance," Bill Newsom remembered about the young couple, who set up housekeeping in Marin County, where they had their first child, J. Paul Getty III, in November 1956.

Everything changed when the young Californians landed in Rome in 1958, just as Federico Fellini began preproduction for *La Dolce Vita*, which would immortalize the decadent, ravishing world of the ancient capital in its postwar years when it was released in 1960.

They had been summoned to Italy by the patriarch, in order for Paul Jr. to begin working at Getty Oil Italiana. But by 1964 the younger Getty had lost interest in business. He began to embrace the counterculture movement—complete with long hair, beard, and a hippie wardrobe that exasperated his father. And the couple had drifted apart. Gail had fallen in love with Lang Jeffries, a handsome American actor who had come to Rome to shoot a television show. (Gail and Lang were married in Rome in 1966, and divorced five years later.)

Though Paul was saddened, their separation was amicable. Bill Willis, a handsome, lanky, gay Tennessean, heard a knock on the door of the antiques emporium he'd opened at the top of the Spanish Steps in the early 1960s. "I'm Paul Getty Junior and this is my wife, Gail," the oil heir said cheerfully. "I'm looking for an apartment for her, because we're separating."

Gail wanted no alimony, but things were more complicated when it came to ironing out details of financial support for their four small children—Paul III, Mark, Aileen, and Ariadne. To figure it out, Paul Jr. and Gail asked Bill Newsom to journey to Rome from San Francisco. Bill—who was also Paul III's godfather—had just graduated from Stanford Law School and become an associate at Lillick,

Geary, Wheat, Adams & Charles. Now he had to choose between staying at the law firm or coming to Rome.

He never regretted his decision to resign. "I saw the world and really got around and had a marvelous time," Newsom said in a series of oral history interviews he recorded in 2008 and 2009 for the Bancroft Library of the University of California, Berkeley. During his several months in Rome, he recalled meeting "some crazy interesting people," such as writer Gore Vidal, and "a lot of freakish people," including the circle of actors around Fellini. "I'm glad I didn't stay at Lillick, Wheat," he said.

The business of negotiating the settlement was resolved pretty easily, on the backs of a few envelopes, over some pleasant dinners. Coming up with rational numbers was challenging, though. Paul's annual trust income was then just $56,000 after taxes. But calculating a sliding-scale percentage of the income he would one day inherit, the figures became "astronomical."

Gail remained a frequent visitor to Sutton Place and in high standing with her former father-in-law: *I am very pleased with Gail and her children*, wrote Paul Sr. in his journal. And on other occasions: *Gail and Paul, Mark, Aileen, and Ariadne arr at 6 from Rome. I admire them. We pass time happily. I am proud of my darlings.*

On a trip to England in 1965, Paul Jr., then thirty-three, met Talitha Pol. She had been born twenty-five years earlier in Java, where her Dutch parents, Willem and Adine Pol, were traveling. When the Nazis invaded the Netherlands, the couple were unable to return home. In Bali, where they sought refuge, they were captured by the Japanese and interned in atrocious prisoner-of-war camps. After their release, Adine died in 1948. Willem then married Poppet John, daughter of the Welsh postimpressionist painter Augustus John.

Poppet was a warm stepmother as Talitha grew up in the family's homes in London and Ramatuelle, in the South of France. Talitha's beauty—almond eyes, alabaster skin, and red-gold hair—blossomed. But people sensed a fragile, wounded quality in her.

After studying acting and dance at the Royal Academy of Dramatic Art, she landed a few parts. She was an extra—one of the thousands—in *Cleopatra* (1963) and had a credible role in Michael Winner's drama *The System* (1964).

About town in London, people were enthralled with Talitha. "Everyone fell in love with her," tastemaker Nicky Haslam recalled.

Talitha even transfixed men not normally attracted to women. She was the only woman who ever "erotically stirred" Rudolf Nureyev. According to the legendary dancer's biographer, Julie Kavanagh, he told several friends he wanted to marry Talitha. "What he was actually seeing was an exquisite, androgynous reflection of himself," Kavanagh wrote.

It was thanks to Nureyev that Talitha and Paul Jr. met, at a dinner party in London hosted by Claus von Bülow, right-hand man to Paul Jr.'s father. When Nureyev couldn't make it at the last minute, von Bülow filled his seat with Paul Jr.—who was instantly smitten by Talitha. Their wedding, a year later in Rome, took place in the same damask-lined room inside the Palazzo Senatorio, atop the Campidoglio, where Gail had married Lang four months before and where Paul's father had married Teddy three decades previously. Talitha wore a white hooded minidress trimmed in mink and carried a white lily, a symbol of purity and commitment; Paul, in a dark suit, sported a silk tie with a large lily printed on it. (Six months earlier, von Bülow himself had headed to the altar, with the former Martha "Sunny" Crawford. Two decades later, when he was on trial for attempting to murder her in Newport, Rhode Island, Getty provided him with millions for his bail and defense costs.)

Bill Newsom recalled his first encounter with Talitha, in the terraced penthouse she and Paul Jr. had moved into in one of Rome's most ancient quarters:

"They had a beautiful place on the fifth story in a narrow, narrow sixteenth-century building. I arrived there and there was a canary out of a cage and Talitha . . . shushed me and said, 'Quiet.' And for the next five minutes crawled around in a skimpy costume, very skimpy indeed. A bikini or something. And crawled around trying to trap the canary and finally did it. And then only after that did everybody say hello.

"She was perhaps the most beautiful woman I've ever seen. That sounds extravagant. Put it this way: I've never seen a better-looking woman. And she was very, very nice. A lovely woman."

Newsom's new acquaintances also included Getty's close friend Alessandro Ruspoli. "A strange, strange fellow. An older man with a teenage wife and a lot of rich stories about them," the lawyer recalled.

Dado, as this gentleman was called by his legion of friends and admirers, was born to a plethora of hereditary titles. To name a few, he was 9th Prince of Cerveteri, 9th Marquis of Riano, and 14th Count of Vignanello. He was also, it was widely believed, the inspiration for the lead character in Fellini's 1960 film *La Dolce Vita*, played by Marcello Mastroianni.

Reared in his family's stupendous palazzo on the Via del Corso and at their massive, moated castle in Lazio that dates back to 847, he bestrode many worlds. While respecting the strict codes of the "black aristocracy"—nobles historically aligned with the pope, particularly in an 1870 conflict—from which his family descended, with its lineage of saints, popes, and warriors, Dado glided stylishly through café society, the culturati, and the opium dens of the Far East, where he also was a student of yoga, transcendentalism, and the occult. (Orson Welles gave him lessons in hypnotism.)

At one point, Ruspoli shared a villa on the Côte d'Azur with director Roger Vadim and Jane Fonda, where Paul Jr. and Talitha were guests. Fonda described the group as "some of the most decadent types I'd ever met—lovely, charming and sensual." From Dado's three marriages and another relationship, he produced five children, one of whom, Bartolomeo, later married Paul Jr.'s daughter Aileen.

"Dado was the best-looking man of his generation, the ultimate prince-intellectual," recalls his friend Taki. "He was extremely well-read, poetic, a big seducer."

Bill Willis, who became great friends with Paul Jr. and Talitha, not only planned the couple's honeymoon in Morocco, he tagged along. When it was over, "none of us wanted to leave," Willis recalled. Perhaps it was he who located the Palais de la Zahia, built in the pink-walled city of Marrakech centuries before by the ruling pashas. Its sumptuous days were long gone—it was then a maze of disheveled rooms, courtyards, terraces, and gardens—but Paul decided it would make a good wedding present for his bride, and that Bill could fix it up for them.

Willis, who had studied briefly at both Columbia University and Stella Adler's acting school in New York, was yet another American who sailed to Europe with dreams. "Bill yearned for civilization," influential antiques dealer Christopher Gibbs said. In Morocco, he found his calling. La Zahia was soon magically restored at his hands, its rooms faced in *zellige* (glittering, richly patterned mosaic tiles) and *tadelakt* (glazed and pigmented plaster).

Zahia means "pleasure" in Berber. Now the palace was living up to its name again. Up and running, it was imbued with that splendid combination of decadence and efficiency that only the very rich can pull off. "There was a marvelous secretary," remembered a woman who lived in a neighboring house. "She ran the house with such precision, at the same time she'd also be there cutting up hash cakes for us all. There was hash for the novices, opium for the advanced."

La Zahia was only used for holidays, though. Home was still the couple's penthouse in Rome, now filled with many treasures from their frequent travels to Thailand and elsewhere in Asia. It was on these trips that the couple descended deeper into drugs.

La Zahia became the ultimate destination for haute hippies and some of the singular people of the era. The Gettys' guests included the Doors' Jim Morrison and his girlfriend Pamela Courson, Yves Saint Laurent and Pierre Bergé, writers William S. Burroughs and Gore Vidal, director Michelangelo Antonioni, and Marlon Brando, who stayed for months. Paul and Talitha's "One Thousand and One Nights" parties sometimes carried on for days.

For the Rolling Stones, it was practically a home away from home. In the mid- to late sixties, Morocco was to them what India was to the Beatles. While John, Paul, George, and Ringo ventured to the ashram of the Maharishi Mahesh Yogi in Rishikesh, Mick, Keith, and Brian gravitated to La Zahia, burnishing its legend.

Brian Jones arrived first, with his girlfriend Anita Pallenberg, a German-Italian force of nature who had grown up in Rome. Keith Richards and Mick Jagger followed. The stoned Stones found bliss at La Zahia. "We would climb up on the roof, where we could see the snowy mountains above and the garden below, full of palm trees, squawking birds, and fish in tanks," recalled Gibbs, their close companion. Paul and Talitha "had the best and finest opium," wrote Keith. "We enjoyed being transported."

Paul and Talitha were catalytic figures within a circle of remarkable people. But who met who first? Paul and Anita knew each other as youngsters in Rome; through her boyfriend, the avant-garde painter Mario Schifano, she got the jump on meeting the most celebrated people of the day, including the two pivotal figures who arguably invented "Swinging London"—Gibbs, and his great mate Robert Fraser. Tastemakers extraordinaire, both were gay, drug-toting, Eton-educated, upper-class rebels. Anybody really cool in town, including the Beatles and the Stones, as well as artists visiting from New York and Los Angeles, hung out in Mayfair at Fraser's art gallery and flat, and in Chelsea at Gibbs's shop and his apartment on Cheyne Walk.

And who found which drugs first? Willis was the discoverer of cocaine; he turned Fraser on to it, who in turn introduced the Stones and the Beatles to it. When it came to LSD, Fraser led the way. "Robert was your gentleman junkie," said Richards. "With Robert, it was always the crème de la crème, it was pure."

Fraser, whom Paul Jr. called "an icon of his time . . . the most infuriating friend I've ever had," turned everybody on to the new movements in art—pop art, particularly—which galvanized their creativity. "He was the best art eye I've ever met," said Paul McCartney in *Groovy Bob: The Life and Times of Robert Fraser*, by Harriet Vyner.

In the late 1960s, this group, through their combustible, often drug-fueled interactions, helped usher in a new era of social liberation. They led the way in breaking down the class barriers and distinctions that had long stood, particularly in England. A key ingredient in this new social mobility was music, and musicians.

"Suddenly we were being courted by half of the aristocracy," Richards recalled in his autobiography, *Life*. "I've never known if they were slumming or if we were snobbing. They were very nice people. I decided it was no skin off my nose. If somebody's interested, they're welcome. . . .

"It was the first time I know of when that lot actively sought out musicians in such large numbers. They realized there was something blowin' in the wind, to quote Bob [Dylan]. . . . They felt they were being left out of things if they didn't join in. So, there was this weird mixture of aristos and gangsters, the fascination that the higher end of society had with the more brutish end. . . . The rough mixed with the smooth."

A key figure in it was snappy young Tara Browne, a son of Dominick, the 4th Baron Oranmore and Browne, who sat in the House of Lords, and the fabulously wealthy brewing heiress Oonagh Guinness.

Guinnesses and Gettys—scions of beer and oil fortunes—could relate well to one another. Over generations, addictions and tragedies have plagued both of these astronomically rich, accomplished, and eccentric dynasties.

While still a teenager, the precocious Tara socialized with Truman Capote, Salvador Dalí, Samuel Beckett, Jean Cocteau, Lucian Freud, John Huston, and Humphrey Bogart as well as Jimi Hendrix, David Bowie, the Stones, and the Beatles. (Paul McCartney dropped acid for the first time in his London townhouse.)

"Tara was absolutely central to it," said Jane Ormsby-Gore, daughter of the 5th Baron Harlech, about the contemporary scene. "We were meeting people from different walks of life, but we needed someone in the middle saying, 'Oh, so-and-so, have you met such and such?' And that was what Tara did."

Tara's twenty-first birthday, in March 1966 at Luggala, his mother's glorious 5,000-acre estate in County Wicklow, Ireland, drew two hundred of Britain's brightest young things, including most of the above named (and the Lovin' Spoonful, who performed). A photograph of Paul, Talitha, Bill Willis, Anita Pallenberg, Brian Jones, and Tara on the emerald mountaintop, with silvery Lough Tay far below, shows them bursting with glee, and stoned out of their minds, as the wind howled. It was a defining moment.

One evening around midnight a few months later, the Lotus Elan convertible that Tara was behind the wheel of smashed into another vehicle in London. Shortly afterward, at home in his country house, John Lennon read the coroner's report in the *Daily Mail*. He sat down at his piano and began writing "A Day in the Life":

> *I read the news today, oh boy*
> *About a lucky man who made the grade . . .*
> *He blew his mind out in a car*
> *He didn't notice that the lights had changed*
> *Nobody was really sure if he was from the House of Lords . . .*

It was the final song on what has been called the band's greatest creative achievement and the best album of all time, *Sgt. Pepper's Lonely Hearts Club Band*, which was released in May 1967 with a cover art-directed by Fraser.

In the view of many of those who knew him, Tara Browne's death augured a sea change.

"It was like a death knell sounding all over London," said Marianne Faithfull in *I Read the News Today, Oh Boy*, a biography of Browne by Paul Howard.

The good vibes—the freewheeling, optimistic, sunnier, London-centric portion of the sixties—gave way to an American-driven youth culture, which was darkened by Vietnam, Charles Manson, Altamont, assassinations, and the really destructive kind of drug usage.

Earlier in 1967, a police raid at Redlands, Keith Richards's house in England, left him, Mick, and Fraser facing serious drug charges as well as a hostile press. They bolted to Morocco. Brian and Anita joined them. En route, she fell into Keith's arms, the start of their twelve-year relationship; while tripping on LSD, they all ran into Cecil Beaton, who photographed them, and then came along to the Gettys'. "While watching the native dancers, Mick was convulsed by the rhythm, every fiber of his body responding to the intricacies," Beaton wrote in his diary.

Brian was captivated by Berber music, full of chanting and complex percussive rhythms. After he found a large troupe from the Gnawa tribe in the Atlas Mountains, Paul invited them all to come to dinner and to perform in Zahia's banquet hall. But Brian was so stoned for most of his stay he barely got out of bed; then, enraged after a fight with Anita, he ripped out La Zahia's one phone line.

The celebration Paul and Talitha threw to usher in 1968 was particularly epic. It drew Stones and Beatles. "Paul McCartney and John Lennon were there, flat on their backs. They couldn't get off the floor, let alone talk. I've never seen so many people out of control," the American writer John Hopkins recorded in his diary on January 1.

That May, Talitha, then twenty-seven, gave birth to the couple's son, whom they christened Tara Gabriel Galaxy Gramophone Getty. It was the Age of Aquarius, but the name still elicited chuckles worldwide. "Rich Kid with Silly Name," ran a headline in the *San Francisco Examiner.* In the story underneath, Talitha explained: "Every name has a precise significance and my son will be very proud of them when he grows up. Tara is an Irish aristocratic name; Galaxy means galaxy and he was born under the stars. He will be undoubtedly fond of music so we named him Gramaphone [*sic*]." (His first name was an homage to Tara Browne, who was also the namesake of Tara Richards, Keith and Anita's third child, who died in infancy.)

In October, Talitha appeared in an uncredited cameo in *Barbarella*, the camp sci-fi sensation directed by Vadim, starring Fonda, and featuring Pallenberg in the role of "the Great Tyrant."

In 1969, *Vogue* dispatched a team to La Zahia, including photographer Patrick Lichfield, a cousin of Queen Elizabeth's. "During their brief Moroccan vacations the Gettys' house comes sensuously alive," *Vogue* reported. "Orangewood burning . . . music of Strauss, Wagner, The Beatles . . . cushions embroidered a century ago by Christian slaves in Essaouira . . . dancers, acrobats, storytellers, geomancers, and magicians . . . never fewer than fifteen or twenty for dinner . . . by the light of candles ('the shadows have to be alive') among roses wound with mint and pyramids of tuberoses. While Salome is playing in the background, snake charmers charm and tea boys dance, balancing on their feet trays freighted with mint tea and burning candles."

Nothing secured the couple's mythic stature more than the picture that Lichfield shot on the roof; it became one of most iconic photographs of the twentieth century—an image seemingly no fashion designer since has not tacked onto his or her mood board. With the minaret in the distance and the sky darkening, Talitha crouches in the foreground, clad in a vibrant coat over white harem pants and boots, rings on every finger. Paul Jr. lurks in the background, brooding in a hooded sand-colored djellaba, out of which he peers inscrutably.

That's the take from the portrait session that has been most widely reproduced (licensed by Getty Images). The shot that *Vogue* actually ran in the January 1970 issue is markedly different: he is in the foreground, standing next to Talitha, smiling broadly and wearing a hoodless and very colorful printed silk robe.

But the portrait is really about her. It captured her look—her bohemian chic and posh-hippie style; her extravagant eclecticism, with its mix of couture pieces and ethnic finds, which has become an essential reference point for innumerable fashion designers in the last half century.

As the January *Vogue* hit the stands, Talitha and Paul were spiraling further downward due to their drug addictions. They separated, and Talitha embraced sobriety back in London, where she and infant Tara moved into a house that Paul Jr. acquired on Cheyne Walk, along the Thames. Queen's House, as it was called, was built in 1707 and had a haunted, romantic aura.

In July 1971, she flew to Rome to talk things over with Paul Jr. Paul woke up in the apartment one morning to find Talitha unresponsive. Cardiac arrest was listed as the cause of death, but, according to most media reports, she died of a heroin overdose. She was thirty years old. (In the months just before and after her death, Jim Morrison, Janis Joplin, Jimi Hendrix, and Edie Sedgwick would self-destruct as well.)

Talitha and Paul's impact on style has been strong and enduring.

In 1967, when thirty-one-year-old Yves Saint Laurent first met her in Morocco, the youthquake that had shaken London had yet to hit Paris; couture still maintained a certain rigidity.

He was enthralled by Talitha's air of sexual freedom, the easy, fluid movement of her body; he had never seen anything like her. "My vision completely changed," he said, after her death.

Both he and Pierre Bergé were then still "terribly square," Thadée

Klossowski, a member of YSL's inner circle, told author Alicia Drake in her book *The Beautiful Fall*. "Yves was shocked and immensely titillated."

In 1983, when Diana Vreeland mounted her landmark Yves Saint Laurent show at the Metropolitan Museum in New York, the first exhibition the institution had ever devoted to a living fashion designer, Saint Laurent paid homage to Talitha and Paul in his catalog essay:

"Like F. Scott Fitzgerald, I love a dying frenzy. . . . Decadence attracts me. It suggests a new world. . . . In my own life, I've seen the last afterglow of the sumptuous Paris of before the war. . . . And then I knew the youthfulness of the sixties: Talitha and Paul Getty lying on a starlit terrace in Marrakech, beautiful and damned, and a whole generation assembled as if for eternity where the curtain of the past seemed to lift before an extraordinary future."

The fascination has only continued. "Forty-six years later, we still seek to emulate her mysterious allure," *Vogue* observed recently.

In addition to altering the direction of fashion, these Gettys put their stamp on interior design. Yves and Pierre were so captivated by La Zahia that they bought properties in Marrakech and asked Bill Willis to decorate them: Dar es Saada ("House of Happiness," in Arabic) and then Villa Oasis (on which Willis collaborated with Jacques Grange, the eminent Paris decorator). Willis became a revered figure in Marrakech, where he remained until his death in 2009 at age seventy-two. He worked his magic there for a very select list of clients—Marella Agnelli, Marie-Hélène de Rothschild, and a few other grandees. While his name never became widely known—something to do with his relatively small body of work along with his love of cocaine and his willfulness—his influence traveled far: the international style-setters who visited his clients' houses were paying close attention.

"Bill created the Marrakech look, and it started with that house," said Grange, referring to La Zahia.

According to Bergé, Moroccan history can be divided into two epochs: "'Before' and 'after' Bill Willis," as he wrote in his foreword to *Bill Willis,* a 2011 monograph written by Marian McEvoy. "Today there is not a single Moroccan house that does not owe something to him. He became a tireless student of Morocco, laying bare the country's soul like almost no one else."

(La Zahia has belonged to French *intellectuel engagé* Bernard-Henri Lévy since 1998, when he bought it from actor Alain Delon.)

Following Talitha's death, J. Paul Getty Jr. withdrew from the world. Debilitated by addictions, depression, and a growing list of physical ailments, he secluded himself on Cheyne Walk, when he wasn't checked into the private London Clinic. When Paul III was kidnapped in 1973, and when the young man suffered his stroke eight years later and required expensive care, Paul Jr. was so enfeebled that he couldn't deal with his responsibilities. The ever-valiant Gail held everyone together. She moved into Queen's House with Paul for a time, while the three younger children went to schools in England.

After the death of his father in 1976 and the 1984 sale of Getty Oil, Paul was not just another peculiar, reclusive invalid: he was a filthy-rich one. As he struggled to regain his health, much of the time still at the London Clinic, he began making donations of all stripes, large and small. He sent checks to battered women's shelters, striking coal miners, a down-on-his-luck concert pianist. He sent his Bentley to the north of England to pick up a cat burglar's dog made homeless after its owner was sent to prison. Much of the giving was done very quietly.

But in 1985 Great Britain collectively gasped at the news that he had given £50 million to the National Gallery. Other gigantic gifts followed: £20 million pounds to the British Film Institute; £5 million to St. Paul's Cathedral, the masterpiece of Sir Christopher Wren.

Paul made a number of other gifts that enabled important works of art to remain in Britain, out of the clutches of wealthy foreign collectors and museums—the J. Paul Getty Museum included. *The Three Graces,* an exquisite sculpture that the 6th Duke of Bedford commissioned Antonio Canova to create in 1814 for Woburn Abbey, his family seat, was one such example. In the early 1980s, the heir of the 13th Duke of Bedford (who had been J. Paul Getty's close friend) tried to give the statue to Britain in lieu of taxes. After his offer was rejected, the Cayman Islands–based company that bought it sold it to the Getty Museum for about $12 million. Public outcry and a tumultuous, five-year-long legal battle followed, during which the government withheld its export license while various parties tried to raise funds to buy it. Paul Getty Jr. offered to contribute $1.5 million toward its purchase on behalf of the Victoria and Albert Museum and the Scottish National Gallery. This transpired at the height of the paranoia in the art world over the so-called Getty factor, whereby—as some feared and others hoped—the newly loaded Malibu museum would send art prices soaring as it veritably plundered Europe of its patrimony. When Paul Jr. stepped up to help keep the Canova and other treasures in Britain, the London papers had a field day. Some reports suggested that he was motivated by spite for his late father and his museum. Just as it seemed the deal to "save" the Canova was sealed, the director of the Scottish National Gallery gave credence to this view in a television interview. Outraged, Getty rescinded his offer. After the director apologized profusely, Getty reinstated his pledge, and the marble remained in Britain.

A new Maecenas had appeared in the land; he was still a fragile one, though. But one day in 1985, one Briton took Paul in hand: Prime Minister Margaret Thatcher marched into the London Clinic and dispensed a dose of her particular brand of strong medicine: "My dear Mr. Getty. Now, what is the matter? We must have you out of here."

Within the next two years, Getty received an honorary knighthood from the Queen and was named Arts Patron of the Year; he was to receive the award from the Prince of Wales during a gala dinner at the Savoy Hotel. Still wobbly, Getty got cold feet. Just forty-five minutes before he was due to arrive, Christopher Gibbs had to call the organizers to break the news that Mr. Getty couldn't make it. Nineteen-year-old Tara was deputized to accept the award on his father's behalf.

Eventually J. Paul Getty Jr. did come out of his shell. His rehabilitation finally jelled, thanks in large part to a woman. But an English country estate, a boat, and the game of cricket also helped make the last decade of his life pretty glorious.

The woman was Victoria Holdsworth, a willowy beauty he had known for many years who became his close companion. The daughter of a Suffolk farmer who had been a commander in World War II, she had been married three times previously and had two sons. In 1994, they boarded a Concorde to Barbados (his first trip outside Britain in eighteen years), where they embarked on the *Talitha G*. Six years earlier, Paul Jr. had purchased the 262-foot superyacht, which had been commissioned in the 1920s. Only now was she emerging from the restoration he'd ordered—one of the most painstaking in the annals of yachting. In December 1994, on her teak deck, Paul, then age sixty-two, and Victoria were married.

By then, Getty also owned Wormsley Park, an ancient manor in Buckinghamshire on 2,700 sublime acres. Dating from 1086, it passed in 1574 into the hands of the Scropes, a noble family, and belonged to their descendants, the Fanes, until 1985, when Paul bought it, at Gibbs's suggestion. Gibbs and a dream team of talent including interior decorator David Mlinaric spent seven years bringing the neglected property back to its original glory, and then some. With the addition of some extraordinary new elements, including a four-acre lake and one of the finest private libraries anywhere, Wormsley was a magnificent country seat ready for a new dynasty.

The library, constructed of flint, was built from scratch in the style of an ancient castle, though it includes state-of-the-art climate control and other technologies. Inside its baronial reading room, the fifteenth-century-style hammerbeam roof of English oak is painted in gilt and midnight blue, depicting the conjunction of the planets at the hour of Paul's birth, at sea off the coast of Italy.

It was a worthy home for his peerless collection of rare books and manuscripts. In the 1960s, before he came into his fortune, Paul Jr. started to collect seriously, sometimes buying from dealers on credit. Whatever money he had seemed to go to books. After his father died, he had the wherewithal to fully pursue his obsession. His collection, one of the best in the world, spans the seventh to the late twentieth centuries; it includes illuminated manuscripts, early printed books, and historic bookbindings. Highlights include the First Folio of Shakespeare's *Comedies, Histories, and Tragedies* (which he bought from Oriel College, Oxford, for £3.5 million), the first printed edition of Chaucer, and the psalter used by Anne Boleyn (a guest at Sutton Place, remember).

In 1999, over one hundred masterpieces from the collection traveled to New York, where the Morgan Library showcased them in a major exhibition, *The Wormsley Library: A Personal Selection by Sir Paul Getty, KBE*.

For many of its visitors, however, Wormsley's greatest delight is its cricket ground.

Cricket became much more than a game to Paul. It was a big part of his recovery, and his reemergence into society. "I came upon cricket at a time when I was deeply depressed and it had a lot to do with bringing me out of that state," he said in a rare interview, with ESPN.

Mick Jagger introduced him to the sport when Getty was still secluded on Cheyne Walk. Jagger, who lived a few doors away, was one of the few visitors allowed into the house. If cricket was on the telly, Mick wanted to watch. Over cups of tea, he began to explain the game's many subtle idiosyncrasies and arcane rules. Paul was hooked. And it wasn't just the game itself. He loved the surroundings of this quintessentially English pursuit. "There's a whole way of life about it which I adore," he said.

England's great aristocratic estates traditionally included cricket grounds, along with a team supported by the lord of the manor. But no one had built one of these costly follies since the war years—until Getty. Then he outdid everybody. He had his modeled on the Oval, the nation's most sacrosanct pitch, in south London. At Wormsley, it is flanked on three sides by glorious countryside. The fourth side, looking toward the wooded Chiltern Hills, is elevated on a large grassy bank, allowing perfect viewing, with a delightful mock-Tudor pavilion for the players.

"It's so perfectly cut into the landscape," says one English lord who is a regular there. "It's not just one of the most beautiful cricket pitches. It's one of the most beautiful things. Full stop." (Getty was so mad for the game, it was even played on the deck of the *Talitha G.*)

The inaugural match in 1992 was attended by Her Majesty the Queen Mother and Prime Minister John Major. An invitation to one of its summer matches, particularly to see the home team, the Sir Paul Getty XI, at bat, remains one of the most coveted in the realm— "The most enchanting, exclusive, and enthralling place in England to hear willow on leather," as *Tatler* recently declared. (Cricket bats are made of wood from willow trees.)

In March 1998, three months after he was granted British citizenship, J. Paul Getty Jr. became a full-fledged knight of the realm. "Now you can use your title. Isn't that nice?" the Queen said to him after she dubbed him with her sword, making him a Knight Commander of the Most Excellent Order of the British Empire, for his services to charity. A photo of Sir Paul and Lady Getty outside Buckingham Palace after his investiture appeared the next day on the front page of the *Times* of London. Getty was even the subject of an editorial inside the paper under the headline "Model Billionaire," which read: "This reclusive Briton, once trapped in the world of wealth and family tragedy, has imperceptibly become an English institution himself."

6

Mark

One morning in 2005, Londoners woke to find one of their most beloved icons massacred.

A classic red British Telecom box lay overturned in Soho Square, half of it bent almost ninety degrees, a pickaxe protruding from it. It appeared to be bleeding.

The "blood" pooled around it was paint. It was all the handiwork of then little-known street artist Banksy. His pranks would soon escalate about as fast as his prices. Without ado, however, the Westminster City Council ordered the nuisance carted away. Whether the piece amounted to a violent attack on a cherished national institution or a cheeky satire on modern life and technology was a question pondered by a few.

Three years later—Valentine's Day 2008—*Vandalized Phone Box* (lot 33A) appeared on the block at Sotheby's in New York during the (RED) Auction, a gala event spearheaded by musician Bono and artist Damien Hirst, to raise funds for AIDS programs in Africa. (The biggest charity auction ever, it collected $42.5 million.)

Lot 33A, carrying an estimate of $200,000 to $300,000, sparked heated competition. A determined anonymous bidder fended off all challengers until the hammer fell at $605,000.

It took another three years for the item to resurface, on the grounds of Wormsley, not far from the cricket ground.

"I had to have it . . . it was killing the phone box story with a phone box that was being killed," Mark Getty—Paul Jr. and Gail's third-born child—eventually confessed. "A marvelous joke and metaphor."

Indeed, in the public imagination, the much-mythologized Sutton Place pay phone had become synonymous with "the tragic dynasty." Putting a stake through the heart of *that* was well worth the 600K (and the money did go to charity).

The timing of its purchase that night at Sotheby's was propitious too. Just ten days later, Mark, then forty-seven, accepted a $2.4 billion buyout offer from a private equity firm for Getty Images, the scrappy start-up he cofounded in 1995, which revolutionized the photography industry. Gettys were not just inheriting fortunes now, they were making them again.

Broad-shouldered, red-haired, Rome-born Mark (whose first language was Italian) had become a pillar of the British Establishment. But every summer in Tuscany, he's still "Marco." He's gone since he was five, when his mother bought a primitive farmhouse. Weekends and summers there in the remote wooded hills near the village of Orgia provided a safe haven and a sense of normalcy, especially during the maelstroms that hit the family. In July 1973, Mark happened to be away in San Francisco visiting his maternal grandparents when his brother was abducted.

From age fourteen onward, he was educated in England—at Taunton, a relatively relaxed prep school in Somerset, and then at Oxford, where he studied politics and philosophy.

As Mark's father recovered his health and became one of the leading philanthropists in Great Britain, Mark and his siblings mixed easily among different strata of British society, including the aristocracy. "They just swam in, seamlessly, which is very rare for Americans," observed one peeress. "People liked them because they were just themselves. The kids were all very nice and cool. But the Gettys also knew the rules of England. They made the right decisions about which schools to go to. They had all those cricket matches. It was all very pukka. The Gettys just got it."

Mark, an Anglo-Saxon and Italian mash-up, found his match when he met Domitilla Harding in 1980 in Rome. Born in New York (in 1960, like Mark), she was brought up in Rome by an American father, a businessman, and an Italian mother who descends from one of Italy's great papal dynasties, the Lante della Roveres. Their family tree includes Pope Sixtus, who built the Sistine Chapel, and his nephew, Julius II, who commissioned Michelangelo's frescoes. Julius also restored part of the ancient Basilica dei Santi XII Apostoli, where Domi, as she is known, and Mark were married in 1982.

The couple spent the first years of their marriage in New York, where Mark worked in investment banking at Kidder, Peabody. In 1986, they acquired their own summer property in Orgia, close to Gail's. Atop a steep hill, they found a hamlet of six rustic farmhouses—a *borgo*, as it's called in Italy. It had been abandoned for years, except for an elderly, eccentric hermit squatter. After buying one of the stone houses, they slowly—over fifteen years—were able to acquire the entire property, as they tracked down the various owners and gained the deeds. As they spread out from house to house, the family expanded too. After Alexander, who was born in 1984, the couple had Joseph in 1988 and Julius two years later.

As the boys grew up, Getty cousins and other relatives descended on the property every July and August. A bit of work was mixed in during the holidays—the kids were given Italian lessons, and a number of family members pitched in to help Domitilla with Miss Italy, the fashion line that she operated for a decade. Anna, her niece, was the fit model; Gisela, Anna's mother, and Ariadne, Mark's sister, took the photographs that were posted on the website, which Alexander set up.

Traditionally, wealthy Anglo-American expatriate families in Italy, like the Actons in Florence, have kept fairly aloof from Italians and spoken the language poorly, if they did at all. The Gettys all speak beautiful Italian (Mark speaks with a Sienese accent) and they mix with a wide variety of Italians—aristocrats, locals, artists, and intellectuals.

For everyone in the family, but for Mark in particular, the high point of summer was (and still is) the Palio di Siena. Held in the Piazza del Campo, Siena's magnificent medieval square, it lasts only about ninety seconds as ten jockeys—each representing one of the city's *contrade* (districts)—careen bareback for three laps. Possibly the most dangerous horse race in the world, it is doubtless the most splendid.

Brief as the races are—one is held in July and one in August— the Palio consumes the passions of the Sienese all year long, as they scheme and prepare for the competition, an eight-hundred-year-old tradition full of intrigue and pageantry. Only citizens of Siena can fully participate, but an outsider is allowed to take part as a *cavallaio*, a horse breeder. When he was about twenty-five, Mark bought his first horses, a pair of Anglo-Arabians named Amore and Barbarella. For the next nearly thirty years, with fifty-some horses, he never missed a year—or won a race.

By the early 1990s, Mark and Domitilla were living primarily in London, where he worked in the corporate finance department of Hambros Bank. Not that he needed the work. By now, the Gettys were all awash in cash, as their trusts swelled following the sale of Getty Oil. But without a family business, and with each of four branches now managing its own trust, they had become a splintered tribe, and there was a sense of loss.

At the same time, Mark and a Hambros colleague, South African–born Jonathan Klein, hatched plans to launch an investment fund of their own. Mark persuaded relatives from three of the four Getty family branches (George's daughters being the exception) to back them. His father, his uncles Gordon and Ronald, and thirteen cousins put up about $30 million in seed capital. (Other investors joined them, including Hambros Bank and RIT Capital Partners, the investment trust run by Lord Rothschild.) The idea was to make money, but at the same time it presented an opportunity to knit the family back together.

An initial investment in Conservation Corporation Africa, a fledgling game-reserve and ecotourism operator based in South Africa, got off to a good start, for the business and the Gettys: the relatives got along, and Mark's role as the peacemaker in the family solidified.

Looking for something big to make a splash in, Mark and Jonathan homed in on the stock photography business, then an inefficient but lucrative seller's market.

Getty Images got off the ground in March 1995, when they paid $40 million for Britain's Tony Stone Images, with its library of 1.1 million photos. Building on that cornerstone, they snapped up one stock firm or archival collection after another, in a bid to consolidate the fragmented field.

With the digital era in its toddler years, photo researchers still located images by dint of cumbersome quests through mazes of independent photo stock agencies. After it consolidated collections, Getty Images enabled researchers to use computers to retrieve images—initially in the form of snail-mailed glossy prints, later via digital technology.

In October 1995, Getty gained stiff competition from Bill Gates: Corbis, a firm he had founded in 1989 to make digital artworks to decorate people's homes, acquired the vast Bettmann Archive, making the two companies archrivals.

Two years later, *Forbes* published an interview with Mark about his new company and "the arcane field of stock photography." The article's quizzical tone suggests that the public, and some journalists, didn't yet understand what Getty was onto: "You may chuckle when you hear what industry the younger Getty has delved into: stock photos. This is the business of pulling used photographs out of file folders and lending them to book publishers, movie studios, advertising agencies, and the like."

With Getty Images now in possession of about 25 million images, their costly challenge was how to distribute and market them. It was not unlike the situation Mark's grandfather faced when he first struck oil in the Neutral Zone. Where he had to build railroads, supertankers, and refineries, Mark had to digitalize his images and build thick cables and data centers for downloading them.

"Intellectual property is the oil of the twenty-first century," Mark told the *Economist*. "In the oil business, the capital is in the ground; in the intellectual-property business, it is in people's heads."

Late in 1997, Getty Images' quest to build out its digital infrastructure was jump-started with its purchase of Seattle-based Photo-Disc, a pioneer in web-based photos, which also led the company to relocate its headquarters from London to Seattle, joining the emerging tech megalopolis.

The same year, far from any digital domain, photographer Slim Aarons, eighty-one, heard a knock on the door of his farmhouse in Bedford, New York. It was Mark. "He was wearing this little windbreaker and I thought he was a guy looking for a landscaping job," Slim recalled in a *Vanity Fair* profile.

After a storied career photographing old money scions and high society ringleaders for such publications as *Holiday*, *Town & Country*, and *Life*, Aarons was retired, his work little valued. When *A Wonderful Time*, his photo album of the rich at play, was published in 1974, it sank. Vietnam, Nixon's resignation . . . Slim was out of step with the times.

When he realized that this young "fella" wasn't a gardener, he invited Getty up to his attic to look at his life's work. Mark made an offer on the spot for the entire collection, and the deal was sealed with a handshake. "He gave me what I call 'fuck you' money," the photographer said happily.

With Getty Images' distribution and marketing, Aarons's oeuvre became another touchstone for the fashion world. Not unlike Mark's stepmother, Talitha, in fact. Style-wise, they were just polar opposites. While Talitha became a patron saint of posh hippiedom, Aarons—"the Jimmy Stewart of photography," as fellow lensman Jonathan Becker called him—made WASP style look crisp and cool. "I don't think there's any American designer who doesn't have a copy [of *A Wonderful Time*]," said designer Michael Kors.

"Wonderful guy," said Slim about Mark. "Grandson of the old man himself. Direct line right down."

In 2001, Mark and his uncle Gordon made a £10 million donation to the National Gallery in London, in honor of Paul Jr., who had virtually saved the institution sixteen years before with his £50 million gift. Shy as he was, his name wasn't carved anywhere on the building. Now, after this new donation from his son and his brother, one of the main entrances on Trafalgar Square was remodeled and named the Sir Paul Getty Entrance. A bronze bust of him there greets visitors. (In 2009, Mark was appointed chair of the institution's board of trustees, considered the most prestigious charitable post in Britain.)

The next year, the family name returned to the Big Board, after a decades-long absence, when stock in Getty Images began trading on the New York Stock Exchange under the ticker symbol GYI.

In April 2003, Sir Paul Getty, age seventy, died at the London Clinic, where he had been undergoing treatment for a chest infection. Five months later, an epic memorial mass for him took place at Westminster Cathedral. The 1,500 attendees comprised a who's who of the British Establishment—including Baroness Thatcher and scores of English cricket champions.

The Getty family—all branches—appeared in full force. In addition to Mark, Domitilla, and their three sons, there was Paul's first wife, Gail, and his widow, Victoria; Gordon and Ann with their son Peter; Donna Long, Gordon and Paul's half sister; Gloria, Paul's brother George's first wife, with her daughter Caroline; brother Ronald's son Christopher with his wife, Pia; Paul III and his former wife, Gisela, with their daughter, Anna; Caleb Wilding, Aileen's son; and Ariadne with husband Justin and their children, Nats and August.

In his eulogy, Christopher Gibbs spoke about Paul's battles with addictions and depression: "While we must not ignore the woes of his life, it is how he turned them around and put them to work which deserves fanfare."

Having inherited Wormsley, Mark took the reins and moved into the massive estate with his family, though the younger boys were off at boarding school (the esteemed Dragon School in Oxford), and Alexander soon left the nest. He set off first for Africa, where he helped out at Conservation Corporation's Zuka Private Game Reserve, then moved to New York, where he studied at the School of Visual Arts and worked as a video technician for Getty Images.

As Getty Images expanded, the digital media landscape continued to shift. With the rise of the internet came demand for lower-resolution, and lower-priced, images. Madison Avenue went into a slump and the financial crisis was looming. Thinking that the company would fare better under private ownership, without public investor pressure, Getty Images in 2008 accepted a $2.4 billion buyout from Hellman & Friedman, a private equity firm. Mark remained as chairman, and collected about $38 million. His relatives also became even richer—with their collective stake, they reaped a $281 million windfall. All of them remained as minority shareholders.

Four years later, the company accepted a $3.3 billion buyout from the Carlyle Group, the Washington-based private equity firm, which provided capital to continue competing against rivals old and new.

Despite being an information-age chief, Mark has no social media accounts and guards his privacy acutely. He considers the press a necessary evil to which he occasionally speaks. Inevitably, every article about him includes "the tragic background paragraph," as he peremptorily termed it to a reporter for *Management Today*, a British business publication, with whom he sat down for an interview. Then there's "the trite association of money and tragedy," he added. "It's all so profoundly boring."

Being measured by what his grandfather accomplished is of no interest to him either: "I always wanted to do something that was purely mine and I never wanted my life to be one where I lived in the shadow of . . . my grandfather. He did a lot of extraordinary things, but that was him and it wasn't me."

At Wormsley, Mark put his stamp on things. In addition to *Vandalized Phone Box*, a collection of other modern sculptures, including pieces by Jeff Koons and Keith Sonnier, appeared on the landscape. And in the spring of 2011, a gleaming steel and glass structure rose, the six-hundred-seat Opera Pavilion. It was built as a home for the Garsington Opera, one of England's summer companies, which had recently lost its longtime home on an aristocratic estate in Oxfordshire.

"I love opera . . . and, when I heard that they were looking for a new home through a friend of mine, I thought it would be a terrific thing to happen here," he told a reporter from the *Telegraph* before Garsington's debut at Wormsley.

How did such a private person feel about thousands of strangers entering his gates? "Well, it's a big place, and the idea that one person should occupy it all, all the time, alone, is kind of absurd," he said with a laugh. (According to a family friend, the estate's level of security is high: "It's like getting into Fort Knox.")

When he spoke, the reporter detected "a touch of loneliness." That year, he and Domitilla divorced. Now a ceramicist and glassmaker, she lives full-time in Orgia, which has continued to be a magnet for Gettys from far and wide every summer, thanks to her as well as to Gail, still the matriarch of her branch of the clan.

Alexander, tall and dark-haired, moved to California for several years. Settling first in Los Angeles, he volunteered at Gettlove, his

aunt Aileen's homeless shelter, while he pursued his interest in photography. He had been taking pictures since he was ten, when his
father launched Getty Images. But it was his mother who gave him
a camera and taught him how to use it. "He's the normal one in the
family," says a friend. "Very down-to-earth. Spartan."

While photographing landscapes and architectural subjects,
he worked for Airbnb, shooting homes for its website. He also met
Tatum Yount, a bright MBA candidate at USC. The pair married
in 2012 and moved to San Francisco. As their children, Jasper and
Olivia, were born, she worked as a brand consultant for the health
and wellness industry and he continued his fine-art photography.
An exhibition of his landscapes, *Human/Nature*, appeared in 2013 at
the Gauntlet Gallery, in the Tenderloin. Its opening night was full of
Getty cousins, aunts, and uncles.

Joseph, Mark and Domitilla's second son, moved to Rhode Island
for college, as a member of Brown University's Class of 2013, with a
major in history. A clever teddy bear with perfect manners and an
easygoing disposition, he is the bridge builder in his generation of
the Getty tribe—fitting, for a middle child. In Providence one day,
he discovered a stockpile of old red-and-orange Getty Oil signs at
an abandoned gas station. (A drop of oil fills in the *G*.) The next day
he had them picked up and shipped around the world to his various
relatives, in whose houses and offices they now proudly hang.

At a dinner party one weekend in New York, he met Sabine
Ghanem. Born in Geneva to a Lebanese father and an Egyptian
mother, she was enrolled at the Gemological Institute of America
in New York. Long-limbed, green-eyed, with a bob of flaxen hair,
she has a commanding personality and a cosmopolitan air. "I'm
certain we'll be happy together, so you should be my girlfriend," he
told her right off.

After earning their diplomas, they moved into a flat in London's
Pimlico. He pursued a career in finance (later opening his own
hedge fund, Getty Capital) and she launched her line of fine jew-

elry, Sabine G. Her fanciful pieces were soon adorning the likes of Celine Dion, Rihanna, Nicole Kidman, and Catherine Deneuve. Given her own extravagant style and outsize personality, glossy magazines began to avidly cover her. She also gained a large following on Instagram, where she showcased her jewelry and also provided peeks inside the Getty world.

On a trip to Harbour Island in the Bahamas in spring 2014, Joseph popped the question. It wasn't such a surprise—she had told him she should design her engagement ring because "you're going to mess this up." But she was thrilled with the 1920s emerald mounted with diamonds that he picked out for her at S.J. Phillips, the venerable Mayfair jeweler. Reportedly, when he previewed the ring to his mother, she told him it was beautiful, but wondered, "Isn't it a bit grand?" Which confirmed for him that he'd made the right choice for his bride-to-be.

For Sabine's thirtieth birthday that August, Joseph threw her a fabulous two-day party aboard the *Talitha*, the family superyacht (her name now trimmed of its initial *G*). She chose the theme: *The Party*, the 1960s Peter Sellers classic. She wore a vintage hot-pink dress by Azzaro, and the plunge pool was filled with bubble bath, which naturally she ended up in, as the *Talitha* floated off Porto Ercole on the Tuscan coast.

Sabine likes a theme party. For a Halloween dinner, she picked *Auntie Mame*, for which she wore a purple 1960s Pierre Cardin haute couture gown. Fashion-mad, she has described her style as Bob Mackie meets Catherine Deneuve. "I find clothes are very empowering. You have to live up to the magnificence of the piece you are wearing," she told *British Vogue*.

On a brilliant morning in late May 2015, a pack of paparazzi swarmed outside of Basilica dei Santi XII Apostoli in Rome. Thirty-three years after Mark and Domitilla were wed inside the sixth-century basilica, Joseph and Sabine chose to exchange their vows there.

A parade of young royals and *jeunesse dorée* arrived for the ceremony: Princess Beatrice, in pink pastels from her fanciful hat on down; Monaco's dashing Pierre Casiraghi with his fiancée, Beatrice Borromeo; and others with such names as Thurn und Taxis, Niarchos, Agnelli, Santo Domingo, and Brandolini.

But where was the bride, and where was her hooded cape? Since the latter stretched twenty-three feet and featured 500,000 sequins (hand-embroidered by Maison Lesage) shaped into an image of a radiating sun, it required its own minder and car, which threaded its way through Rome's tortuous traffic. At last the garment arrived and was fastened to the bride, who was already clad in a figure-hugging, long-sleeved duchess-silk dress—the handiwork, like the cape, of Schiaparelli Haute Couture.

Some 375 of the guests had barely recovered from the costume ball the night before—the theme being *Liaisons Dangereuses*—at the seventeenth-century Palazzo Taverna. Immediately following the ceremony, waiters in liveried tailcoats served lunch at that most hallowed hall, the Circolo della Caccia, where Joseph's great-grandfather, despite being the richest man in the world, had been denied membership. That night, on the seaside west of the city, there was another ball, at Castello Orsini-Odescalchi, where a *Spiegeltent*—a 1900s circus tent—was erected for a wild circus-meets-cabaret-themed celebration. Looming a stone's throw away was La Posta Vecchia, J. Paul Getty's former villa, now a luxury hotel.

That August, in Siena's Piazza del Campo, Mark Getty's losing streak finally ended. Polonski, his seven-year-old Sardinian Anglo-Arabian, ridden by a jockey named Giovanni "Tittia" Atzeni, got an early lead and veritably flew to the finish line, setting a new Palio speed record (1 minute, 12 seconds) and making Mark the first foreigner ever to run a winning horse. It only took eight centuries. "I lost all of my Anglo-Saxon reserve," he later said of his euphoria.

Capping this momentous year, in December Her Majesty the Queen awarded Mark (an Irish passport holder) an honorary knighthood, in recognition of his services to the arts and philanthropy.

Around this time, he began a new relationship with Caterina Nahberg, a Spanish-born beauty who resided in Rome, where she had been married to the scion of an ancient Italian noble family, Prince Filippo del Drago.

On the business front, in January 2016, Getty Images declared victory over their Seattle rival when the company acquired the distribution rights to Corbis's vast library of images, though in a roundabout way. When a Beijing-based company, Visual China Group (VCG), bought Corbis, Getty Images struck a deal with VCG to license those images around the world, except in China. "Almost twenty-one years but we got it. Lovely to get the milk, the cream, cheese, yogurt, and the meat without buying the cow," Jonathan Klein crowed.

In 2018, the Getty family acquired Carlyle's 51 percent equity stake for around $250 million (and rolled over the company's roughly $2.35 billion debt), taking back control. Three years later, in December 2021, the company came full circle when it announced plans to list itself again on the New York Stock Exchange, following a merger with CC Neuberger Principal Holdings II, a deal valued at $4.8 billion. As a public company, Getty Images would be able to "aggressively invest in more product," announced Mark, who remains the chairman. With annual revenues of nearly $900 million, the company's 300 million "assets," in addition to photos, included videos and music, as well as a stable of assignment photographers such as Getty Images' royal photographer Chris Jackson. A shot of Kate Middleton can move from his lens to news-media sites around the world almost instantly.

Arguably, Mark Getty had cornered the world photography market. "He's the Amazon of images," as one photographer put it. But not everybody is a fan of Getty Images, of course. It prospered as it undercut the prices for pictures, which reduced and, in some cases, wiped out the livelihoods of many photo stock agencies and photographers.

A year after the release of *All the Money in the World*, a documentary called *Gettys: The World's Richest Art Dynasty* was broadcast on the BBC. Featuring interviews with Mark and Gordon, as well as with a few intimates such as Christopher Gibbs, it seemed to be a united Getty family rejoinder to the movie. It burnished J. Paul Getty's legacy as a philanthropist and art collector, but Mark briefly addressed Ridley Scott's film. It "turned it into a story where he's the bad guy," he said, referring to his grandfather. "The kidnappers were the bad guys."

"I do lose a lot of sleep thinking about what the experience was like for my brother," he also said.

But happiness prevailed in 2018. Mark and Caterina, parents of an infant daughter, Sol, were married in the Walled Garden at Wormsley. Two acres of enchantment, the garden was begun in the 1700s but fell into disrepair for much of the twentieth century, before celebrated garden designer Penelope Hobhouse brought it back to life for Mark's father. It is divided into four distinct spaces, enabling visitors to move from "room to room."

Mark and Caterina began to spend much of the year in Rome, in a palazzo that he rented near the Borghese Gardens. He also published his first book, *Like Wildfire Blazing*, a fable-like novel about a group of beings at the beginning of the world, a tale of the elemental struggle between darkness and light. "I always wanted to write and found the process incredibly liberating. . . . I thought by writing about some of the issues people might face when they're creating a society, I would get closer to understanding what makes good and evil. Even in the current climate, I'm an optimist and believe that good will always triumph," Mark told the London *Sunday Times* about the book, which was published by Adelphi, a small press. Getty oversaw all aspects of the book's production, including its dark-blue cloth spine and endpapers, which he designed himself.

The younger generation were now deepening their roots at

Wormsley, and multiplying. Alexander, Tatum, and their children moved from San Francisco to the property, where he became the estate manager. There's a lot to manage: in addition to the opera, cricket, garden, and library, the property sometimes opens its grounds for weddings and events, as other aristocratic English country houses often do. While overseeing all that, Alexander and Tatum keep a low profile. "They lead a very simple life," says a friend. "No excesses of any kind. He hates anything showy."

Sabine and Joseph are a different story. "She's the most Getty of them all!" says a longtime Getty watcher, alluding to Sabine's dramatic style. Indeed, *Tatler*, the English society bible, ranked the couple number three in its 2019 "Social Power Index," behind the Duke and Duchess of Cambridge and just ahead of Harper Beckham, the in-demand, then seven-year-old daughter of David and Victoria. "She's easily the best-dressed at any event," the magazine commented of Sabine. A case in point: the pink Emilia Wickstead skirt suit, paired with a matching turban-like hat, that she wore to Princess Eugenie's wedding at Windsor Castle. In another issue of the same publication, Sabine poked good fun at the notion of dynasties when she and hotel heiress Nicky Hilton Rothschild posed for a lavish fashion spread and accompanying video wearing ball gowns and vamping it up à la Alexis and Krystle, in the style of the iconic 1980s TV soap *Dynasty*.

The couple, with their daughter Gene, born in 2017, and son Jupiter, born in 2019, weekend at Wormsley. In London, they moved to a capacious duplex facing Green Park, which previously belonged to Joseph's grandfather; Sir Paul acquired it in 1986, when he vacated his melancholy Cheyne Walk townhouse. Gibbs and David Mlinaric decorated it for him; the Tudor-era paneling that they installed (salvaged from Raby Castle in County Durham) set a baronial tone. For their young family, Sabine and Joseph refreshed it themselves— brightening it up with coats of tangerine, yellow, and other brightly hued paints, as well as with contemporary art and photography.

Hanging prominently in the drawing room is a large red Getty Oil sign. For furnishings, in addition to their own bold 1960s and '70s items, they were able to pick out antiques—including a number of pieces that once graced Paul and Talitha's Moroccan palace—from the Getty family's storage facilities. ("They never sell anything. They have warehouses around the world," said one family associate.)

And Julius, the youngest brother, emerged into the spotlight. The sensitive, cool one in the family, he sometimes sports floppy dark hair and sometimes a peroxide-blond buzz cut. Fond of art and books, he opened a pop-up art gallery in London's Fitzrovia, where the inaugural group show of groovy young artists was entitled *Dangerous Stuff*. Plans for a clothing and jewelry line, to be called Jetty, are on his drawing board. When *Tatler* compiled its list of 2020's "It Boys" ("today's crop of society studs"), he was included. His category: "Dynastic Dudes."

Appealing and colorful as members of the young generation are, they nonetheless seem tame compared to their really wild antecedents. "I know all the old-school gos [gossip]," one old hand reminisced. "But the young ones aren't very gossipy. They're just happily married."

7

Aileen

On a chilly afternoon in December 2019 in Washington, DC, Aileen Getty, then sixty, and Jane Fonda—just hours shy of her eighty-second birthday—had their hands zip-tied by the Capitol Police. They were arrested while attempting to occupy the Hart Senate Office Building.

It was another raucous Fire Drill Friday—a weekly protest against congressional inaction on climate change, which Fonda had started a few months previously, with major funding from Aileen Getty. (FDF arrestees that season also included Gloria Steinem, Sally Field, Lily Tomlin, and Viva Vadim, Jane's teenage granddaughter.)

As cops hauled off Fonda and Getty, both were defiant, and looking considerably younger than their years. Jane was in a long, operatic, crimson-colored cloth coat, while Aileen wore a student-like nylon anorak, with jeans, sneakers, and a knit cap.

It had been a productive year for Paul Jr.'s second-born child. Over the course of many weeks, her efforts had helped bring rush-hour traffic in parts of central London, Washington, and other major cities to a standstill. The blockages were orchestrated for a good cause: to call people's attention to the climate emergency. With the situation as dire as it is, the more measured, gradualist approaches traditionally employed by mainstream environmental groups didn't cut it anymore, she decided. Among her initiatives, she became the lead donor behind Extinction Rebellion, an international organization that uses extreme, disruptive tactics and civil disobedience to spark change.

Stopping traffic in Piccadilly Circus and Dupont Circle: pretty impressive, especially for a five-foot-four wisp who long ago had been described in the media as a "junkie." Twenty-eight years earlier, she'd even been declared to be all but dead.

"Elizabeth Taylor's former daughter-in-law is dying of AIDS, *A Current Affair* will report Friday," *USA Today* wrote in 1991. "Doctors now tell her she has from six months to a year to live."

Growing up in Rome and Tuscany, Aileen was the delicate child. A few terms at Hatchlands, a posh girls' finishing school in England, turned her into a rebel, and an avid consumer of alcohol. She kept a stash of hard liquor in her room. Weekend visits with her grandfather at Sutton Place provided a measure of stability. "He was one of the more nurturing members of the family," she recalled. And when Teresa, his pet lion, gave birth, Aileen was accorded a special treat— the cubs would be brought up to her room, one by one.

Leaving Hatchlands before graduation (lessons in contract bridge and how to curtsy to the Queen didn't interest her), Getty moved to Los Angeles. In 1981, at age twenty-two, she married into Hollywood royalty when she eloped with Christopher Wilding, the second son born to Elizabeth Taylor and her second husband, Michael Wilding. Aileen and Christopher, who had been dating for a few years, said "I do" in a chapel on the Sunset Strip. Beforehand, Gail hosted a star-studded engagement party for the couple at her house in Brentwood. Carol Burnett, Roddy McDowall, Sissy Spacek, Dudley Moore, and Timothy Leary were among the guests. Miss Taylor— then Mrs. John Warner—shimmered in pearls, while Aileen flashed an engagement ring of imperial jade encircled by diamonds. Christopher, a photographer and film editor, wore a gold hoop and diamond studs in his left ear.

Several pregnancies ended in miscarriages, and Aileen battled depression. The couple adopted their son Caleb in 1983, when he was twenty-two hours old; a year later, Christopher and his mother accompanied Aileen to the delivery room when she gave birth to Andrew. Then she descended deeper into depression.

To lift Aileen's spirits, her mother-in-law invited her to come along with her to Paris, where she was fund-raising for the American Foundation for AIDS Research (amfAR), which she had helped found earlier in 1985. In her hotel room, Aileen woke one morning drenched in sweat. "I got it," she thought with dread. A test soon confirmed that she was HIV-positive. She'd contracted it while having unprotected sex during an extramarital affair.

Six years went by before she publicly acknowledged her diagnosis, but she soon broke the news to her relatives. Her own kin initially had a difficult time expressing their emotions; they were still overwhelmed by their own multiple tragedies. With her mother-in-law, who was reeling from the death of her friend Rock Hudson, emotions poured out when Aileen and Chris went to her house in Bel-Air to tell her. "We all cried and cried," Aileen recalled. She later moved in with "Mom," as she called Taylor, who cradled a sobbing Aileen in her arms for many a night.

Panicked nonetheless, Aileen bolted with her young sons to New York, where she binged on coke. She lost custody of the boys, and the couple ultimately divorced in 1989. Taylor remained steadfast throughout. "I will always love Aileen as if she were my own child," she said.

Over the next several years, Aileen was in and out of clinics, hospitals, and psych wards (where she endured twelve shock treatments), as she battled her addictions, nervous breakdowns, and other issues, including anorexia and self-mutilation. By November 1991, she was in pretty good shape—she regained partial custody of the boys, along with a good relationship with Wilding. Even so, she was not quite ready to reveal her HIV status to the world. But producers of *A Current Affair*, the scandalmongering TV news show, outed her in an episode that was broadcast a week after basketball star Magic Johnson announced that he was positive.

Aileen found herself splashed on the covers of the *National Enquirer* and other tabloids. Not surprisingly, they didn't report her story the way she would have liked, which led her to sit down with writer Kevin Sessums. "The worst symptom of AIDS is denial," she said in the profile he wrote for the March 1992 issue of *Vanity Fair*.

She unloaded on the tabloids: "They totally trashed me. They bring all the rubbish in. So . . . I thought, Well, shit, just a second. Fuck that. I'm alive. I'm a fucking living miracle, man. What am I ashamed about?"

A few weeks later, she spoke at a press conference sponsored by the National Community on AIDS Partnership, the start of her new career as activist, in which she worked closely with her former mother-in-law. The first celebrity AIDS ally, Taylor spoke up forcefully, to presidents and everyone on down, to raise funds for research as well as to dispel the stigma and prejudice that carriers of the disease were contending with. (Aileen could attest to this personally. In spite of her being a Getty, a hospital in Los Angeles where she sought treatment had turned her away.)

Despite her own still-fragile state, Aileen gained a sense of purpose and self-worth through her work as a public advocate. "My grandfather probably would have been proud that I did something," she told *People* in April 1992. "He had a real hard time with people not using what they had. And I didn't use what I had for years and years."

In August 1993, Aileen and Elizabeth appeared on the cover of *Hello!* magazine with the cover line "How the Woman Who Has Fought Most for the AIDS Cause Faces the Illness in Her Own Family: Elizabeth Taylor at Home with Aileen Getty Who Has AIDS."

"I still feel like she's my daughter," Taylor told the magazine. "I think we are both survivors . . . very much so."

Still, before Aileen achieved lasting sobriety, there were relapses. Cocaine was her primary drug. She also did heroin, at one point reportedly with her nephew Balthazar. After one overdose, she went into a coma for twenty-four hours. In 1994, after the Northridge earthquake damaged her house, she and her sons moved in with Timothy Leary, the guru of psychedelic drugs. She accompanied him cross-country on a string of speaking engagements, as he promoted his VHS video *How to Operate Your Brain*. They also made some short films together.

In 2005, Aileen founded her first nonprofit, Gettlove, to provide meals for the homeless of Los Angeles. It grew into a full-service organization dedicated to meeting the spectrum of needs faced by homeless people, with a focus on housing.

"I would see her in the parking lot, distributing meals," recalls a Gettlove volunteer. "She knew every homeless person there by name. She would offer each one a choice of sandwiches—different ones on different days, with funny names, like the Elvis sandwich. It was such a respectful, sweet way to feed people."

About the same time, Aileen renewed some old family ties. In 2001, she began a relationship with Prince Bartolomeo Ruspoli, the third-born child of the celebrated Dado—her father's partying partner in Rome and elsewhere during the sixties.

"Maybe you've seen the following couple tooling around Los Angeles in their Rolls-Royce convertible," gossip columnist Liz Smith wrote about the pair shortly after their marriage in 2004. "He looks like a Botticelli angel and, when he's shirtless, shows his nipple ring and a tattoo across his chest reading 'Notorious.' She's a middle-aged hippie who comes from one of the richest families in America, and she is 'crazee' about her young bridegroom. He's 27; she's 46."

Bartolomeo's mother, Debra Berger, a California-born beauty, arrived in Rome at age seventeen and met Dado, forty-nine, at the home of Roman Polanski. In addition to "Meo," the couple produced another son, Tao, during their ten-year relationship. After it ended,

Debra moved back to California, giving her boys, scions of this charismatic, cultured, and decadent thousand-year-old Italian dynasty, a perch on the Pacific.

Tao studied philosophy at Berkeley, lived for a couple of years on a parking lot in Venice Beach in an old school bus, and was married for nine years to actress Olivia Wilde. A filmmaker, he produced and directed in 2002 a very personal and unflinching documentary, *Just Say Know*, about his parents and his brother. In it, each of them discussed their history of addiction.

"Heroin takes you by the hand, like it's your best life friend, so warm and trusting, and it leads you into the darkness," said Debra, who disclosed that she began using drugs at age twelve.

"When I was young, I shot heroin in my veins, then I realized there was no culture in the needle, so I learned the ritual of opium smoking. . . . Opium is like a beautiful woman," said Dado, describing his forty-five-year relationship with the substance.

Debra had become clean; with Dado, it was somewhat unclear. Meo, on the other hand, was in the throes of withdrawal during his interviews. He spoke as he tossed around in bed.

"I'd rather quit at home than in jail—it's hell laying your ass on a concrete floor," he said, revealing that he had started drinking at age seven and smoking weed at thirteen, before going on to mushrooms, acid, coke, speed, and crack.

Bartolomeo and Aileen, both the products of wealthy, complex, substance-using dynasties, certainly had much in common. Their marriage ended in 2006, but the two remain close (other Getty family members also maintain warm relations with him). "The Gangster Prince," as he called himself on his Instagram profile, enjoys the martial arts, horses, tattoos, cats, and muscle cars. Settled in Los Angeles, he has been sober since August 2017.

Aileen was able to conquer her addictions when she faced up to her underlying issues. "Drugs are about control over fear . . . and when you have AIDS, your lack of control is that much more evident. I tried to make up for that lack of being in control with a lot of cocaine," she said.

"She transformed her life completely. She went from darkness to light," said Princess Claudia Ruspoli, a cousin of Bartolomeo's. "She did it all by herself. She is amazingly strong. She has been completely clean for more than ten years now. And Bartolomeo has been clean more than three years now. They are survivors."

Over the years, Aileen has also suffered a number of the opportunistic infections that AIDS patients commonly face, including fungus and multi-drug-resistant tuberculosis. To overcome them, she went all-in on an organic, vegan diet. "She swapped bad addictions for good ones," according to an old friend in California. "Last time I saw her, she looked better than ever. Not only has she survived, she is fucking thriving."

That feat is all the more impressive considering her family background, as this friend, who is also familiar with other members of the Getty clan, observes: "When you have that kind of money and even a slightly addictive personality, when there is no end to the amount of drugs or sex you can get, and everyone is kissing your ass, nobody is telling you the truth—how do you survive? I am shocked any of them survived. *That's* when money is a burden."

Aileen's sons, now in their midthirties, are sturdy as well as kindly fellows. Caleb Wilding restores and rebuilds cars and motorcycles, in the West. Andrew Wilding, a Los Angeleno, is a filmmaker and musician. *Piano Man*, a black comedy he wrote, shot, and directed—which was produced by his London-based cousin Joseph—was released in 2010. In May 2020, he began releasing singles from an upcoming album, *Come Over*, under the stage name Kowloon (he has avoided any mention of being a Getty or Taylor descendant in promoting his work). Wilding wrote, performed, recorded, and mixed all the tracks in his home studio, blending vintage synthesizer, drum machines, and bass lines with eighties-inspired vocals. "Danceable love songs—albeit love songs set in a time of digital malaise and looming ecological catastrophe, with anxious, dread-filled lyrics that are as timely as they are postapocalyptic," according to Spotify.

Yet it's challenging to feel too angst-ridden when peering into Andrew's luminous, piercing blue eyes, which were well-displayed in a video made for his smooth single "Walk with Me" ("Walk with me, we can make it / Talk with me and let me answer your heart").

In 2012, Aileen established the Aileen Getty Foundation. While continuing to address homelessness, the organization expanded to support multiple causes, including the arts, meditation in schools, and peace-building in the Middle East, as well as HIV/AIDS research, for which it has collaborated with the Elizabeth Taylor AIDS Foundation, amfAR, and the Elton John AIDS Foundation (all of which have showered Aileen with accolades and thanks). Among her recent initiatives is a program to prevent the spread of HIV and AIDS in the American South, zeroing in on disadvantaged youths.

She has chaired some of amfAR's most successful fund-raising events. Her relatives have been supportive. In San Francisco, her aunt and uncle, Ann and Gordon, allowed their palatial mansion to be transformed into a very glamorous casino for an annual Charity Poker Tournament and Game Night. The 2019 edition, which raked in $400,000, was attended by the Bay Area elite, movie stars including Gwyneth Paltrow and Jon Hamm, and Gettys of all generations.

By 2019, Aileen came to the conclusion that one cause has unequivocally become more pressing than any other: the climate crisis. She shifted the bulk of her resources and time to address this existential threat. With her friends Rory Kennedy, the youngest child of the late Robert F. Kennedy, and Trevor Neilson, a well-connected advisor and investor, she cofounded the Climate Emergency Fund (CEF). Getty provided the group with a cornerstone grant of $600,000; it has subsequently raised about $3.5 million more in funding.

This is an all-hands-on-deck moment, they announced on their website: "We believe that only a peaceful planet-wide mobilization on the scale of World War II will give us a chance to avoid the worst-case scenarios and restore a safe climate."

And no more dawdling. "The world's philanthropists need to wake up to the reality that a gradualist approach to the climate emergency is doomed to fail," Trevor wrote in a post on the Medium platform in which he outlined CEF's goals, which include cutting emissions to net zero by 2025, establishing a citizens' assembly that would set climate policy, and urging governments and media to tell the truth about climate change.

While CEF provides grants to grassroots activists who are taking a disruptive approach and using aggressive tactics, such as Extinction Rebellion and Fire Drill Fridays, they draw the line at anything violent. Yet civil disobedience usually involves some degree of law-breaking. Extinction Rebellion was started by two British activists in October 2018. Causing traffic mayhem and gridlock is the best way to get people's attention, they reasoned. Irksome as that can be, it is "necessary because it is evident the public is still not sufficiently engaged," said Aileen. "We can't sugarcoat it anymore." Moreover, if people think *this* is disruptive, it's nothing compared to "the real disruption and the incomprehensible suffering of those that we love" that would result from climate change.

"Even if this approach isn't going to deliver the outcome we're hopeful it will, it's better than doing what we've been doing that hasn't amounted to any change," Aileen added. "However imperfect the actions will be . . . at least they are actions."

Kennedy, a filmmaker, shares Aileen's sense of urgency. "We're very much running out of time here," she said. The two can also relate on family matters. In an interview with the *New York Times*, Kennedy resisted efforts to lump members of her clan together. "There are a lot of us," she said—so best not to speak of them "as a unit." But there are shared values: "As a family, we have appreciated, over the years, the importance of protest," she said.

Early in 2020, it was announced that Aileen would serve as a host—along with Bill Clinton, Elton John, Barbra Streisand, the designer Valentino, Tom Hanks, and others—for what promised to be the most high-wattage charity benefit Los Angeles had seen in a while, the Elizabeth Taylor Ball to End AIDS. The first-ever Los Angeles fund raiser for the Elizabeth Taylor AIDS Foundation, it was to be held on the back lot of Fox, the studio that released *Cleopatra*, Taylor's most epic vehicle—which, naturally, would be the theme of the party. Aileen was two when filming on this colossal picture—the most costly yet made—commenced in Rome in 1961. The sixteen-month-long shoot riveted the Italian capital. Hollywood set designers built a twelve-acre reproduction of the Roman Forum (larger than the real thing), which may well have inspired J. Paul Getty, besotted with ancient Rome, to imagine what he could one day erect in Malibu. Perhaps the toddler Aileen even crossed paths with her future mother-in-law, or, for that matter, her future stepmother (Talitha was an extra). Sixty years later, the invitation to the Elizabeth Taylor Ball to End AIDS sort of encapsulated the sweep of the Gettys' Californian-Italian cross-pollination. Like everything else in 2020, the event went virtual. For her part, Aileen introduced President Clinton.

When Covid hit, Getty, Kennedy, and Neilson realized they could not support sending people to the streets to protest. CEF helped found and fund (with an initial grant of $100,000) the bipartisan Coalition for Sustainable Jobs (CSJ), a sort of rainbow coalition for the climate change community. It includes Republicans from many corners—including evangelicals, hunters, fishers, and young conservatives—all of whom agreed to push for moderate clean-energy and climate change policies.

Late in 2021, Aileen resassumed a more combative stance, coauthoring an opinion piece for the *Guardian* with Rebecca Rockefeller Lambert. "Fossil Fuels made our families rich. Now we want this industry to end" ran the headline. "We can't build back better unless we build back fossil-free," the women wrote.

Over the years, some journalists and commentators reporting on Aileen's philanthropy have predictably harped on the fossil-fuel origins of her fortune, and her not exactly modest lifestyle ("New Face on Climate Activism Scene Is Multimillionaire Who Owns Several Mansions" read a headline on Western Wire, a website funded by an association of oil and gas producers).

"I'm aware that the optics are what they are. I want to do what's correct and what's right," she told the *Chronicle of Philanthropy*. "It's not necessarily restitution, it's what I get to do as a human being. I happen to have resources that I get to bring into the mix."

At the end of the day, we all simply have to do "what's right," Aileen says. "There's legacy, and there's personal responsibility."

8

Ariadne

Ariadne—Gail and J. Paul Getty Jr.'s youngest child—was the shy one. She successfully dodged the public eye for most of her life, while her siblings became the subjects of headlines, though generally not by choice.

When eventually she did appear in the spotlight, she chose a venue as high-powered as it gets: the World Economic Forum in Davos, Switzerland.

On a frosty morning in January 2018, this diminutive fifty-five-year-old blonde, clad in dark blazer, slacks, and shiny Giuseppe Zanotti sneakers, joined the heads of state, captains of industry, and other potentates who gathered for the annual alpine summit.

WEF is where global leaders go to "move the needle" (a Davos catchphrase) on humanity's pressing issues: climate change, income inequality, Mideast peace. LGBTQ rights had never been on the main menu. In recent years, there had been a few "off-piste" events to address the subject, but it remained a fairly taboo topic, not tackled in the official panels.

Acceptance for LGBTQ people became a personal priority for Ari Getty (as she is generally called by friends and family) as soon as her children, Natalia (known as Nats) and August had each come out as gay, loudly and proudly, around 2010. (In 2021, Nats adopted the male pronoun, when he announced his gender transition.) When they advanced into their twenties, both launched careers as fashion designers, and Nats began to date Gigi Gorgeous, a Canadian-born transgender icon. Ariadne rejoiced in their identities. Then Donald Trump got elected. Ariadne grew fearful as his rhetoric and policies generated increasing discrimination and violence against LGBTQ people.

She journeyed to Davos to announce her response: a $15 million gift to GLAAD, the world's foremost LGBTQ media-monitoring organization. (It was founded in 1985, when a group of journalists gathered to protest defamatory, sensationalized AIDS coverage in the *New York Post*; two years later, it persuaded the *New York Times* to begin using the word *gay* in place of *homosexual* or other words that were pejoratives.)

Ariadne's donation—made through her Ariadne Getty Foundation (AGF)—was earmarked to establish the GLAAD Media Institute, which will train an army of ten thousand activists and leaders around the world to communicate accurately the stories of gay, lesbian, and transgender people.

When it was time to announce the new institute, Ariadne, previously a quiet philanthropist, realized she had to show up, and only one location would do. "We need to go to Davos, we need to be on center stage to do this, with the world's biggest companies," she said.

Leveraging the Getty fortune and name, she cosponsored, with GLAAD, a panel entitled "How Business, Philanthropy, and Media Can Lead to Achieving 100 Percent Acceptance for LGBTQ People." The corporate heavyweights who participated included Brad Smith, president of Microsoft; Serge Dumont, then vice chairman of Omnicom; and Jim Fitterling of Dow Chemical, the only openly gay CEO of a large industrial company. After the discussion, moderator Richard Quest, the CNN anchor, announced Ariadne's gift. As claps erupted, she remained in her seat in the audience, still a bit shy. But, in an impassioned voice, she made a declaration: "Take a cause—make it your one cause, make it stand out, make it shout out."

Born in Rome in 1962, Ariadne spent much of her childhood in the Tuscan countryside around La Fuserna, the simple farmhouse that her mother bought after her divorce from Paul and her remarriage, to actor Lang Jeffries. Ariadne's chores included picking out tomatoes, zucchini, and other bounty from the vegetable patch for family meals, and starting the primitive electrical generator that was the farmhouse's only source of power. In her free time, she would walk the two miles to the tiny village of Orgia and go from house to house, helping out the predominantly elderly population with their household tasks. In return, the matriarchs of the community doted on her. "I literally was raised by a village," said Ariadne.

In the mid-1970s, following the kidnapping, Gail and the children moved to England, where Ariadne attended boarding school in Sussex. On weekends and school breaks, she often came to stay at Sutton Place with her grandfather, who was also her godfather. "I think I got lucky, being the youngest," she recalled, over tea in Paris in 2019 before one of August's fashion shows. Initially Ariadne appeared shy, but her natural warmth and effervescence soon surfaced.

Being the baby of the family, she was allowed to sit in her grandfather's study, while he was surrounded by piles of papers, books, and visitors. His work ethic was "bananas," she said. Yet he was great fun. She would tie his shoelaces together, making him giggle, until she finally got too much in the way. Then he would say "Scat!" and send her off to Bullimore and Parkes. She would "help" them polish the silver, efforts that doubtless entailed more work for them.

"He wasn't such a talkative man, but you knew that you were loved and taken care of," she said of her grandfather. "It was horrible for me when my Nonno Getty died." (She was thirteen when he passed away in 1976.)

When it was time for college, she came to America, enrolling at Bennington, the artsy and intense Vermont school, where her contemporaries included future literary stars Bret Easton Ellis, Donna Tartt, and Jonathan Lethem.

Academia wasn't for her. She dropped out and traveled, then lived between New York and Los Angeles. Using an old Pentax camera, she became a photographer, focusing on architectural subjects. Exhibitions of her hand-colored prints, held in galleries in both cities, were well-received. But around that time, the mid-1980s, she drew more notoriety from her choice of roommate—Cher.

Ariadne was Cher's long-term houseguest. She moved into one of the spare rooms in the star's Los Angeles mansion, and stayed about three years. ("Cher said to her, 'Make yourself at home.' So she did," August explained.)

In 1988, Ariadne married Justin Williams, an actor she'd been seeing for a couple years, and the pair moved into a small house in Brentwood. They had Nats in 1992 and August two years later. In his babyhood, August designed his first gowns by draping napkins over forks. Before long, he was repurposing his mother's silk Louboutin shoe bags to make new looks for his Barbie dolls. "Fashion was my first language," he later explained. Nats, on the other hand, was a tomboy, usually skateboarding or climbing trees.

Shy though Ariadne might have been, that didn't mean she wasn't tough and fiercely protective when it came to looking out for her children. They were brought up using their father's surname, Williams; until around the time Nats turned eight, they had no idea they were Gettys, much less what that meant.

In Los Angeles, the Getty name looms large, sometimes literally. When they passed signs for Getty Drive or Getty Circle on the freeways, for example, Ariadne would steer straight ahead without saying a word. Even on school field trips to the J. Paul Getty Museum, the children were unaware they had any connection to it. In retrospect, Nats says he should have had a clue: his mother always chaperoned those class trips.

"I wanted them to grow up without the weight of the name," Ariadne explained.

The Getty name, of course, comes with burdens as well as blessings. Ariadne was ten when her brother was kidnapped. Her young adult years—the early 1990s, when her sister, Aileen, battled AIDS—were also a frightening time. Little was known then about how the disease was spread. Before she went to the hospital to visit Aileen, Ariadne worried about possible transmission to baby Nats. But her pediatrician assured her it was safe for her to go. "Those were really scary days," she recalled.

Around 2000, the Williamses left Hollywood for Buckinghamshire in England, motivated in part by her wish to be close to her father. That's when Ariadne told her children about their Getty blood. She couldn't keep it from them any longer, as they would be going to schools with their cousins. (As adults, Nats and August chose to use the Getty surname.)

During the decade the family lived in England, where they resided in a house very close to Wormsley, Nats and August attended elite boarding schools, including St. Edward's and Dragon. Nats did well academically, but school was never for August. He did, however, find inspiration at Wormsley, in the Walled Garden.

Roaming alone through the mazes of flowers, inspired by beauty and decay, August (who described himself at the time as "a chubby, ginger, American gay kid") created imaginary scenarios and characters—including one he calls the Getty Girl, a sort of phantasm and muse. The bowered sanctuary was formative. "I like to live my life somewhere between fantasy and reality at all times," he said.

In 2004, around which time Ariadne and Justin divorced, she began to establish herself as a philanthropist when she started the Fuserna Foundation (she later renamed it the Ariadne Getty Foundation). Its mission statement was two words long: "Unpopular causes." She distributed money to worthy but underfunded initiatives, including a reading program for prisoners. Inmates were given books and offered £5 to finish them, with the funds going to a charity of their choice. Later she traveled to refugee camps in Uganda to supply generators known as "solar suitcases," which medical personnel used in areas without electricity.

She was also able to enjoy a good relationship with her father. After having been incapacitated by depression and illnesses for decades, he had finally overcome many of his problems. "It was wonderful . . . to watch him emerge. I feel we got very lucky," she said. "He found a much more expansive life. . . . For a family that was initially fragmented, we became a much closer family."

Around 2010, Ariadne and the kids moved back to Los Angeles. Nats flew to California a few months ahead of his mother and brother. Academically he was doing fine, but he needed to escape the boarding-school social scene, where he'd fallen into trouble. He was drinking and struggling with body-image issues, which would challenge him for years to come.

During those months in LA, his aunt Aileen looked after him. After her own battles with drugs and HIV, Aileen was now in a good place and running Gettlove, her nonprofit to aid the homeless. When Nats arrived, he and Aileen lived in a building attached to a men's sober-living center. "We would wake up at five every morning, make three hundred lunch bags, do the breakfast line, then we would drive around LA handing out bags with blankets and toothbrushes to homeless people," Nats recalled.

"It was hard-core, but one of the most meaningful and important things I've ever done, and it really set the tone for my life back in LA. It turned me into a mini version of my mom and my aunt."

Around the same time, 2,500 miles away in Mississauga, Ontario, Gregory Lazzarato was a high school athlete (a nationally ranked diver) with a secret. Lazzarato—who was born the same year as Nats and who later became Gigi Gorgeous—had discovered makeup.

Lazzarato began making videos in which she offered makeup tutorials, posting them on YouTube. They quickly gained viewers; in the process, she earned self-esteem. "I never felt beautiful earlier in my life. Makeup was a confidence tool for me, and it helped me identify with my femininity," she said.

But she was still embarrassed enough to hide her posts from her family. Eventually a relative saw them, and informed Gigi's mother, Judy. "She confronted me," recalled Gigi. "I thought she would be mad. Instead, she said, 'I'm your biggest fan. But we should probably keep this from your father for now.'" Soon enough, David, her dad, found out. His reaction: "Just be safe." Before long, Gigi began to receive checks from advertisers on her YouTube channel, and later from brands she partnered with. Her two brothers, one older, one younger, were supportive too.

In Los Angeles, Nats enrolled at Mount Saint Mary's University, where he double-majored in political science and business; August entered New Roads School. After he was asked to repeat freshman year, he dropped out. He began homeschooling, while teaching himself how to be a fashion designer. "I decided to take a whack at what I'd been doing since I was three," he said. "I was kind of the oddball in the family. I have a fascination with an absurd amount of glam. No one knows where it came from. I'm from a family of tomboys."

As the trio settled into a 6,000-square-foot penthouse atop the Montage Hotel in Beverly Hills, the kids were finding their identities. August's coming-out story, at age fifteen, involved a room service waiter at the Sunset Tower Hotel, as he later told the *New York Times*. Nats began to date girls. When they both told their mother about their orientations, it was no surprise, as Nats recollected: "When I told her I was gay, she looked at me and said, 'Nats, I gave birth to you. I knew the minute you came out of me.' I was like, 'Thanks, but, dude, Mom, you could have given me a heads-up!'" Said Ariadne, "I kept waiting for them to tell me, because I didn't want to tell them."

As her children explored gay life in Los Angeles, Ariadne welcomed their friends and lovers. She became a den mother to much of the city's queer community, members of which took to warmly calling her Mama G. One typical night, August stepped out of his bedroom around midnight and found six drag queens in the kitchen with Ariadne, who was making them bowls of pasta. "They were like, 'We're here to see your mom. Go back to bed,'" he recalled.

Even while rolling out hospitality, Ariadne was fretting about the darkening political climate and the threats it presented to Nats and August and people like them. Their coming out encouraged her to come out, as an activist. "That's when she got super involved in the LGBT Center and GLAAD. I think that's when she found her inner fire," said Nats. "It lit a fire under her ass. I'm so proud of her."

In 2012, August—eighteen, lean, tanned, and liberally tattooed—officially launched his career. He opened August Getty Atelier, in a spacious building his mother acquired in Culver City. Two years later, he debuted at New York Fashion Week, becoming one of the youngest designers ever to show there, with a collection of sculpted minidresses and chiffon gowns.

While at Mount Saint Mary's, Nats—gamine, with porcelain-pale skin, sometimes-platinum short hair, and his share of tattoos—began modeling, represented by Next Management. In November 2015, when August staged his next big show—an extravaganza on the Universal Studios lot, in collaboration with photographer David LaChapelle—Nats was cast to walk in it. So was Gigi Gorgeous; two years earlier, when Gregory announced her transgender status on social media, she'd adopted the name (legally, she changed it to Gigi Loren Lazzarato). About the same time she moved to LA, where, through mutual acquaintances, she met August. Self-described as "boy crazy," Gigi was dating men and identified as gay.

Already a tall, striking blonde with full breasts, she was still in her transition process, which had started quietly a few years before. Her path began when she met a transgender girl for the first time. "It clicked for me," Gigi said. "From that day on, in my mind I started living as a trans woman. It just took everyone else a little longer to find out." It also involved years of hormone treatments and surgeries, in locations ranging from Los Angeles to Bangkok. Every step of the way she documented her transition on social media. In the process, she gained some eight million followers across YouTube and other platforms, and a reputation as a trans role model.

Even though Gigi and Nats were both part of August's Universal Studios show, they didn't meet there. There were sixty models, and it was a huge, immersive production. (The Old West lot was transformed into "Heaven" and "Hell." Among the props in the latter were televisions rolling Fox News footage of presidential candidate Trump.)

They met a few months later, when they flew to Paris to walk in a show for August there.

At Charles de Gaulle Airport, Nats fell for Gigi. "I pretty much knew the second I saw her. She radiated an infectious amount of positive energy and happiness. She is this amazing bright light. I pretty much laid it on the table to her. I said, 'We're not going to be just friends. I'm obsessed with you. Can we go out on a date?'"

"Then, sooner rather than later, we both said, 'I love you,'" said Gigi. She came out as lesbian.

Gigi got an immediate stamp of approval from Ariadne. "I liked her straightaway. She's so full of life, you can't resist her," she said.

As the couple was finding happiness together, August Getty Atelier, with about twenty employees, was taking off. Rachel McAdams wore a slinky emerald-green satin halter-neck gown August designed for her to the 2016 Academy Awards, where her film *Spotlight* won Best Picture. His ever more extravagant custom creations were also being worn by Lady Gaga, Katy Perry, Miley Cyrus, and others.

"I just want to make the world a shinier place—one sequin at a time," said August, summing up his philosophy.

More accomplishments came in 2017. A feature-length documentary, *This Is Everything: Gigi Gorgeous*, directed by two-time Oscar winner Barbara Kopple, premiered at the Sundance Film Festival. For the occasion, Gigi wore an especially dazzling August Getty Atelier creation, which came to be known as the "Million Dollar Dress." Constructed from metal mesh, it was embroidered with 500,000 Swarovski crystals. Six artisans spent three months making it. A couple months later, Paris Hilton wore it to the Hollywood Beauty Awards. (Its name notwithstanding, it was estimated to be worth some $270,000.)

That September, August showed his Spring 2018 collection at the Four Seasons Hotel in Milan. "His vision translated well: models wore glamorous looks with red carpet appeal such as a silver and gold beaded white strapless gown," wrote *WWD*.

Next, it was Nats's turn to take the wraps off his fashion line. He began it in secret, as he completed his studies at Mount Saint Mary's. His grades were perfect, and he planned to become a lawyer. "But there was another side of me, and I didn't know how to express it," he said. His aha moment came via an Yves Saint Laurent jacket. "It was white leather. I had wanted it forever, and finally treated myself to it. I was so stoked."

But the joy was short-lived. "I went out with it on, and there were, like, five other people wearing it. I thought, *You've got to be kidding*. I had spent so much on it and now it didn't feel special." He remedied that by taking paint pens and Sharpies to it. His customized jacket was soon drawing praise from friends, who asked him to perform similar interventions on garments for them. Following some Instagram posts and word of mouth, his pieces—hoodies, trucker hats, and other staples of streetwear to which he gave an arty, luxe spin—became "a thing," as he recalled.

In the beginning, he financed it from his allowance and kept it a secret from his mother. "I was super insecure about it. It took a lot for me to say, 'Look at this' . . . because it's a representation of me." He needn't have worried. Actress Bella Thorne and singer Halsey were among the first customers who began snapping up the merch online.

The business, Strike Oil, launched officially in 2018 out of the Culver City building where August operates. Its large, stark-white rooms feature contemporary art, as well as a sizable vintage Getty Oil sign, a gift from cousin Joseph in London. Ariadne serves as CEO of both companies. The name Nats chose for his is a tribute to his great-grandfather and his famous statement that the key to success was "Rise early, work hard, and strike oil."

"It's one of my favorite rules to live by. I have it tattooed on my right ankle," he said. "So, when it came time to name my empire, if you will, I chose it as an homage to the family I have now and the ones that came before. It's my DNA.

"I always looked at leather as the black gold of fashion," he added, borrowing the term for oil. "When I start painting on a leather jacket, it feels like I am painting on oil, like I am striking oil."

(Great-grandfatherly inspiration and pride also run deep for his brother. "Whenever I am feeling sad or uninspired, I go to his grave. I sit and ponder, surrounded by nature, and think, *WWJPGD*—*what would J. Paul Getty do?*" said August. Recently, when he Instagrammed an image of the Getty Center's hilltop campus, he captioned it simply, "Feeling prideful AF.")

Many of the sketches Nats prints on his pieces are inspired by artists he was exposed to as a child—a number of whom Ariadne collects, including Keith Haring, Andy Warhol, Jean-Michel Basquiat, Jeff Koons, and Raymond Pettibon. The extended family, abounding with collectors, also provides inspiration. "Everybody kind of has their own vibe and taste," he explained. "Being surrounded by that even without knowing I was being exposed to it really shaped my love and appreciation of art."

At the same time, he had some harrowing experiences. In his social media posts, he has talked forthrightly about his battles. During the Covid lockdown in 2020, he reflected: "I never realized how ill I truly was. Between drugs, eating disorders, and mental health issues I honestly was knocking on deaths door. . . . After multiple over doses, a near coma, broken bones, and a body weight of under 80lbs I still returned to a life of drugs, darkness and self hate. . . . It has taken me years to recover and it is still a daily struggle."

Gigi helped him find the light. She was the first person he had dated "who saw me for me," he said. In March 2018, Nats proposed. The pair flew to Paris, where they boarded a helicopter. They hovered above the forests of the Île-de-France and landed at Château de Vaux-le-Vicomte, which Nats had rented for the occasion. Designed in the seventeenth century by Louis Le Vau, architect of Versailles, it is widely considered the most ideal château in France. (J. Paul Getty admired it too: he contemplated buying it, as he wrote in his diary.)

WILL YOU MARRY ME? appeared in large lights on the building's façade as the couple descended. Ariadne, August, and other family and friends were awaiting them inside with champagne. Cue the fireworks.

The jubilant scene inside was captured in a video that Gigi posted on YouTube. "I'm going to have a daughter-in-law!" said Ariadne, who was accompanied by her partner of more than a decade, Louie Rubio, a music producer. (His credits include soundtracks for numerous movies and TV shows, including *Baywatch* and *Brothers and Sisters*.)

Soon after, Gigi met most of the Getty clan when she traveled with Nats to Wormsley, to attend uncle Mark's wedding to Caterina Nahberg in the Walled Garden. On a podcast with Gigi, Nats later spoke of how well everybody got on, which he likened to "the icing on the cake" of their engagement: "When you met my entire extended family, it was like, 'Damn, if you can keep up with *this*—getting into it with them, and being able to hang—I am so down.'"

In June 2018, Ariadne, along with Nats and August, gave a pretty remarkable interview to Brooks Barnes, LA correspondent of the *New York Times*, for the profile entitled "Growing Up Getty."

Ariadne was nervous at the start: "I'm a super-shy introvert—this is not my comfort zone," she said, over sips of chicken soup in her apartment at the Montage, where she was also flanked by Bandit, her brown chihuahua, and a pair of Jeff Koons balloon dogs.

Talking about why she gave $15 million to GLAAD, which had been announced in Davos a few months earlier, she decried the Trump administration's assaults on gay rights—they were affronts to her family and others like theirs. At the same time, her family was dealing with a unique onslaught, from the new movie *All the Money in the World* and the TV series *Trust*, both of which plumbed the grisly details of her brother's kidnapping. "Our family has been under attack," she said. August and Nats, for their parts, called the films "demonizing" and "disgusting."

The Ridley Scott–directed movie, starring Christopher Plummer and Michelle Williams, had been released six months earlier. Danny Boyle's series, starring Donald Sutherland and Hilary Swank, was currently on FX—the ten episodes of Season One. Two more seasons had been envisioned by the producers. For Ariadne, a single season was more than enough. She not only vocalized her unhappiness (while the rest of her extended family largely opted not to comment), she hired Martin Singer, one of Hollywood's toughest and most powerful attorneys. A letter he sent to FX and Boyle stated that the series "falsified the dreadful story of Ariadne's brother's kidnapping to turn it into a cruel and mean-spirited depiction of the Getty family, maliciously and recklessly portraying them as greedily cooperating in and/or facilitating a kidnapping that left a family member mutilated." Seasons Two and Three did not go into production.

That September, the Los Angeles LGBT Center presented her with its Distinguished Achievement Award—her first-ever award for philanthropy. (A $4.5 million gift from Getty enabled construction of the organization's new Ariadne Getty Foundation Youth Academy and the forthcoming Ariadne Getty Foundation Senior Housing.) "I'm shaking like a leaf," she said when she got to the stage in the ballroom of the Beverly Hilton, even though her children had warmed up the 1,500 guests with a humorous introduction. In August's part, he offered details of his coming-out story: "I never came out. I just said one day, 'Mom, I'm going on a date with the room service guy.' All she said was, 'Which one?'" (Ari did go out later that night in search of one of the health-service vans that operate around West Hollywood; she loaded up on information packets and condoms, which she gave to her son.)

"I have recently stepped out of the shadows of my donating and my philanthropic work, which hasn't been that easy," said Ariadne in her remarks. "I've done it to encourage others to step forward and understand the impact of what it means to give . . . and to participate on a larger platform, to have things resonate. I encourage everybody to get connected, start being active, and don't be shy like me for all the years that I have been."

She also thanked one of August's ex-boyfriends for introducing her to the LGBT Center. "My office is filled with all of August's exes," she said.

In January 2019, August vaulted to fashion's stratosphere when he showed a collection he entitled "Confetti" alongside the haute couture collections during Paris Fashion Week. Inside the Salon d'Été, a glass-conservatory-like space at the Ritz Hotel, models in white silk, satin, and lace lounged around a grand piano. "Bridging the Old Hollywood glamour of his hometown with Parisian Grace," *WWD* wrote.

Showing his work during the Paris season at such a tender age wasn't stressful for him. "It was a natural progression. I don't get nervous. This is what I do," he said.

As soon as the presentation was over, August flew to Davos to join his sibling, Gigi, and Ariadne. Returning to the World Economic Forum, AGF and GLAAD sponsored another panel with top corporate executives, "Making Equality Equal: The Next Move Forward for LGBT Rights." The emphasis on corporate social responsibility reflects Ariadne's view that while governments—in the US and around the world—are lagging behind on human rights and moral leadership, big businesses can be more responsive and effective agents to advance social equity issues (something that became more fully apparent to others a couple years later, in the wake of battles over election laws and Black Lives Matter). "So, basically, we're here to strong-arm the corporate world, to make sure they do the right thing. Shame them, if necessary," she said.

A particularly moving moment came when Dr. Corinna Lathan, CEO of AnthroTronix, a robotics and biotech firm, spoke. AGF/GLAAD is helping to foster "a culture of LGBTQ acceptance" at Davos, she said; its panels were having unexpected impact. The previous year at Davos, she recounted, her main purpose had been to moderate a panel on the Earth BioGenome Project. Yet "the most powerful conversation that I had was with pop culture icon Gigi Gorgeous." Gigi, as it happens, is "the idol" of Lathan's own eleven-year-old transgender daughter, Eliza. A letter that Gigi subsequently wrote to Eliza was enormously inspirational to her. "The professional became personal," Lathan said.

When spring 2019 arrived, the spotlight was on Gigi. Harmony Books published her memoir, *He Said, She Said: Lessons, Stories, and Mistakes from My Transgender Journey.* In it, she disclosed that she had not yet proceeded with gender reassignment surgery. She was conflicted about having the procedure to remove her penis and construct a vagina. "Part of me wonders if I'm holding onto my anatomy so that Nats and I can have children," she wrote.

Shortly after the book appeared, she divulged in a YouTube video that she had flown to Bangkok for the operation but canceled it the day before, due to fears that the operation might not be totally successful: "I have had lots of friends who have gotten the surgery. I've seen a lot of vaginas—post-vaginas—and some are gorge and functioning and some are not so gorge. Obviously, it goes without saying, I want a gorge, functioning vagina." She and Nats, she added, were actively trying to conceive a child together.

July was a blockbuster month for the whole family. August returned to the Paris Ritz to present his next couture collection. With "Enigma," his theme was darkness. A gorgeous, gothic spectacle, it unfolded as models slowly began to materialize through an allée of pleached linden trees, planted in Versailles boxes, in the hotel's Grand Jardin. The procession of extravagant if macabre looks ranged from an armor-plated minidress molded from resin to look like a tombstone, to a boat-sized pannier skirt and bodice of black lace. Clad in a black sleeveless T-shirt, black jeans, studded belt, and boots, August beckoned the models forth as waiters served champagne to guests, classical music played, and a breeze rustled through the trees.

"I like to tell stories," he later explained. "With 'Enigma,' I wrote about tragedy and morbid love."

Nonetheless, the atmosphere was lively, in part thanks to more than a dozen friends who August flew to Paris to see the show. The multicultural group, most of whom live in West Hollywood and had not been to Paris before, included drag queens and transgender persons. It was definitely some fresh air at the Ritz.

At the same time, seasoned couture aficionados in the audiences were impressed. "Extraordinary. I've seen something today I've never seen before," said Houston doyenne Becca Cason Thrash, who has seen quite a bit in her time.

For August, there were just two opinions that really counted: his mom's and the French. "Both are a little scary because they are both hard-hitters," he said. He held his breath, then, when he saw Ari in the Grand Jardin: "I get nervous for my mom. She means the world to me."

Before the month was out, Ariadne celebrated her fifty-seventh birthday, *Variety* honored her as Philanthropist of the Year in a dinner at the Montage Hotel back in Beverly Hills, and Nats and Gigi were married.

The ceremony, July 12, had all the pomp one would expect for the marriage of a great-grandchild of J. Paul Getty. Two hundred twenty formally clad guests gathered on the lawn of the Rosewood Miramar Beach Hotel in Montecito, California, overlooking the Santa Barbara Channel. Pink and white rose petals were strewn everywhere as a violinist drew her bow and commenced the ceremony with the notes of Celine Dion's "Because You Loved Me."

Nats, wearing a white suit with a tailcoat that he had designed, waited by the altar with Ariadne and Louie. Gigi, in a white flowing gown by Michael Costello, walked down the white velvet carpet bordered with white cherry blossom trees, accompanied by her father.

After the couple was pronounced Gigi and Nats Getty, the guests (including Caitlyn Jenner) dined on pan-roasted filet mignon and chicken piccata. Video toasts to the newlyweds came from, among others, Katy Perry and Orlando Bloom ("Show us how it's done!") and Gavin Newsom, California's governor and Nats's godfather ("I'm proud of you and I'm proud of Gigi").

When 2020 began, the family returned to Davos, this time with one more Getty. Ariadne's brother Mark announced that his company, Getty Images, was partnering with GLAAD to build a new digital glossary and set of guidelines that prioritize intersectionality, allowing LGBTQ-related images shot by Getty's 250,000 photographers to be more easily found. "There's a huge opportunity here to break stereotypes, tell stories that haven't been told before," he said. The Ariadne Getty Foundation later posted photos of the brother and sister captioned: "We moved the needle in Davos. . . . Siblings changing the world."

As Covid-19 took hold, the Gettys, like most of the population, went relatively quiet. Nats took the opportunity to examine his life and reflect. In January 2021, he posted a photo of himself bare-chested on Instagram. His breasts had been removed. "I am transgender, nonbinary," he announced.

All his life, he explained, he had felt "not in sync with the body I was born with. . . . So I decided to start my physical transformation and get top surgery."

He also acknowledged the advantages he enjoys, which others might not. "While I feel so blessed to be able to start my transition surrounded by love and support, it's not lost on me the many people who are having to navigate this alone and in silence."

"I didn't fall in love with Nats because of his gender, I fell in love with the person that he is," said Gigi shortly afterward when, at the same time, she announced her new status as pansexual.

As the pandemic began to wane, the family got back to business. With its new "Oil Spill Tee," Strike Oil continued to attract buzz (Machine Gun Kelly was spotted wearing one). At the same time, the fledgling company recognized the ills of fossil-fuel extraction (15 percent of the sales proceeds went to the Marine Conservation Institute). And Ariadne awaited the opening of the Los Angeles LGBT Center's Ariadne Getty Foundation Senior Housing, a 70,000-square-foot, five-story tower adjacent to the two-year-old Ariadne Getty Foundation Youth Academy. Fostering a community where young and old cohabitate—where each can support and learn from the other— reminded her of her childhood in Orgia, she told *Los Angeles Blade*. "That's definitely the thing that makes me the happiest," she said of this coming together. "There's no room for loneliness."

9

Paul III

The Janiculum is the second-tallest hill in Rome. From its heights, the ancient capital stretches out below. The splendor and wonder of it all only increases when you gaze down from the Fontana dell'Acqua Paola, the monumental marble fountain atop the Janiculum, built in 1612 by Pope Paul V. Viewers of Paolo Sorrentino's masterful film *The Great Beauty* will recognize it from the opening scene.

Late one warm summer night in 1972, two teenagers jumped into the fountain's semicircular pool.

"We sat in it for hours. We were gazing down at the city, waiting for the light," remembered one of the boys, Pietro Cicognani. "When the sun came up, it was so glorious—the whole city was at our feet."

Cicognani would eventually move to New York and become a successful architect whose work was widely publicized. The last name of his companion that night was already world-famous, but few people outside Rome knew anything yet about red-haired, freckle-faced Paul himself.

Cicognani had been introduced to J. Paul Getty III by a cousin. "We hit it right off. He was a sweetheart—very gentle, sensitive," he recalled. "He wouldn't talk about his family. He just wanted to live life. He had a desire to feel the moment."

While his younger siblings seemed to flourish more in the Tuscan countryside, Paul was thoroughly at home in Rome. Over six feet tall and lithe, he loved speeding through every neighborhood and corner of the city on his motorbikes. Schools were seemingly the only places he didn't take well to. Creative but rebellious, he cycled through seven or eight educational institutions before, at sixteen, he convinced his mother, Gail, to let him leave school and focus on painting. (Paul III's father kept in sporadic contact with him from England or Morocco.)

Rome had changed a great deal since the days when his parents arrived, when the city was in its elegant *Dolce Vita* heyday. By the early 1970s, it had become a countercultural melting pot, filled with students from Latin America who had fled fascist regimes and hippies from around the world who were seeking some combination of enlightenment and escape.

Among them were a pair of beautiful German twins, Gisela and Jutta. After arriving in Rome in 1972, they spent a night on the beach at nearby Sperlonga where they dropped acid, a consciousness-altering experience that also served to introduce them to members of Rome's creative community.

As soon as Paul met them—both paled-skinned and dark-haired—the trio became inseparable; they moved into a basement apartment in Trastevere. Seven years Paul's senior, the young women were budding actresses, filmmakers, artists, and activists. Gisela—who for a time went by the name Martine—had recently given birth to a daughter, Anna, with her second husband, a German actor, from whom she soon parted. Anna was being cared for by the twins' family in Germany.

One of Paul's good friends was Carlo Scimone. The son of a proper Roman family, he was pursuing his interest in photography—often using Paul as a model. Among the portraits he took of Paul were artistic nudes, some of which appeared, rather scandalously, in *Playmen*, a fashionable Italian magazine. In their youth, Paul and his siblings would come to his house for meals and to hang out, and vice versa.

In the spring of 1973, Paul visited Cinecittà, where Paul Morrissey was shooting *Flesh for Frankenstein*. On the set, Paul met Andy Warhol, a friend of his father's. Andy had recently been in Milan, where he was transfixed by Leonardo da Vinci's mural *The Last Supper*. It would make a great movie, he told the young Getty.

Excited, Paul proposed the idea to Carlo. Filming soon began in the Trastevere basement. Carlo shot it with a Super 8 camera. With frizzy red hair, red lipstick, and mascara, Paul played an androgynous Jesus Christ, while a group of their friends served as the apostles. Instead of being crucified, Jesus was electrocuted.

The film was never shown. It was lost in the chaos that began to unfold a few weeks later when Paul was abducted, in the early-morning hours of July 10, 1973. He was walking home from Piazza Navona, where he'd been with friends, when three men jumped out and pulled him into a white car. Pistol-whipped, blindfolded, and chloroformed, he was driven 240 miles south, into the desolate reaches of Calabria.

Two days later, the kidnappers, members of the Calabrian mafia, phoned Gail and told her they had her son, and she should await their ransom demands. The Italian police and the press initially dismissed the story as a hoax. After the kidnappers demanded $17 million, J. Paul Getty issued his statement from Sutton Place: "If I pay a penny of ransom, I'll have fourteen kidnapped grandchildren."

Over the next five months, Paul III endured horrors, as he was dragged between a series of huts, caves, and bunkers. Much of the time he was chained like an animal, and plied with cheap whiskey, cognac, and other liquor to keep him docile (the beginning of his addiction to alcohol). In October, his captors brutally sliced off his right ear and sent it to a newspaper in Rome. Due to a postal strike, it took five weeks to arrive. After negotiations with the kidnappers, the Gettys agreed to a payment of $3.2 million, which was flown from California to Italy by Bill Newsom. After it was delivered to the kidnappers, Paul was released on a remote roadside in a snowstorm the night of December 15, 1973, and later found by police.

Afterward, Gail took Paul and his siblings away to the Austrian Alps for two months to help them all recover. But life was changed forever, for all the Gettys. Their "story" would be told and retold so many times, but rarely, if ever, by the people who were there.

Scimone, who went on to have a distinguished career in the Italian Foreign Ministry and make a family with his wife, Margherita Rostworowski, never spoke publicly about his childhood friend for more than forty years. But after seeing the portrayal of Paul in *All the Money in the World*—as an idle boy, at the mercy of events—Scimone agreed to talk to me.

"Paul was intelligent, vital, full of life," he recalled. "He would have done a lot, if he could have had a normal kid's life. I'm speaking now, giving the memory I have of Paul, because I want to give him back his dignity."

Paul "was not allowed to have a normal life," he continued. His siblings faced similar challenges: "They were burdened and overwhelmed by the weight of their last name. They wanted to be normal, simple—in jeans and T-shirts. But the minute people found out who they were, attitudes toward them changed. I remember being at a dinner with Paul and Mark. The whole atmosphere at the table suddenly changed when people found out their last name.

"They were golden kids. They had an aura around them. They were very empathetic. You wanted to be with them. Aileen . . . *cara ragazza* [dear girl]! . . . Gail was tender and sweet."

A few years ago, Scimone ran into Mark on a street in Rome. "I'd last seen him when he was a boy, in the country," he recalled. "I hugged him. I was glad to see a boy who was saved."

After his release, Paul didn't issue a statement. But several months later he gave an interview to Joe Eszterhas, which was published in the May 9, 1974, issue of *Rolling Stone*. A close-up portrait of a brooding Paul, shot by Annie Leibovitz, made the cover.

In an almost matter-of-fact fashion, Paul recalled many details of his ordeal. Just before the abduction, he remembered, he bought some newspapers and a Mickey Mouse comic book.

He described the pandemonium the night of his release, at the police station in Rome, where hordes of screaming reporters and photographers jostled. "It was madness," he said. And in the months following, he had no calm: "Everytime I went somewhere in Rome, I had a police escort. Motorcycles, sirens. I really couldn't go anywhere."

He became numb: "I felt it very difficult to talk, even to my family. . . . I said only essential things—'Pass the salt, pass the bread.'

"My mother and I talked a few times, but didn't say very much. . . . She keeps telling me that we have to sit down and talk about it, but—Oh, what in the world for? We should cry on each other's shoulders?

"I find I don't like speed anymore. It scares me. The other day I was in a taxi and the guy drove like a madman and I had to tell him to slow down."

In September 1974—nine months after the end of the kidnapping ordeal—J. Paul Getty III married Gisela at the town hall in Sovicille, near his mother's house in Tuscany. The bride was four months pregnant. At eighteen, the groom was four years below the age at which Gettys were permitted to marry, according to the terms of the trust that Paul Jr. and Gail, upon their divorce, set up for their children. The clause was meant to protect the girls from fortune hunters, but Paul III was nonetheless cut off financially.

His grandfather did agree to give him a small allowance. It was also decided that California would be a safer place for the newlyweds.

Weeks after the couple landed in Los Angeles, carrying hopes of putting hell behind them, their child, Paul Balthazar, was born at Tarzana Medical Center in January 1975. Soon after, Jutta arrived from Germany with three-year-old Anna. Paul legally adopted Anna several years later.

There was never going to be anything remotely conventional about Balthazar's and Anna's childhoods. The family set up housekeeping at the Chateau Marmont. The faux-Gothic hostelry, perched above Sunset Boulevard, had long been a favorite of Hollywood stars. ("If you must get into trouble, do it at the Chateau Marmont," Columbia Pictures boss Harry Cohn advised.) But in the mid-seventies, the establishment had fallen into disrepair; its threadbare rooms could be had for as little as $14 a night.

When the Gettys moved to a small house in Laurel Canyon, the electricity was sometimes turned off due to unpaid bills. The kids mingled with their parents' crowd, which included Warhol, Keith Richards, Leonard Cohen, Allen Ginsberg, William Burroughs, and Bob Dylan. Their babysitters included a teenage Sean Penn and Timothy Leary, the godfather of LSD.

Despite Paul's track record at school, his grandfather insisted he go to college. At Pepperdine University, where he studied Chinese history, he lasted one semester.

The trauma of his kidnapping overwhelmed him. Emotionally unable to talk about it, he turned to heroin, cocaine, and alcohol. His marriage suffered too. He had affairs, with musician Patti Smith among others, while Gisela became involved with actor Dennis Hopper.

In the late 1970s, Gisela relocated with the kids to the San Francisco Bay Area. Their dwellings there included a teepee at the Green Gulch Center in Marin County, one of the first Zen communities in America, where meditation began at dawn and the monks lovingly farmed organic fruits and vegetables. When the trio moved to a simple apartment in San Francisco, they slept on futons and Gisela made meals using lentils, whole wheat pasta, nutritional yeast flakes, and other organic ingredients then almost unheard of in most American households.

An artist, Gisela also engaged in a multitude of creative endeavors, from dervish dancing to esoteric Japanese drumming based on Zen thought.

In the apartment, there was no television. Instead, the kids put on plays, for which they wrote the scripts and made the costumes.

Everything was handmade, following the precepts of the Austrian philosopher and educator Rudolf Steiner, who believed that children should develop their intellectual, artistic, and practical skills in a holistic manner, a philosophy that spawned an independent school system known as Waldorf schools.

Even by the liberal standards of the Waldorf school that Balthazar and Anna attended, Gisela sometimes stood out. There was the day she came to pick up her kids with her head freshly shaven, and a spiked punk-rock collar around her neck.

Troubled as Paul was, friends recall him as someone with a lively, intelligent mind and great charm. "He was *truly* bright, curious, full of ideas and game for adventure," said photographer Jonathan Becker, who saw Paul often in Los Angeles in the late 1970s, after they met in 1976 in New York at Elaine's.

"He was very present in the here and now, he enjoyed life, he could focus on things, he was highly intuitive," Becker remembered.

"And naughty. He was sadly druggy—on and off the hard stuff and whatever. Around him were a lot of people with the same habits. In those days, people tended to do whatever the hell they wanted, and it was funny. Until you saw the consequences.

"There were days when Paul seemed checked out, but for the most part he enjoyed life, with a tremendous sense of humor about people. He got it."

Getty was also brave, Becker adds, recounting the story of a near-fatal sailing trip from Los Angeles to Catalina Island in 1977. Along with a few of Paul's friends, they rented a thirty-six-foot sloop for the voyage. Halfway back to the city, they encountered heavy seas: "A real squall, with thirty-knot winds growling, huge waves, the troughs as deep as the mast," said Becker, who was skippering. "We had to haul in and head up the face of every wave, otherwise the wave can roll you. It was eight hours like that. I was beyond exhaustion.

Paul was below barfing endlessly in the cabin with his friends. Stoned, useless, spoiled brats, I kept thinking. Finally, Paul came up alone and took the mainsheet—and we got there. Paul saved the day."

In 1981, Paul was working as a director's assistant and an actor (he appeared in Wim Wenders's *The State of Things*, which was released the following year). Trying to get himself together, he gave up drinking. To help him cope, doctors prescribed a variety of medications. After his years of drug and alcohol abuse, his liver shut down and he collapsed into a coma for six weeks. When he awoke, he was paralyzed from the neck down, and had lost much of his sight and ability to speak. Whole words were beyond him, but he could get out syllables, in a grunting fashion, which those close to him learned to decipher. Yet his brain and his emotions continued to function well. "He lives the life of the mind. He's a good poet. He loves music," said Bill Newsom, his godfather. "He's a great, great fellow."

He required round-the-clock care. At Gail's house in Brentwood, where he lived for a time, state-of-the-art medical and therapeutic facilities were installed. When he did go out, it was an elaborate production. "He was accompanied by two or three male nurses, and he was wheeled around the galleries in a sort of hospital trolley," a staff member at the J. Paul Getty Museum recalled of his occasional visits.

In 1986, Paul and Gisela officially separated. Around that time, Gail made some decisions for her grandchildren. "Enough of this hippie shit," she is said to have declared. At her instigation, Balthazar transferred to a school that was Waldorf's polar opposite—Gordonstoun, in Scotland. Famously severe and cold, it has educated generations of British aristocrats and royals, many of whom have testified to how miserable they were there. Prince Charles described it as "hell" and a "prison."

Balthazar fared surprisingly well. "You had to learn how to survive in the woods. I enjoyed it very much," he said.

Anna, meanwhile, continued her education in San Francisco at the Hamlin School for Girls, a prestigious academy in Pacific

Heights, then at the Sorbonne in Paris, where she studied for three years. "She had beautiful, long brown hair—her style was earthy and bohemian. She always seemed effortlessly glamorous," recalled a Hamlin classmate.

By the late eighties, Balthazar was back in California, enrolled at Bel Air Prep. One afternoon in 1988, a casting agent spotted the thirteen-year-old in detention (something about throwing a desk at a teacher).

English director Harry Hook was searching for the leads for his upcoming film adaptation of *Lord of the Flies*, William Golding's 1954 novel about a group of schoolboys stranded on an island. Hook didn't want to use professional actors. "I wanted fresh faces. I wanted to find kids who were real," the director said. Out of hundreds of candidates they interviewed, he felt Balthazar was the only one right for the part of Ralph, the voice of order and civilization. "With Balthazar, I felt there was an intensity and sense of morality to him, and that he was a very likable child."

Returning to LA later in 1988 from the intense four-month, hurricane-beset shoot in Jamaica, Balthazar had money in his pocket and an agent who was lining up new roles for him, beginning with *Young Guns II*. By the time both films were released in 1990, he was living the high life. He was unabashed about enjoying the bling. In interviews, he explained that *this* Getty wasn't born with a silver spoon. "I grew up scrappy. . . . The money wasn't there," he later reminisced on a podcast with actor Dean Delray.

At fifteen, he moved in with a twenty-year-old girlfriend, then dated Drew Barrymore; he went clubbing all night with friends including the Beastie Boys. Yet even with continued success—in such films as Oliver Stone's *Natural Born Killers* (1994) and David Lynch's *Lost Highway* (1997)—family sorrows took their toll. His father's misfortune wasn't just a private family matter; it was yet another manifestation of "the Getty curse," as the press repeated time and again. "That's a lot to cope with when you're growing up and I didn't handle it well," Balthazar said. "I got angry."

He became a third-generation heroin addict.

"For me the drugs were never about getting high, they were about adventure . . . the search for higher consciousness," he said.

"Without Mom's guidance, I'd be dead. In fact, I did die, several times. I was just lucky," he later told the London *Times* ("Member of a Troubled Dynasty" read the headline). "Normally these things don't have a happy ending, but my family are together and they made me want to be a better person."

Gisela and Paul divorced in 1993 and she moved to Europe. Living between a cottage in the Austrian Alps and an apartment in Munich, she has pursued fine art photography, writing, and documentary filmmaking. But she returned regularly to California to visit her children and Paul, with whom she remained close.

After finishing at the Sorbonne, Anna relocated to Los Angeles, where she pursued an acting career. She landed parts in a few independent films as well as in some of the 1990s' buzziest TV series, including *ER* and *Malibu, CA.*

On the eve of the new millennium, Balthazar met Rosetta Millington, with whom he found mutual understanding. The second of three children born to two hippie-artists, she grew up in an itinerant commune her family belonged to in Southern California. While it was a loving environment, "there weren't any boundaries," she recalled.

At fourteen, she began an international modeling career, which included campaigns for Azzedine Alaïa and shoots with Bruce Weber. Then she launched herself as a fashion designer and entrepreneur, with a children's wear line that had grown into a success by the time she met Balthazar.

"It was love at first sight, but it was also perfect in that all of our friends were the same and he was raised in a similar way," she said.

Their circle included the Arquette siblings. One of his closest friends is David; she has been best friends with Patricia since early childhood. At age eight, the girls had predicted their respective career paths, in fashion design and acting. "We were ambitious even then," said Rosetta, an elegant brunette with a precise manner.

She and Balthazar married at Los Angeles City Hall in 2000. Cassius (named after Muhammad Ali, a hero of Balthazar's) was born to the couple that year. Grace, Violet, and June came in 2001, 2003, and 2007, respectively.

They moved into a sprawling six-bedroom 1920s Spanish-style house with a lush garden, above Sunset Boulevard not far from the Chateau Marmont. On her visits from Germany, Gisela continued to drop into the old stamping ground, photos of which she sometimes posted on her Instagram page. ("And always the Chateau M," she captioned one picture.)

After her own wandering childhood, Rosetta prioritized providing a sense of stability for her children—a lively brood. Family dinners are served every night at six thirty. Fridays, the family observes Shabbat; Balthazar has studied the Kabbalah since 2009. The previous year had been tumultuous; a brief affair he had with the actress Sienna Miller was widely reported.

The Gettys' residence became a new nexus of hipster Hollywood. "Anyone who is anyone has been at the house," said Balthazar. (Jack Nicholson and Al Pacino are among the many who have attended the couple's parties and gatherings.)

Cassius once expressed to his mother a wish for his family to be "regular."

"I don't quite know what regular means," she said.

Meanwhile, husband and wife were succeeding in their creative endeavors. In 2006, Balthazar joined the cast of *Brothers and Sisters*, the hit series that ran for five tear-inducing seasons, in which he played Tommy Walker, scion of a wealthy California family.

After the birth of June, her youngest, Rosetta turned their guesthouse into an atelier and began producing a small collection of gowns and cocktail dresses under the label Riser Goodwyn. It was meant to be a line for just friends, but when you have friends like Demi Moore and Kirsten Dunst, word travels, and orders came in.

Between her film jobs, Anna was supporting herself as a caterer. She became an assistant to Akasha Richmond, organic chef to the stars (Michael Jackson and Barbra Streisand among them). The work reconnected Anna to her childhood cuisine. As a teenager, she had fallen off the organic wagon, rebelling against yeast flakes and the like.

Anna's August 2003 wedding in Tuscany, to screenwriter Gregory Pruss, brought together much of the Getty family, and spanned East and West. Some three hundred guests gathered for the hilltop cere-mony. Balthazar walked Anna—resplendent in an antique diamond choker lent to her by her aunt Ariadne—down the aisle. She stopped to give a kiss to her wheelchair-bound father, Paul III, before she and Pruss were pronounced husband and wife by Gurmukh Kaur Khalsa, yoga guru to the stars (including Madonna and Courtney Love). She chanted "Sat Nam" ("I am truth") three times.

In Los Angeles, where the couple raised their children, India and Dante, born in 2004 and 2009, Anna forged a career as an advocate of holistic healthy living. Certified as an instructor in kundalini and prenatal yoga, she produced a DVD collection: *Anna Getty's Pre and Post Natal Yoga Workout*. But organic food became her primary focus. In 2010, Chronicle Books published *Anna Getty's Easy Green Organic: Cook Well—Eat Well—Live Well*.

In addition to recipes, it contained recollections of her mother's cooking as well as memories of the monks at Green Gulch tending their fruits and vegetables. "That's where my food education began," she wrote.

A healthy diet is the key to life, she stressed: "Reconnect to food and its power to nourish your mind, body, and spirit. Empower your-self through your kitchen and the food you prepare."

In the early 2010s, she crossed paths again with Scott Oster. They had met twenty-five years before at a West Hollywood nightclub, when he was beginning his career as a pro skateboarder and was about to be married. Now they were both recently divorced. They began dating, as he pursued his new career as an interior designer and she delved further into organic cooking. In 2014, they had a son, Roman. Later that year on a trip to Paris, when they were cycling by the Eiffel Tower, Scott proposed. Attendants at their 2015 ocean-side wedding in Big Sur included India, eleven, the maid of honor, and Dante, six, the ringbearer. This time, Anna walked herself down the aisle. The following year the family, including newborn Bodhi, settled in the idyllic valley town of Ojai, where Anna's aunt Aileen lived at the time. (When the *New York Times* Styles section published a somewhat snarky piece on the scene there in 2015, it described the two Getty women as "offbeat heiresses.")

Anna explained in another article, in *Greener Living Today*. "We've always worked," she said, speaking at least for herself and her brother. "People have passed on in my family and things have changed a bit, but not drastically. Even though my aunts and uncles live a very wonderful lifestyle, most of them drive Priuses and they're putting in solar panels at their properties.

"One thing that I constantly have to remind people of is that when you are an heir, you get money when people die," she added.

In 2011, J. Paul Getty III died at the age of fifty-four. He had been living with his mother in Ireland, at Gurthalougha House on a 100-acre lakefront estate in County Tipperary, but he passed away at Wormsley, with Gail and Gisela by his side.

Balthazar issued a statement: "[He] taught us how to live our lives and overcome obstacles and extreme adversity and we shall miss him dearly."

Even with Paul's physical limitations, he and Balthazar had found ways to open up to each other emotionally. "He would tell me he loved me. We had regular father-son moments," Balthazar recalled. "He would worry and he would cry. . . . To the day he died I would hop in bed next to him and tell stories or watch a film."

Thanks to his own earnings, as well as the Sarah C. Getty Trust, Balthazar's "scrappy" days were long gone. A weekend beach house in Malibu, a whopping gold Rolex, private jets, and a fleet of fancy cars became part of the lifestyle. His ground transport included a Lamborghini and a Porsche Turbo ("My first 'fuck you' car. I haven't normally done that. And that's part of being okay with 'it,'" he said in 2016—"it" meaning, presumably, being a Getty).

Music became his focus now. He made beats for a rock band, Ringside, and he formed a rap duo, the Wow, with South African rapper K.O. Using Pro Tools, a digital audio workstation (a birthday gift from Rosetta and their friend Joaquin Phoenix), he turned the guesthouse into his music studio, where he produced an album, *Solardrive*. Under his rap name, Balt Getty, he began DJing around the country—sometimes spinning several nights a week.

A turning point for Rosetta came in 2015. Patricia Arquette appeared at the Academy Awards wearing an elegant black and white column dress Rosetta had designed for her. Nominated as Best Supporting Actress for her role in Richard Linklater's *Boyhood*, Patricia took home the statue, and Rosetta garnered considerable buzz.

With June now in kindergarten, Rosetta took her work as a fashion designer to the next level and launched her eponymous line out of the pool house. Reflecting her minimalist sensibility, she created understated but beautifully cut pieces, made of superlative-quality silk, cashmere, and other materials. Devotees of the Rosetta Getty label soon included the likes of Margot Robbie, Tracee Ellis Ross, Dakota Johnson, Claire Foy, and Rihanna, while *Vogue* and *WWD* gave glowing coverage.

Each season she produces a limited number of wardrobe fundamentals—an assortment as rigorously curated as a museum collection. When she begins a collection, she usually chooses an artist or an architect to study and draw inspiration from (Louise Bourgeois and Louis Kahn are favorites), or she picks a young contemporary artist to collaborate with (such as Kayode Ojo or Anna-Sophie Berger).

Looming ahead in 2016 was the fortieth anniversary of the death of Balthazar's great-grandfather. By now, many of the millions who visited the J. Paul Getty Museum's sites in Brentwood and Pacific Palisades had no idea who J. Paul Getty was. Among the general public, the Getty name had come to be better associated with drugs, decadence, and tragedy. At the same time, to the youngest Gettys, their patriarch had become a fairly remote historical figure.

As the anniversary approached, both the museum and the Getty family delved into their history. At the Getty Center, curators prepared a permanent, interactive installation, *J. Paul Getty: Life and Legacy*, to tell the story of their patron's life as a businessman and an art collector; at the Getty family meetings in Italy, Balthazar and his uncle Mark put together lessons for the youngsters. Starting with their Scots-Irish roots and the pioneering days in Bartlesville, the tutorials explored the work ethic and unconventional thinking that enabled Getty to become the richest man of his time, and to create one of the world's greatest cultural assets. In addition to the museum, which has never charged an admission fee to any visitor, the J. Paul Getty Trust operates the Getty Conservation Institute and the Getty Research Institute, preeminent centers of scholarship and preservation.

As the museum put the finishing touches on its installation, the curators asked Balthazar to come and test the beta version of the interactive touch screens. In September 2016, just before it opened to the public, director Timothy Potts welcomed twenty-three Gettys to a private preview. Five generations, they ranged from age 8 (Veronica, Billy and Vanessa's youngest child) to 103 (Teddy, J. Paul Getty's last wife).

Aileen thanked Potts and his staff for "unearthing and shedding a more natural light on my grandfather" and for "making it possible to strip away some of the myth that was setting like stone."

As Balthazar said in an interview with *The Iris*, the blog of the J. Paul Getty Trust, it was an opportunity to reconnect with a legacy he had once shunned, and for his family as a whole to bolster its pride: "I think you rebel against these sorts of things because you want to create your identity and nobody wants to be seen as the great-grandson, or grandson, or son of anybody. You want to be your own man and create your own legacy . . . but the older I get the more pride I'm able to have in my family's history. As a family we feel incredibly proud. It's not about showing off. It's not about gloating. It's really just having pride in what Nonno was able to do. I do feel an incredible connection."

"Stand back—it's about to get wack!"

"Single droppin' in a couple hours. Wack—Balt Getty—wack."

Behind a turntable set up in the parking lot of a strip mall on Fairfax Avenue in Los Angeles, on an evening in June 2019, Paul Balthazar Getty was whipping up the crowd. At his invitation, a couple hundred hipsters and local characters—including Tommy the Clown, the freestyle-dancing LA legend—had gathered for a block party. Getty had multiple reasons to celebrate: Monk Punk, his luxe streetwear line, was debuting; his retail store (housed in a former RadioShack outlet) was opening; and his latest hip-hop track—which was entitled "Wack," if you hadn't guessed—was about to drop.

As the night progressed, the exuberant forty-four-year-old father of four also shared news of a significant milestone reached by his eldest, Cassius Paul: "What up, everybody, I'm Balt Getty. My son just graduated fucking high school. Man, I was cryin' like a baby, it was crazy."

Balthazar was now one of Hollywood's most multi-multi-hyphenates: actor–producer–director–DJ–musician–artist–fashion designer–shopkeeper.

His trajectory into fashion began when he started customizing items of clothing with his own sketches as well as with variations of the old Getty Oil logo. Not unlike what happened when his cousin Nats began her business, requests from friends came in. He began producing a line of affordable streetwear under a label he called Purplehaus (it's his favorite color). Then he took his designs to the next level, with a luxury range of accessories and clothing, including "the Paul," a long, collarless shirt inspired by his grandfather Paul Jr.'s Moroccan djellabas. He christened this line Monk Punk.

"It came to me one night," he explained to me inside the store, as friends such as actor David Arquette (in a bright-orange track suit and huge gold chain) milled about. "It makes you think of spirituality, being in touch with your emotional side, let's say. But then, you're still a punk. So—I'm not a pussy, you're not going to push me around. It's about embodying both sides, both of which I think are important."

Balthazar proceeded to point out images from Monk Punk's new look book. The models were not the usual fashion types, but former members of the Rollin 60's Neighborhood Crips, the fearsome street gang; they were photographed around Crenshaw and Sixtieth, epicenter of gang conflict in LA. "Instead of models, I said, 'Let's do something authentic. No styling.' I just said, 'You guys, just rock it how you would rock it,'" said Getty, who was clad in an oversized white Monk Punk T-shirt, a large gold chain, and a pink knit cap. (Before the photo shoot, he made a donation to Crenshaw Rams, a program that helps neighborhood youth, "because I believe in community and starting again," he told the *Hollywood Reporter*. "Not to mention how fly they looked in season one of my line Monk Punk.")

As she prepares her fashion collections, Rosetta often does research at the Getty Center. Her 2019 collaboration with the Getty Research Institute (GRI), was particularly resonant. That spring she immersed herself with the curators there as they prepared a landmark exhibition, *Bauhaus Beginnings*, a reexamination of the founding principles of that influential German art school, which had been established a century before.

While the show featured items by Bauhaus stars such as Wassily Kandinsky and Walter Gropius, Rosetta was captivated particularly with work produced by some of the school's lesser-known female students, such as a curtain fabric with interlocking red, black, and white lines. Rosetta alchemized that into a plaid she used in a double-breasted peak-lapel jacket.

Just before the opening of the exhibition, which Rosetta sponsored, she photographed her look book at the Getty Center. Models posed throughout the stark Richard Meier–designed campus, even in the hushed stacks of the GRI library. Coincidentally, just as she was shooting in this cerebral environment, her husband was shooting *his* look book at Sixtieth and Crenshaw, with a very different mood and cast.

About the same time, Anna launched her new project, Amalgam Kitchen, a website and Instagram account focused on mainly plant-based, low-sugar recipes that she creates. As its name suggests, Amalgam presents a blend of her knowledge of many different diets and ways of healthy eating.

Under the umbrella of his multimedia platform Purplehaus, Balthazar continued to expand his horizons. He launched collaborations with the fashion brands Moncler and Chrome Hearts. He produced a cycle of three-minute-long videos for a series he entitled *A Day in the Life*, which he described as "a reality show for people with ADD." In one, Balt, Rosetta, and the kids touch down in San Francisco and attend one of his great-uncle Gordon's lavish birthday parties; in another, they all descend on the Piazza del Campo in Siena for a running of the Palio. (Typically, the family spends six weeks each summer in Tuscany, communing with nature and their fellow Gettys.)

On the music front, Balthazar released a series of tracks. On some of them, he playfully grappled with the subject of wealth. One of the songs he wrote was entitled "Money."

To print some cash
Fuck that I think we'll pass . . .
Gettin' in for free
Even though I got my money
We wear the wreckage like a crown don't give a fuck can't take us down
Running through the streets livin' off monopoly money

"I like to poke fun at myself and the irony of it all . . . this material world we live in. . . . It's like warning people about a drug, but doing it too," Balthazar commented about the track. Yet he sees his output being in line with family tradition. "I think I'm a chip off the old block, in the sense—my grandfather, my great-grandfather—we're workers. I don't want to rest on my laurels. We all want to make our own names."

When the long period of Covid-induced home confinement ended, a member of the youngest generation of the family made the first splash. Seventeen-year-old Violet Getty, photographed by Collier Schorr, appeared on the cover of the Spring/Summer 2021 issue of *Self Service*, the extremely cool Paris-based fashion and culture biannual publication. Wearing a boyish brown silk jacket by YSL over a T-shirt of her own, she had an androgynous look, with her short brown hair and brown eyes.

Since she was small, Violet has opted to wear primarily boys' clothes. In her high school years, she identified as gay and introduced girlfriends to her supportive family. "She's so confident—such a doll with so much charisma," said a family friend. "She is going to become a big model."

Another chip off the old block, as Balthazar would say.

10

Tara

Tara Gabriel Galaxy Gramophone Getty—Paul Jr.'s fifth child, whom he had with Talitha, his second wife—is sometimes described as the "normal" Getty. In this family, of course, "normal" is relative. But considering the tumultuous circumstances of his childhood, his equilibrium is striking. He was three when his mother died tragically in Rome in 1971. In the aftermath, his father fled to London and spiraled downward into drug addiction and depression, while Gail took care of Tara, along with his four half siblings, in their apartment in Rome. Two years later, amidst the turmoil of Paul III's kidnapping, Tara's kindly maternal grandparents, Willem and Poppet Pol, became his surrogate parents.

They raised him in Ramatuelle, an idyllic French village in the hills above Saint-Tropez, where he went to a local school and took up sailing. There he got his hands on the tillers of Mirrors, Lasers, and other dinghies, before he graduated to more substantial boats. The sea, after all, was in his genes, his father having been born aboard ship off the coast of Liguria.

At fifteen, when Tara was in boarding school in England, more turbulence hit, with the eruption of the titanic legal battles between

Getty Oil and Gordon as well as between some extended family members and Gordon, the sole trustee. Unwittingly, Tara was thrust into the middle of these conflicts. In their campaign to avoid a sale of Getty Oil, the company's board members, executives, and lawyers in California concocted a complex scheme to dilute Gordon's voting power. This plan required a family member to petition the Superior Court for Los Angeles County to name a cotrustee. The lawyers decided a minor child would make the best plaintiff in this suit, and they chose Tara. Unlike some of his elder cousins, he didn't have a relationship with Gordon, or a strong parent like Gail, who, being fond of Gordon, was not likely to permit any of her children to sue their uncle. But Paul Jr., still in a weakened state, signed off on Tara's participation, after which a Getty Oil–aligned lawyer, appointed as his guardian ad litem, pressed the case in court. Tara was told that his interests were being looked after and he should not be concerned if his name began to appear in the newspapers. Even after Getty Oil was sold, this suit was at the crux of the legal squabbles that persisted for several years among some family members over Gordon's management of the Sarah C. Getty Trust, which ultimately led to its being partitioned into four separate trusts.

Per the Getty way, family relations continued amicably for Tara. Shortly after the trust litigation was resolved in 1986, he went to stay with his paternal grandmother, Ann Light (Gordon and Paul Jr.'s mother), in Palm Beach. "It is his first visit to the island," the *Palm Beach Daily News* reported.

Tara was nineteen when he stood in for his father at the Arts Benefactor of the Year gala dinner at the Savoy Hotel, accepting an award from Prince Charles on his father's behalf after Paul got cold feet. "My father has got [an] extremely bad toothache," Tara told the audience.

He had recently returned from Kenya, where he spent most of his gap year between boarding school and university working at a rhinoceros sanctuary. The African continent captivated him. "I did feel like Africa was going to be in my future from then on," he reminisced many years later.

Even as Tara began his studies at the Royal Agricultural University in bucolic Gloucestershire, a meeting in a London boardroom one day around 1990 ultimately brought him back to Africa.

At Hambros Bank, David Varty, a South African, was trying to raise funds to expand his fledgling company, Conservation Corporation Africa (CC Africa), one of the earliest exponents of ecotourism. Tara's half brother Mark (eight years his elder), a member of Hambros's corporate finance department, sat in on Varty's pitch meeting. Mark recognized the company's potential to be profitable as well as environmentally and socially beneficial (apartheid was coming to an end). He knew, too, that his younger brother could contribute to it.

Mark brought the proposition to his extended family. As they considered investing in it, Varty was run through the gauntlet of Getty financial advisors (including Judge Newsom) in New York and San Francisco. After he passed muster, a family delegation headed by Gordon flew to South Africa to make the final decision. Their large entourage descended on Varty's nascent game reserve, which was called Phinda (the Zulu word for "the return"). Close to the Indian Ocean in KwaZulu-Natal, it was located on 32,000 acres that had been devastated by decades of overfarming and hunting; the idea was to restore the land, repopulate it with animals, and help the local community in the process.

"There is one thing you should know," Mark told Varty as they set off on their inspection tour. "My uncle has arachnophobia. . . . If he sees a spider he'll leave."

"There's spiders everywhere you look," said a panicked Varty.

Indeed, their convoy of Land Rovers halted when the lead car came upon an impressive web strung across the road by a golden orb spider. Just then, as fate would have it, a spider-hunting wasp flew in and stung the arachnid to death in front of Gordon's eyes. Overjoyed by this good omen, he was now well-inclined to make the investment.

The deal was sealed a short time later when, with everyone sitting on overturned beer crates outside a staff hut, a local teacher articulated how the investment could contribute to the emerging democracy in South Africa led by Nelson Mandela. Newsom leaned in to his old school pal. "Gordon, we've got to support this," he said. The Getty family became CC Africa's majority shareholders.

In the years to come, various Gettys would intern there and contribute in different ways, but Tara moved there and put down roots. He began pitching in just after he finished his studies. "I was a dogsbody, just doing anything and everything that was around for me to do," he recalled. "I was like a stand-in ranger, but I was mainly a porter, carrying people's bags to their rooms."

Even as he settled into the bush, Tara—tanned, sandy-haired, and easygoing—was still captivated by the sea. And for a sailor, there was little that could be more exciting than the launch, in 1993, of his father's new superyacht.

A 262-foot art deco gem, she was commissioned in the 1920s by the chairman of the Packard Motor Car Company, who christened her *Reveler*. Later owners included Charles McCann—a lawyer and son-in-law of dime-store magnate F. W. Woolworth—who renamed her *Chalena*, and movie producer Robert Stigwood, for whom she was *Jezebel*. After Paul Getty Jr. acquired her in 1988, he entrusted a stern-to-bow refit to the preeminent naval architect Jon Bannenberg, whose celebrated commissions have included Saudi billionaire Adnan Khashoggi's *Nabila*, Malcolm Forbes's *Highlander*, and Microsoft cofounder Paul Allen's *Rising Sun* (now owned by music and movie mogul David Geffen). The five-year-long restoration of Getty's boat was so painstaking that steelworkers had to learn welding techniques that hadn't been used since World War II. Its saloons and six staterooms feature Lalique glass doors, skylights salvaged from a 1920s City of London bank, and open fireplaces, along with period art and furnishings sourced by Christopher Gibbs. "It's like being in a Noël Coward play or an Agatha Christie novel," according to one delighted passenger.

A twin-funneled, clipper-bowed beauty with a crew of eighteen, the *Talitha G*, as Paul renamed her, quickly set a new gold standard in superyacht design and service; she became a floating emblem of Getty glamour. In the eyes of many who care about these things, she remains peerless. The mere mention of her name can send pulses racing. "Utterly incomparable. . . . There is no other yacht in the world that can match the magnificence of this extraordinary vessel," said the late taste arbiter David Tang, a family friend. "Every detail of this yacht is unswitchable. Every detail balances into harmony. . . . To float and glide on *Talitha G* is like being on Solomon's carpet over water, breakfasting at Damascus and supping at Medina."

With Paul still in delicate health, however, getting him aboard was a challenge. He and Tara talked about crossing the Atlantic, but that voyage never happened. There were holidays on the Mediterranean and the Caribbean, though.

It was on a skiing holiday of his own, in Verbier, Switzerland, that Tara met Jessica Kelly. The daughter of a Sussex farmer, she was soft-spoken and down-to-earth, with brilliant blue eyes and blond hair. Tara gave Jessica her first look at the Phinda Private Game Reserve in 1995, when he invited her for a vacation. The next year, she joined him there full-time.

The whole operation was then still quite rough, which didn't bother her. "Africa seduced me, and I defected for good," recalled Jessica, who took a job as a bush-camp cook. "It was a real baptism-by-fire. Kind of sink or swim. My farm-girl background probably helped a bit. Tara and I, between us, are both very connected to the natural world."

As CC Africa acquired other properties and grew, Tara took on increasing responsibilities, managing the development of new lodges and serving as a nonexecutive director. (Eventually, when the company expanded its footprint outside Africa, it was renamed &Beyond;

the Enthoven family of South Africa became partners with the Gettys.) Together, Tara and Jessica began to steer the Africa Foundation, the business's nonprofit arm.

In 1998, the couple tied the knot—first in London, at the Chelsea Register Office off King's Road. Their church wedding took place soon afterward, in Ramatuelle. Upon their return to South Africa, they resided in a series of four thatched-roof cottages at Phinda, as well as a house in Cape Town. Two years later, their life expanded significantly. Their first child, born in August of 2001, was christened Orlando Willem Pol. "It's unusual without being crazy," Tara explained at the time, given the inevitable comparisons to the string of names his parents had chosen for him, prompting that memorable headline in San Francisco. Two months later, they added about 3,400 acres to their property portfolio when, with the backing of the Getty family trust, they acquired a property adjacent to Phinda called Zuka.

There, on the slope of a 200-million-year-old volcano crater, they built a 5,400-square-foot lodge using 200-year-old sandstone, its floor-to-ceiling windows affording spectacular views of the vast grassland and bushveld populated with elephants, zebras, giraffes, wildebeests, white rhinos, black rhinos, lions, leopards, and cheetahs, among other creatures. By the time they settled in, Orlando could tell a black rhino from a white one (the latter have square mouths), and "cheetah" was one of the first words that his baby brother, Caspar, learned to pronounce.

The Zuka Private Game Reserve—which within a few years expanded to encompass more than 25,000 acres—joined forces with Phinda and with another neighborhing property to form an immense protected nature reserve, the Mun-Ya-Wana Conservancy, named after the river that bisects the territory. Now a Big Five game reserve, it comprises some 70,000 acres.

Over the decades, Tara's relatives in California have been supportive of his Africa Foundation. Uncle Gordon and his wife, Ann, hosted fund-raising dinners and auctions at their mansion (Gavin

Newsom sometimes did the gaveling, and Gordon often bid). The senior member of the Getty clan has also paid return visits to Phinda, leading intergenerational family posses that have included his grand-nephew Balthazar and his granddaughter Ivy, who have assisted in conservation drives. For a number of years, Tara's sister Aileen has been a generous donor to the Africa Foundation.

Tara and Jessica remain the driving forces behind the Africa Foundation, which has funded hundreds of rural development projects in Botswana, Kenya, Mozambique, Namibia, South Africa, Tanzania, and Zanzibar. Bringing a new model of philanthropy to the continent, the organization has sought to work from the ground up, consulting and collaborating with local stakeholders, empowering them to develop their own communities on a sustainable scale.

&Beyond, led by CEO Joss Kent, has continued to expand. In 2020, it owned and operated twenty-nine deluxe lodges and camps in thirteen countries in Africa and Asia, which enables the company to positively impact more than 9 million acres of wildlife land and 2,000 kilometers of coastlines.

Together, the business and its nonprofit arm have provided a model in Africa for how to restore abused lands, and how to run wildlife and community projects side by side.

"If you want to take care of the wildlife, you have to take care of the people," said Tara. "There's no point in preserving rhinos if you don't care for the people who surround them. There'll be poaching and all sorts of problems. But if there's harmony and employment, and people can see the benefit of game to them, they'll protect it."

The Phinda Private Game Reserve—&Beyond's flagship property—employs some eighty full-time field rangers, as well as an arsenal of advanced technology, including artificial intelligence and big data. It's a smart camp: drones conduct twenty-four-hour surveillance over the reserve's acreage, picking up signals from ultrahigh-frequency ear tags that have been attached to the creatures. By tracking them in real time, the reserve hopes to keep them safe from poachers.

Protecting the reserve's crashes of extremely rare black rhinos is particularly challenging. Thanks to a seemingly insatiable black market for rhino horn, poaching of these animals has risen exponentially. The species is nearly decimated. But at Phinda, their numbers have actually been on the increase. A program to dehorn the animals has largely stopped the poaching. Dehorning a black rhino is a major production, involving helicopters and an array of vets, experts, rangers, and immobilizing drugs. The horns grow back every two to two and a half years, so these missions operate frequently.

Since ancient times, the bluebird has been a symbol of happiness, a reminder that joy is often just under our noses—but it can flutter away when one tries to grasp it.

One day in March 2004, Tara received a phone call letting him know that a bluebird of sorts was available, though half the world away. From the bushveld of KwaZulu-Natal, he scrambled to get on a plane. After landing in Amsterdam, he drove straight to a small Dutch port, where the object of his quest came into view.

"*Blue Bird* was in a very bad way and it was apparent that she was near the end of her days, but underneath the rust and ungainly add-ons one could make out the unmistakably sweet lines of a true classic. Clearly, she needed someone to rescue her," Tara recalled afterward in a book he commissioned, *Blue Bird: Seven Decades at Sea*.

This once-magnificent one-hundred-foot motor yacht had been launched in 1938 by Sir Malcolm Campbell, a British racing hero known as "the fastest man on earth." He had it built for a specific purpose—a voyage to Cocos, a remote, minuscule Pacific Island, where he hoped to dig up a legendary hoard of gold stolen in 1820 by pirates in Peru, which was the template for Robert Louis Stevenson's *Treasure Island*. War thwarted Campbell's plans. Requisitioned by the Admiralty, *Blue Bird* instead performed valiant service for king and country, most notably as one of the Little Ships that chugged from Southeast England in 1940 to evacuate soldiers trapped in Dunkirk—the "miracle of deliverance" without which Hitler would have surely prevailed.

She was considerably worse for wear when Campbell, himself in failing health, got her back after the war. He died in 1948, before he could undertake his intended voyage. Over the next decades, *Blue Bird* passed between various owners, under new names—*Sterope, Janick*, and then *Rescator*. In the 1980s, dilapidation set in, along with unpaid bills. By court order, she was chained to a quay on the Riviera, leading to a fire sale. When the US consul in Nice sealed the transfer of ownership to an American purchaser, a California trucking executive, perhaps titleship of the vessel seemed murky; in any event, the consul's document stated that the vessel "is henceforth to be known as *Blue Bird*."

By the time she ended up in the Dutch boatyard, she was on the verge of being sold for scrap. Tara Getty bought her on the spot. "I always liked older things. I quite like restoring things versus building from scratch," he explained. "That probably comes from my father, who was a great collector and also a restorer in his own way." ("It's a big driver for Tara," said Jessica of his urge to restore. "It's a strong thread in our lives, whether it's boats, houses, or land.")

When Tara bought *Blue Bird*, he was not lacking for nautical equipment. Getty had a collection of smaller motor- and sailboats, in addition to *Talitha*, which he and Mark, along with their siblings, inherited (when they did, they streamlined her name—dropping the *G*). Their sisters later opted to allocate their shares in the vessel to their brothers. But members of the entire family continue to pile aboard *Talitha* as she plies the seas—the Mediterranean and Caribbean, most commonly.

Gorgeous as the superyacht is, sometimes big is not better. Making it into some of the family's favorite bays was often a struggle. Tara wanted something that would suit his young family. *Blue Bird* was just right: a pocket superyacht.

The dream team that he assembled to restore her included the sto-

ried Scottish firm that built her, G. L. Watson, which was still in possession of the *Blue Bird*'s original plans. For the interiors, he went to
Dickie Bannenberg, who'd taken over the family firm when his father
died in 2002, a year before Sir Paul Getty. (In September 2003, Tara
read the lesson at the bravura memorial mass for his father at Westminster Cathedral.)

Another Getty-Bannenberg collaboration was gratifying for both
sons. "I'm sure this was in the back of Tara's mind when he came to
us as a continuation," Dickie commented.

Bannenberg Senior had often been asked to name his favorite
boat. His stock answer was always "the next one." His true favorite
was *Talitha G*: "She was the benchmark in the family for a classic
yacht," said Dickie.

Yet with *Blue Bird*, there were "different vibes," the designer
added. "She carried a 1930s DNA . . . but it was all underpinned by
a contemporary level of detailing. . . . It's a combination of things . . .
for a young family with three kids, in that barefoot, easy-living way,
but at the same time looking tailored, crisp, and rich in detail. It's a
magnetic combination."

The saloon is outfitted with walnut paneling that reflects the ship's
original interiors, while white-painted paneling strikes a modern
note. On a table, there is a framed print of Lichfield's seminal 1969
portrait of Tara's parents in Marrakech. "It's a beautiful picture, and
it sort of represents the wild sixties," Tara said of it.

The décor, however, was a breeze compared to the challenges of
giving her a totally new superstructure from the main deck up, incor-
porating the latest engineering and technology into a 1930s vessel of
this size, and, furthermore, meeting the exacting standards required
for class certification by Lloyd's. Nobody had managed a similar feat
before; *Blue Bird* pulled it off.

After more than three years of painstaking labor, Tara's new
boat was christened amid much fanfare from family and friends in
Saint-Tropez on May 30, 2007, his thirty-ninth birthday.

Tara and Jessica, whose third child, Talitha Leonora Pol, was born in 2008, spend some of the warm months in Ramatuelle in Tara's childhood house. "I consider myself very lucky that I came from here. . . . It's an amazing place to be brought up," he said.

They also pass time in England, where Tara, an Irish passport holder (as are several of his cousins), owns an estate adjacent to Wormsley. Their schedule is often dictated by the yachting calendar. In May 2010, *Blue Bird* joined some fifty of the other surviving Little Ships for the crossing from Ramsgate to Dunkirk, in commemoration of the seventieth anniversary of Operation Dynamo. Prince Michael of Kent, who was a passenger aboard *Blue Bird* with Tara and a group of friends, reflected on this unique flotilla in the foreword he wrote for *Blue Bird*: "Enemy action, obscurity, and even the relentless march of time have failed to dim their light. They all have stories to tell, but not many bring us such a varied and dramatic tale as *Blue Bird*." His Royal Highness also commended the quality of the boat's restoration: "Tara Getty and his team have brooked no compromise."

In 2011, Getty, now with a short, sea captain–worthy beard, took possession, following an eight-year-long restoration, of *Skylark*, a deliriously beautiful fifty-three-foot inboard yawl designed in 1937 by the storied Newport, Rhode Island, naval architects Sparkman & Stephens and built in Wiscasset, Maine.

He takes part in about eight regattas a year, including the two most elegant: the Corsica Classic and Les Voiles de Saint-Tropez. "The best part is when you're out at sea racing a steady ten knots on a beam reach with all sails set," he said.

When the magnificently restored *Skylark* made her debut in Mediterranean waters, at the 2011 Les Voiles, Getty hatched the idea to sponsor a new perpetual cup on the Thursday, a day that had traditionally been without an official race. Filling the void, he announced a challenge between *Skylark* and any one boat brave enough to race her. "Let's call it the Blue Bird Cup," he said. "Let's just have a fun day with a race and lunch."

Tara got his lunch handed to him that inaugural matchup. While *Skylark* led most of the way around the course, actor Griff Rhys Jones, in his Sparkman & Stephens yacht *Argyll*, picked his shifts well as breezes turned fickle. Overtaking Getty, Jones thus took possession of the silver Blue Bird Cup (made by Garrard of London in 1937 and presented to Malcolm Campbell).

The following year, Tara triumphed. After getting off to a commanding lead, *Skylark* sailed well ahead for the entire race, even with seven-year-old Caspar helming for a time. With every passing year (except for becalmed 2020), the Blue Bird Cup has gained momentum and cachet. "It's supercompetitive. Dog-eat-dog. Brutal. And everybody wants to be in it," said Jessica.

Tara also belongs to Pugs, self-described (by its founder, Taki Theodoracopulos) as "the most exclusive club in the world." There is no clubhouse or rulebook per se, just the proviso that no more than twenty-one gentlemen can belong. Owning a big boat seems to be prerequisite too.

Tara was elected to its ranks in 2014, joining Mark Getty; the maharaja of Jodhpur; Heinrich, Prince of Fürstenberg; Greek shipowner George Livanos; Sir Bob Geldof; Roger Taylor (the drummer of Queen); Crown Prince Pavlos of Greece; and Pavlos's father-in-law, tycoon Robert Miller, among others.

Each year the Pugs hold their own regatta, the location of which rotates between the Med's salubrious coasts. The *Talitha* and *Blue Bird* often serve as their "committee" boats. "These are by far the two best boats around. They have nothing to do with that modern shit—those refrigerators on steroids out there," Taki told me. "The Getty boats have all the modern things, but they've kept their original lines and classic style."

He added, speaking about the Gettys themselves: "They're quiet—they don't show off. A good-looking family. Nice. They don't bother anybody."

In 2015, *Blue Bird* fulfilled its destiny. That March, Tara and Jessica set off from Antigua on a three-month odyssey with Talitha, Caspar, and Orlando, who had just graduated from high school in South Africa and was about to move to England to attend Wellington College. The family's ultimate destination was Cocos. The five-mile-long island remains uninhabited and arduous to reach, owing to fierce seas and limited shelter. Even for an experienced sailor like Tara, it was a daunting voyage. He admits to having been "a bit concerned" about the eighty-year-old ship's prospects. "A hundred feet sounds big, but it's not really, when you are out so far in the Pacific."

When at last they reached Cocos, they found majestic waterfalls and mountains and primeval jungle—a scene straight out of *Jurassic Park*, they thought. Alas, no gold was unearthed. But the Gettys got their reward. "We pulled it off," said Tara. "It kind of closed the circle. The circle that hadn't been closed because the war came along."

"I have an adventurous and unconventional husband," commented Jessica.

Blue Bird had barely steamed back into its home port when Tara embarked on another major project. This time it was in a Los Angeles boatyard that he spotted his next rescue: the seventy-two-foot *Baruna*, another Sparkman & Stephens–designed yawl. "She was just languishing," said Getty morosely. "She had won all sorts of races, she was a part of American history. Somebody needed to restore this boat."

Five years later, in July 2021, he offered a progress report: "It's a really tricky one. It's going to be incredible when she launches— which was supposed to be two years ago."

Tara was speaking over Zoom, with Jessica alongside him. Both appeared relaxed, tanned, and a bit wet, which was to be expected, as they were aboard *Talitha*, cruising through the Dodecanese in the southeastern Aegean.

Jessica's holiday was particularly well-earned. She had just finished writing a detailed history of the family's endeavors in Africa and designing a new website, Zuka.earth, on which it can be read.

"Zuka is twenty years old this year," she said. "I decided it was time to tell the story."

Inspired by the anniversary, the couple also founded a new study center and reseach laboratory on the property, the Getty Asterism. They repurposed a collection of thatched-roof and stone cabins to serve as a hub for scientists and conservationists investigating ecology, geology, and marine biology. Even as these scientists plumb the depths of the seas and the earth, the name of the center (an asterism is a prominent pattern or group of stars) hearkened back to the galactic dimensions envisioned by Tara's parents when they christened him.

Over Zoom, he graciously fielded questions pertaining to conservation and sailing. And one of a personal nature: Is he, in fact, the "normal" Getty?

"I don't know whether there is such a thing as a normal one," he deadpanned.

"Am I normal?" he repeated the question, with a trace of a grin. "Possibly I haven't gone off the rails as much as some members of the family have.

"It's a pretty eclectic family. It's got all sorts of branches to it. I would say I'm more on the English side.

"There's not a lot of in-house fighting in any form. I have a very good relationship with my siblings. The whole family tries to get together once a year. A lot of families don't get together for years."

Summing up the state of the Getty clan, he concluded, "It's pretty strong. I don't think it's as dysfunctional as everyone makes out!"

As Tara reflected on his father's life, he touched on an uncanny ability possessed by some Gettys—the ones who've survived—to restore themselves: "After having had that gap, the bad years, he had a great last fifteen years. He managed to put the sad part of his life behind him. He got closer to all his children. It all ended up being really good."

IV.

THE GORDONS

11

Pacific Heights

Gordon Peter Getty's absent-minded, floppy-haired head, hovering well above six feet, often seemed to be lost in the clouds. At the University of San Francisco, a twenty-minute walk from his mother's house on Clay Street where he had grown up with his older brother, Paul Jr., he studied philosophy and literature. Emily Dickinson was his favorite poet. On visits overseas to see his father at Sutton Place, he could be found sitting at one of the two grand pianos in the Long Gallery, playing Schubert or one of his own compositions.

In 1956, with diploma in hand, Gordon entered the real world. J. Paul Getty got his fourth-born son started in the oil business, at the bottom. Gordon pumped gas and changed oil at a Tidewater station near his house. A few months later, thanks to President Eisenhower's Reserve Forces Act, he reported for active duty at Fort Lee, Virginia.

Gordon's next post, once again under his father's orders, was on more punishing ground: the Neutral Zone, the wasteland between Saudi Arabia and Kuwait, where the family fortune was being extracted from the earth. In 1959, after several months, it became apparent that Gordon wasn't cut out to be a line officer—somebody responsible for running things day-to-day. After one blunder—principally, a failure to understand the nuances of the Middle East's culture of *baksheesh* (bribery)—Gordon had to take the fall for a Getty Oil underling who had accidentally rammed a pipeline with his truck. The local emir sentenced Gordon to two weeks' house arrest, during which he read Shakespeare and Keats.

Upon his return to San Francisco, Gordon dared to pursue his real passion, music. In 1961, he enrolled at the San Francisco Conservatory of Music, where he studied harmony and counterpoint. According to Robina Lund, his father was "understandably disappointed" when Gordon left the family business, but he was nonetheless happy for him to aspire to a musical career. "Paul was immensely proud of Gordon's ability as a pianist and composer. . . . When Gordon came to stay, Paul would look forward all day to hearing him play."

During his time at the conservatory, Gordon succeeded in composing and publishing five short piano pieces. Just after, writer's block halted his creativity for nearly twenty years.

Despite San Francisco's small-town nature, it took a few years for him to meet Ann Gilbert, a striking five-foot-ten redhead who had arrived in 1958 at the age of seventeen. A native of California's Central Valley, she had picked peaches, packed walnuts, and driven tractors alongside her two brothers on their father's ranch; after graduating from East Nicolaus High School, she moved from her hometown of Wheatland to the Bay Area, where she studied anthropology and biology at UC Berkeley and worked at the cosmetics counter of Joseph Magnin, the fashionable department store near Union Square.

Gordon's and Ann's paths crossed one evening in 1964 at La Rocca's Corner, a popular North Beach tavern. She matched him in a blind beer-tasting game. A few months later, on Christmas Day 1964, they eloped to Las Vegas.

Ann's combination of practicality and charm helped propel the Getty fortune. In 1971, as Gordon's lawsuit over the terms of the Sarah C. Getty Trust dragged into its seventh year, Ann played an instrumental role in brokering a settlement. "See here, Mr. Getty, let's have an end to this," she said to her father-in-law, in a tone that was at once beguiling and assertive.

Even as she became one of the most extravagant women of her time, Ann kept her feet planted on the ground. Notwithstanding the couture wardrobe, private jets, and other accoutrements of wealth that she acquired, she liked to say she was still at heart a farmer.

Following J. Paul Getty's death in 1976, Gordon's income from the trust rose dramatically. Unlike most other Gettys, Ann wasn't shy about spending it. The couple purchased a magnificent five-story neoclassical mansion, designed by architect Willis Polk shortly after the 1906 earthquake. Perched atop Pacific Heights, with stunning views of San Francisco Bay, it sits on a two-and-a-half-block stretch of Outer Broadway, the bastion of San Francisco's gold rush and old money families.

To help her decorate it, Ann hired the blue-chip firm of Parish-Hadley, a partnership between the indomitable WASP grande dame Mrs. Henry "Sister" Parish II and Tennessee-born Albert Hadley, the nice one. Their client roster, a who's who of American aristocracy, included Jackie and John F. Kennedy, Babe and Bill Paley, and Betsey and Jock Whitney.

After many months and shopping trips to England—Ann became a top customer at London's auction houses and antiquaries—the Broadway mansion was transformed into one of the loveliest English-style houses in America. Sister was in charge, but Ann deployed the expertise and taste she'd sharpened from all her stays at Sutton Place. She also benefited from the guidance of Gillian Wilson, the decorative arts curator at the J. Paul Getty Museum (where Gordon was on the acquisitions committee). At the same time, Ann made sure Wilson was properly outfitted for her job. During one meeting, Ann clocked Wilson's cloth coat; she went upstairs to her closet and returned with a fur. "If you are going to these dealers in London and Paris, you need a good coat," she said as she handed the garment to Wilson, who wore it proudly for years to come and referred to it as "the curatorial mink." (Until her retirement in 2003, Wilson remained one of the museum's last living links to its founder.)

Ann and Gordon's mansion was fully operational by December 1979, when a feature story, "Christmas with the Gettys," appeared in *Town & Country*, with photographs by Slim Aarons. Nine-year-old William Paul—"Billy"—the baby of the family, was pictured valiantly hoisting a pole twice as tall as he was to light the candles on the eighteenth-century Russian crystal and gilded bronze chandelier in the unelectrified dining room, which was lined with eighteenth-century Chinese wallpaper. Meanwhile, his brothers—John Gilbert, eleven, Andrew Rork, twelve, and Gordon Peter Jr., fourteen (who is called Peter)—performed tree-trimming tasks.

According to the article's author, the men of the house knew who was boss: "She is in absolute control. Nothing daunts her and nine times out of ten, her way is the only way."

But she didn't do it all alone. Her seven-person staff included a French-Basque chef, Alphonse, as well as a couple familiar faces: Bullimore and Parkes had crossed over from Sutton Place. With them came a sense of continuity and family history—plus they could handle four rambunctious young boys.

In San Francisco, Bullimore ran the house with his customary dry wit, exacting standards, and field marshal manner. He was "imposing and impervious," one visitor observed. Dressed in a waistcoat, he appraised all visitors before they entered. He became a local notable himself, a figure quoted by Herb Caen, dean of San Francisco's columnists (who popularized the word *hippie*, during 1967's Summer of Love). Bullimore was underwhelmed by San Francisco society, Caen reported. "Not much going on, eh?" the butler said to him on a few occasions. In 1970s America, however, there was no more tolerant place for a gay man than San Francisco, which must have been a welcome change from England, where homosexuality was decriminalized only in 1967. According to Christopher Getty, Bullimore had been caught by police in London's Hyde Park while engaging in some amorous activity with another man. "Grandfather took care of it, as one does," he said.

Around 1970, Ann and Gordon attended a small gathering in San Francisco. Dr. Louis Leakey, the pioneering paleoanthropologist and archeologist, had come from Kenya to share with Americans news of his progress searching for evidence of the origins of man. (Drumming up funds to continue his research was certainly on his agenda too.)

Gordon had read of Leakey's work in newspaper articles and was eager to learn more. So, too, were friends Ron and Belinda "Barbara" Pelosi, as well as Ron's brother, Paul, and his wife, Nancy.

Since moving with her husband to the Pelosis' hometown in 1969, Baltimore-born Nancy, née D'Alesandro, had her hands full taking care of their four children; the fifth was born in 1970. (Though she'd grown up in a political household, the idea of herself taking office was still nearly two decades off.)

At the time, Ron and Barbara had the highest political profiles of any in the gang. Ron served on the San Francisco Board of Supervisors; Barbara, a third-generation San Franciscan, grew up steeped in Irish-Democratic politics, being one of six children born to William A. Newsom II, a real estate developer who was a close confidant and campaign manager for Edmund G. "Pat" Brown, who served as governor of California from 1959 to 1967; his son Jerry subsequently reclaimed the office in 1974 for the first of his four terms.

Barbara was born in 1935, a year before her brother William A. Newsom III—Bill, the St. Ignatius classmate of Gordon and his brother Paul. The Getty boys often hung out at Bill's lively Jefferson Street house. With their own father absent, the Getty brothers found a surrogate dad in the genial Newsom *père*. Their affection for him endured. (After Paul Jr. died in 2003, Bill found a framed photograph of his own father in Paul's bedroom at Wormsley.)

The three young couples became ardent supporters of the L. S. B. Leakey Foundation, which had been founded in 1968 to support the anthropologist's groundbreaking fieldwork and research. In that capacity, they honed their skills as they organized large public symposia, reviewed applications for grants the foundation dispensed to researchers, and performed sundry other tasks. Gordon, who became chairman, wrote and edited the brochures, then lugged them to the Central Post Office to make sure they got out on time. He made substantial financial contributions as well. (Dr. Leakey died in October 1972, but his legacy was carried on by his formidable, cigar-smoking widow, Mary.)

A two-day symposium they organized at the Palace of Fine Arts in December 1973 was a triumph. Australian anthropologist Raymond Dart recounted his seminal discovery of *Australopithecus africanus* at a cave in Taung, South Africa, in 1924; Mary Leakey brought the latest news of the digs at Olduvai Gorge in Tanzania; Dian Fossey discussed her study of the mountain gorillas of Rwanda; and Jane Goodall talked about her work with wild chimpanzees at Gombe Stream Research Center in Tanzania.

In the spring of 1975, a Leakey Fellows Day was convened at the Getty Museum in Malibu (attendees included Gloria Getty, George's first wife), where the star attraction was Dr. Donald C. Johanson, fresh from his sensational discovery in Ethiopia of *Australopithecus afarensis*, a 3.5-million-year-old hominoid female who became known as Lucy.

That fall, their conference in Washington, DC, assembled eleven of the world's foremost authorities in the field. Harvard professor Irven DeVore's talk on evolutionary biology and Hamilton's rule—a mathematical formula that provides a basis to explain "survival of the fittest"—captivated Gordon particularly. He developed a keen interest in bioeconomics—the field of social science that uses biology to explain economic events.

In 2013, the Leakey Foundation celebrated Gordon's forty years of service with a four-day celebration in the Bay Area, with toasts from attendees including life trustee Nancy Pelosi and her husband, Paul. According to a citation from Don Dana, president of the foundation, "No person has contributed more to the science of human origins than Gordon Getty."

In the decades after these families met and became intertwined, as they rose to the peaks of wealth and power, there have been inevitable accusations of cronyism. But they bonded over old bones. They were all fascinated by the science—though doubtless learning about survival of the fittest surely came in handy as they tangled with the modern hunter-gatherers of Pacific Heights, Capitol Hill, and beyond.

(Barbara and Ron divorced in 1977, after which she reverted to her maiden name of Newsom and served as the US representative to the United Nations. She remained a staunch supporter of her former sister-in-law and her nephew Gavin until her death from cancer in 2008, at age seventy-three.)

At age nine, Peter Getty, Gordon and Ann's eldest, left for boarding school. He was enrolled at Heatherdown in Berkshire, England. Here, once again, Britain's royals and future ruling class were educated in harsh, peculiar circumstances. His classmates included both Prince Edward and future prime minister David Cameron. "At bath time we had to line up naked in front of a row of Victorian metal baths and wait for the headmaster to blow a whistle before we got in," Cameron reminisced in his memoir, *For the Record*. "Another whistle would indicate that it was time to get out. In between we would have to cope with clouds of smoke from the omnipresent foul-smelling pipe clenched between his teeth."

The decision to send Peter to Heatherdown was no doubt made less out of an urge for him to rub shoulders with royals than a need for security. His cousin in Rome had only recently been released by his abductors; in the Bay Area, the Patricia Hearst drama was still playing out. (Hearst and her four sisters were about a decade older than the Getty boys and raised primarily down the Peninsula in Hillsborough, so the families didn't socialize.)

A few years later, when Billy began school, he stayed in the Bay Area, but for protection he traveled via a limousine driven by a former marine. "He was a sensitive, sweet kid, a gentle boy," recalls a classmate. When it came time for prep school, Billy went to Groton in Massachusetts. Peter and John went east too, to Phillips Exeter Academy in New Hampshire. Andrew stayed in California, attending the Dunn School, near Santa Barbara.

The Getty boys were sometimes portrayed in the media as spoiled brats. ("Peter Getty: Costumed Layabout Scion," read the headline of a *Gawker* piece.) One Exeter classmate of Peter's I spoke to had a different view. "Our classes were very small and discussion-based, so you really got a sense of who a person was. Peter was blazing smart, really well-read and well-rounded, with a lovely dry wit," she said. "He was also a kind person—one of the white hats. Those discussions could get pretty heated. If there was someone struggling, he would be the person to speak up and come to their rescue."

Having a father who was one of the richest men in the country wasn't anything Peter trumpeted. "That kind of thing didn't get you anywhere at Exeter," this classmate added, noting that Firestone and Coors were among their classmates' name-brand last names. "He never made anything of it. He kind of flew under the radar."

"But you knew when his mom was on campus," said a classmate of John Getty, who still vividly recalls the sight of Ann as she dropped John off the first day of school. She was not like the other moms. "She was wearing this short pink raincoat, with a short skirt and very high heels. It was a lot—definitely a bold look for parents' day." John was "popular and very attractive," he adds.

On breaks, the family took adventurous expeditions to Alaska, Nepal, the Galapagos Islands, and other far-flung spots. Billy's close friend Gavin Newsom sometimes went along. Other times, Gavin's father, Bill, took all the boys camping and rafting in the California wilderness. In the early 1970s, after his separation from Gavin's mother, Tessa, Bill moved to the Sierra Nevada foothills, where he opened a law office that specialized in environmental protection, a novelty then. In 1978, Governor Jerry Brown appointed him to the state's superior court bench in Placer County; later Judge Newsom was appointed to the California Courts of Appeal. (After retiring from the judiciary in 1995, he helped Gordon manage his affairs, including his ever-growing fortune.)

In the summer of 1980, Gordon had a breakthrough in Paris, where he was traveling with Ann and the boys. His writer's block lifted when he found a copy of the variorum edition of Emily Dickinson's poems—all 1,775 of them—in the WH Smith English-language bookstore.

When Gordon had studied Dickinson in college in the early fifties, only about a dozen of her poems had been widely published, and they had been bowdlerized. Squabbles among her heirs prevented publication of the bulk of her work until Harvard University Press published the variorum edition in 1955. For Getty, the poems were revelations. He rushed to his hotel suite and began making compositions in his head. Back in San Francisco, he set thirty-two of her poems to music, in a chronology that told the story of the poet's life. It coalesced into a song cycle for piano and female voice that he titled *The White Election*. (One of Dickinson's poems begins, "Mine—by the Right of the White Election! . . .")

Ann began spending an increasing amount of time in New York in the early 1980s, when the family purchased the spectacular seventh-floor apartment at 820 Fifth Avenue, a stately twelve-story limestone building constructed in 1916. Among the handful of cooperative apartment buildings in Manhattan ranked at the very top, 820 Fifth is considered number one by many arbiters. Part of its allure stemmed from Jayne Wrightsman, wife of J. Paul Getty's fellow oilman Charles Wrightsman, who occupied the third floor from 1956 until her death in 2019, at age ninety-nine. (As a collector and connoisseur of eighteenth-century French decorative arts, she had no peer.)

For the Gettys at 820, Parish-Hadley once again went all out on a years-long and costly renovation. A rumor circulated that the curtains alone were running $1 million. In fairness, the windows in the library stretched ten feet high, and the "curtains" in this room were actually made of wood. Inspired by the pelmets that Thomas Chippendale carved in the eighteenth century for the 1st Baron Harewood at Harewood House in Yorkshire, England, Parish-Hadley designers sketched out elaborate, baroque designs, with swags like muttonchops caught and tied with fringed and tasseled cords. The design was then painstakingly carved in wood, which, finally, was gilded and painted. "She wanted the unusual and she could afford it," says a friend of Albert Hadley's. Notwithstanding such opulence, he considered Ann quite down-to-earth: "She's very real. She's the kind of girl who can fix the engine on the tractor."

Yet, as the 1980s progressed, she was a fixture at the Paris couture shows and glittering social functions worldwide. In the *New York Times*, society reporter Charlotte Curtis declared that Ann "is rapidly becoming a superstar." Gordon, who had an aversion to parties, generally stayed home. When they traveled together, it was usually to a music festival—Salzburg, Bayreuth, St. Petersburg; Ann shared his passion for music, opera in particular.

Anywhere she went, Alecko Papamarkou was usually at her side. Now a senior VP at E. F. Hutton in New York, he "walked" Ann. In the parlance of gossip purveyors like *WWD*, "walkers" were always "longtime bachelors"—gays, by inference. Yet in addition to providing Ann with wise business advice, Alecko had a spiritual influence. In 1978, Ann was christened into the Greek Orthodox Church, Papamarkou's faith. Archbishop Iakovos, primate of the Greek

Orthodox Archdiocese of North and South America, performed the service in the chapel of his residence in New York; King Constantine of Greece stood as her godfather.

Papamarkou also kept ties to the inner circle of Ann's late father-in-law, including Paul's closest friend, Heini Thyssen-Bornemisza. In September 1982, Papamarkou cohosted a dinner in his honor, with Gordon and Ann, at the Getty home in San Francisco. Heini stood as he proposed his toast to "a misunderstood man and a great patron of the arts, the late J. Paul Getty."

That fall, Alecko, fifty-two, opened his own firm in New York, A. P. Papamarkou & Co., and the Gettys were among his first investors. Shortly before he hung out his shingle, he treated thirty-six friends to a lavish weeklong stay at the Golden Door, the very fashionable Southern California health spa. In addition to Ann, guests included broadcaster Barbara Walters; Teresa Heinz, wife of the Pennsylvania senator and condiments heir; Infanta Pilar, sister of the king of Spain; and Jonas Salk, the polio vaccine developer, with his wife, Françoise Gilot, Picasso's onetime muse. The Viennese-born British publisher Lord George Weidenfeld, portly and ebullient, was also there. His authors ranged from Vladimir Nabokov to Pope John Paul II; an acquaintance of J. Paul Getty, he had also published the first major catalog of the Getty Museum's collection. Recently he'd launched the literary career of another Golden Door guest, Arianna Stassinopoulos, when he published her biography of Maria Callas. All in all, it was quite a mix that Alecko gathered that week; from it, some substantial ventures would emerge before long.

In the glossy press, 1983 was a banner year for the Gettys. In April, Ann landed on the cover of *Town & Country*, clad in an Emanuel Ungaro couture gown and dripping with David Webb jewels, photographed by Norman Parkinson. On twelve pages inside, she modeled more finery in a succession of fanciful Bavarian castles built by "Mad" King Ludwig II.

In October, Gordon topped *Forbes*'s list of the wealthiest 400 Americans, with a net worth, according to the magazine, of $2.2 billion. At this point his annual income from the trust was reportedly $110 million, on top of which he drew a $20 million fee as the sole trustee. Once again, a Getty was "the richest American." The ranking didn't seem to please him. Gordon locked himself in his soundproof music room and refused to take calls from the Associated Press.

Overnight, there was palpable change in the atmosphere surrounding the Gettys, particularly in the drawing rooms of the Upper East Side. "Mercedes Kellogg [now Bass] used to give these killer Friday lunches in her apartment," recalls a Manhattan gentleman. "They were great fun, everyone came. Right after *Forbes* came out, we were all there one afternoon, whooping it up, when Ann and Gordon appeared at the door. Everybody went dead quiet. You would have thought Moses had come in, that way the room parted for them, like the Red Sea."

As 1983 drew to a close, the simmering tensions between the board of Getty Oil and Gordon exploded. The trigger had been pulled on November 14, when the lawsuit in his nephew Tara Getty's name was filed in Superior Court of Los Angeles County. This action also compelled Harold Williams, the president of the J. Paul Getty Trust, to go into high gear: he had to protect the value of the 12 percent of the stock that the museum owned.

Gordon and Ann flew to New York to meet with new, high-powered members of the Getty Oil board who had been nominated by Gordon but recruited by Ann—including Laurence A. Tisch, chairman of the Loews Corporation, and A. Alfred Taubman, the Detroit real estate developer who had recently acquired Sotheby's auction house.

With the apartment at 820 not yet ready, Ann and Gordon ensconced themselves in a suite at the Pierre Hotel, formerly owned by his father. The fate of Getty Oil hung in the balance. The stakes couldn't have been higher. Just then, Ann gave the most fabulous party New York had seen in ages.

The evening of November 30, a Wednesday, she put on a white satin Dior gown embroidered with gold and welcomed two hundred guests to a dinner in the Temple of Dendur at the Metropolitan Museum of Art, to celebrate Gordon's fiftieth birthday. In addition to a squadron of Gettys, including Gloria, Aileen, Ariadne, and Mark, there was a contingent of forty leading San Franciscans, including the indomitable Denise Hale, all of whom Ann had flown in. Among the notable New Yorkers and Europeans were Brooke Astor, Vicomtesse Jacqueline de Ribes, Lynn Wyatt, Nan Kempner, Bianca Jagger, Ahmet and Mica Ertegun, Carolina and Reinaldo Herrera, Robin Hambro, Pat Buckley, and, of course, Alecko Papamarkou.

After a performance by violinist Isaac Stern, Luciano Pavarotti rushed over from the Metropolitan Opera as soon as the curtain fell on his performance of *Ernani*, and surprised everyone with his rendition of "Happy Birthday."

"It was one of the best parties ever," proclaimed Mrs. Buckley. Five nights later, Buckley presided over the other most glamorous party of the season, under the same roof—the opening of the Yves Saint Laurent retrospective at the Met's Costume Institute, where Gordon's late sister-in-law, Talitha, was extolled.

The very next night, many of the same guests, and about a thousand others, filled Alice Tully Hall at Lincoln Center, to hear soprano Mignon Dunn of the Metropolitan Opera give a recital featuring eighteen songs from *The White Election*.

The drama was only beginning. A couple weeks later, J. Hugh Liedtke, chairman of Houston-based Pennzoil, announced a tender offer for 20 percent of Getty Oil's outstanding stock. The company was officially in play.

In San Francisco, Ann and Gordon had barely unpacked; they rushed back to New York, checking into the Pierre again. An enormous cast of characters representing all sides of the deal took up their positions in the suites and conference rooms of every leading hotel, law firm, and investment bank in town. Following frantic negotiations, Pennzoil raised its offer—it was now a $110 per share leveraged buyout. Considering that GET had been trading at around $50 a year before, it was, in many eyes, a great deal for shareholders—Gettys and non-Gettys alike.

Then things hit an impasse. Liedtke was frustrated because he had been able to deal only with Gordon's battery of bankers, lawyers, and advisors. He announced he would pull out if he couldn't meet with the man himself. "I don't want them telling Mr. Getty what I think or what I'm offering. I want to sit right across the table from him and tell him myself so there won't be any question," said the tough Texan, according to *The Taking of Getty Oil* by Steve Coll.

No way, Gordon's people responded.

Liedtke pondered how to get a message directly to Gordon. On December 30, seeking advice, he phoned fellow Houstonian Fayez Sarofim, a stock fund manager and investment advisor who also owned a big block of Getty Oil. Though he was now a well-established Texan, the Cairo-born Sarofim descended from Egyptian nobility. His ancestry, combined with his tight-lipped inscrutability, had earned him the nickname "the Sphinx" in financial circles.

Sarofim told Liedtke he knew how to handle it: he would call Papamarkou, who could in turn call Ann to ask her to pass Liedtke's meeting request to Gordon.

It worked. Close to midnight on New Year's Eve, the chairman boarded the Pennzoil corporate jet in Houston, bound for New York. His meeting with Gordon was set for New Year's Day.

Liedtke turned his Texan charm on Getty, recalling his wildcatting days in Oklahoma and his acquaintance with J. Paul Getty. His son agreed to a $112.50 a share offer from Pennzoil.

In essence, Ann and Alecko had gotten the biggest corporate acquisition in history back on track.

Then the whole thing jumped to a different track. Gordon's niece Claire got a judge to temporarily block the deal, so she and other family members could evaluate it. During the two-day pause, Texaco chairman John K. McKinley swooped in and offered $125 a share. After wild, round-the-clock negotiations (and after Claire dropped her opposition), Texaco officially won the prize when the papers for the $10 billion deal were signed around 3 a.m. in Gordon's suite at the Pierre.

Pennzoil promptly sued Texaco, claiming it had a deal with Getty Oil even if the contracts weren't signed. Thanks to a clause that Gordon had requested in the negotiations—in which Texaco indemnified the Getty Trust and the J. Paul Getty Museum against any lawsuits that might arise from the sale—the Getty family was not a party to this suit; they banked their billions. After a jury in Houston decided there had been a binding agreement, Texaco was ordered to pay Pennzoil $10.5 billion in damages, the largest jury verdict in history. The two oil companies battled for four more years in court over the judgment. Eventually, Texaco paid a $3 billion settlement to Pennzoil, and went bankrupt.

Getty Oil ceased to exist; twenty thousand employees lost their jobs.

Oil prices plunged. Having cashed out at the top of the market, the Getty family's $4 billion fortune was secure.

That's capitalism—as Gordon explained to an auditorium of University of San Francisco students a couple of years after the sale. "I'm in favor of takeovers, the more hostile the better," he declared. "I like to look at takeovers, and hostile takeovers in particular, as efficiency and economic evolution in action."

Whatever the explanation for their good fortune, the Gettys were, once again, on top.

12

The Richest American, Once Again

In January 1985, one year after the contracts for the largest corporate acquisition in history were signed, Ann and Alecko embarked on a two-week voyage down the Nile. According to some reports, it was about the most fabulous cruise since Cleopatra's golden barge. *Vanity Fair* called it "the most-talked-about sociocultural schlepp of the year."

Aboard the *Nile President* were eighty-three guests Ann and Alecko had flown to Egypt, an eclectic mix that included US ambassador to the United Nations Jeane Kirkpatrick, NYU president John Brademas, Peter Rockefeller (a grandson of Nelson's), King Simeon II of Bulgaria, Prince Alexander Romanov, Evangeline Bruce, Betsy Bloomingdale, Nan Kempner, Jerry Zipkin, George Weidenfeld, Greek shipping magnates galore, and Norna "Miki" Sarofim (Fayez's sister). Before they weighed anchor, Miki treated everyone to a gala dinner in Cairo, at which she informed guests about such ancient wonders as the great palace and temple of Akhenaten, located on land owned by her family. (Though the Sarofim heritage stretches back seemingly to the pharaohs, the family name today is perhaps most widely known thanks to Fayez's live-wire daughter, Allison, who throws New York's most extravagant and exclusive annual Halloween party in her West Village townhouse; Billy Getty's wife, Vanessa, is a regular guest.)

After trooping through innumerable tombs, temples, and pyramids, the party was flown across the desert to Saint Catherine's Monastery in the Sinai to see its icons—one of the greatest collections in Christendom—as well as the burning bush through which God spoke to Moses. "That's strange—I have one just like this in my garden in California," Bloomingdale said to the Greek Orthodox archbishop, their guide. Before the party departed the Nile, they returned to their barge to celebrate Alecko's fifty-fifth birthday, in Egyptian costumes.

A month after bestriding the colossi of ancient Egypt, Ann took on the titans of the New York publishing world. In March 1985, she paid $2 million for Grove Press, the esteemed, boundary-breaking independent house that had brought Samuel Beckett, Jean Genet, D. H. Lawrence, Henry Miller, and Bertolt Brecht to American readers, often after bruising courtroom battles over obscenity laws.

Since her Berkeley days, Ann had been a reader and admirer of Grove books, and *Evergreen Review*, its literary quarterly, which published William Burroughs, Jack Kerouac, and Allen Ginsberg. Over the years, there had been suitors for Grove—conglomerates such as Random House tried to buy it, as did Hugh Hefner. Its iconoclastic president, Barney Rosset, who bought the fledgling publishing house in 1951, fended them off, even though he had been losing money for years, as everyone knew.

In her endeavor, Ann partnered with Lord Weidenfeld. Perhaps the seeds of their alliance were planted that week at the Golden Door (they were seen departing in the same limousine, headed for a well-earned lunch in San Diego). He had long wished to enter the US publishing market; she loved books (and she had the cash). "I'm a publisher because it's a cover for my indulgence," she told the *New York Times* in 1989. "I love to read all day. But I come from nice Puritan stock, and I grew up believing that you have to work all day, so I made reading my work."

After convincing Rosset to sell, they gave him a five-year contract to stay on. Weidenfeld said they hoped to expand the roster of writers, yet "keep the character of a very literary house." From their offices in the Harper & Row Building on East 53rd Street, they also set up Weidenfeld & Nicolson New York, an American arm of the firm he'd founded in London in 1949. Top talent was hired away from other houses, and contracts for about a hundred books were signed in the first five months, many of them accompanied by big checks, such as the reported $1 million paid to Milan Kundera for his next novel. Meanwhile, Ann launched an ambitious nonprofit, the Wheatland Foundation, which organized dazzling conferences on literature and music, in locations around the world. Ann took her new business seriously. "She was always off to the Frankfurt Book Fair, or someplace like that," a New York friend recalled.

While Grove and Weidenfeld & Nicolson published a number of excellent books, including Arthur Miller's memoir, *Timebends: A Life*, and Harold Pinter's only novel, *The Dwarfs*, the ventures did not flourish. After editorial disagreements, Rosset was pushed out within a year. In 1989, Weidenfeld & Nicolson New York and Grove merged into Grove New York; two years later, after the ventures lost a reported $30 million, Getty family financial advisors pressed Ann to pull out. Grove later merged with Atlantic Monthly Press.

"The Gettys are surrounded by financial advisors who they listen to. Rich as they are, Gettys don't like to lose money," said the New York friend. In his memoir, *Remembering My Good Friends*, Weidenfeld explained that the undertaking foundered in part because neither he (who remained anchored in London) nor the San Francisco–based Ann could focus on it fully. He also apportioned some blame to the Getty advisors, who were "already laden with work for the Getty family." But there were no hard feelings, Weidenfeld wrote. After the plug was pulled, Ann and Gordon took him and his new bride, Annabelle, on a cruise along the Anatolian coast of Turkey.

Because she eloped, Ann Getty never had one of those storybook weddings. Perhaps the many extravagant nuptials she hosted for family members and friends over the years were her way of compensating. In any event, no one could throw a wedding like Ann Getty.

When it came time for her new best friend Arianna Stassinopoulos to march down the aisle, she pulled out all the stops.

Ann had, what's more, introduced Arianna to the man she was to marry: Roy Michael Huffington Jr., a quiet, handsome Texas oil heir. Ann had sat down with Arianna and made a list of prospective grooms on a legal pad. Huffington wasn't on it—but then Ann met him on a trip to Japan. *Bingo*, she thought, and phoned Arianna from Tokyo: "I've found him!" She invited both to be her guests at the San Francisco Symphony's opening-night gala in September 1985.

Seven months later, their wedding took place at the Episcopal St. Bartholomew's Church in New York, in a spectacular candlelit ceremony before some four hundred guests (from Shirley MacLaine to Henry Kissinger), followed by a dinner at the Metropolitan Club, all said to be underwritten by Ann to the tune of about $100,000, not counting the bride's gown by James Galanos, which cost $35,000. "In a year of big weddings, including Caroline Kennedy's and Prince Andrew's, the one people are *still* talking about is [Arianna's]," Bob Colacello reported in *Vanity Fair*.

(In 1994, Arianna encouraged Michael, a conservative Republican, to run against incumbent Dianne Feinstein—another close Getty family friend—for one of California's two US Senate seats. Gordon was in a quandary. He made up his mind after Huffington, then a congressman, voted for the Hyde Amendment, which bans federal Medicaid funding to cover almost all abortions. "The Bible-thumping worried me a little," Getty said, explaining his choice of Feinstein. In 1998, a year after Huffington and Arianna were divorced, Huffington revealed that he is gay.)

Having overcome his writer's block, Gordon threw himself into music composition. He set to work on an opera inspired by Sir John Falstaff, Shakespeare's comical yet poignant character from *Henry IV.* Titled *Plump Jack*, it had a lengthy development. Scene I premiered at the San Francisco Symphony in March 1985, Scene II at the Aspen Festival the next year, and Scene III at the University of New Mexico in March 1987. Three months later, the whole thing returned to San Francisco, in a gala concert performance by a 100-piece orchestra and a 60-member chorus. Getty later said the opera was not complete, and he continued to tinker with it.

Gordon faced criticism from the music press that sometimes seemed inordinately hostile. When you are "the world's wealthiest composer," as many articles about him underscored, can your work be judged on its merits?

"It doesn't take much daring to perform an hour of painless, faceless, unabashedly eclectic, pleasantly decorative, sporadically engaging music by a quasi-amateurish but ultra-supportive patron of the arts whom *Forbes* recently labeled the wealthiest man in America," wrote the *Los Angeles Times*'s critic in his review of the 1987 performance. He did offer some faint praise: "Getty, 53, is not without talent."

Gordon maintained a thick skin and a sense of humor about the reviews, and assertions by some that his music was only performed because of his last name: "The disproof of that claim is basically the kind of reviews I get," he commented.

A generational shift occurred on January 23, 1988. Ann Light, née Rork, the much-married matriarch of this branch of the family and the only wife of J. Paul Getty (his fourth) who produced a pair of full siblings—Paul Jr. and Gordon—died at age seventy-nine of emphysema.

In the end, she had equalled J. Paul Getty in trips to the altar. In 1960 she took her fifth march down the aisle, with Dr. Rudolph A. Light, a professor of neurosurgery and an Upjohn Company heir. Following his death ten years later, Ann, with a $25 million inheritance, continued to enjoy a vigorous life between Nashville, San Francisco, and Palm Beach.

At her funeral in St. Edward Catholic Church in Palm Beach, her grandson Mark and her son Gordon both spoke.

"Yes, she was difficult, and I loved her for it," said Mark.

Gordon recounted his mother's final days when she could hardly open her eyes or speak, but she brightened when she heard the voices of her children or grandchildren. "Family," he concluded, "lasts forever."

At a dinner party at home in San Francisco, Gordon later recalled to guests how his mother had taken him to his first opera, at the Hollywood Bowl, when he was seven: "*Madame Butterfly*, and it was so beautiful I wept through it all."

A few months after Ann's funeral, Peter graduated from college. An English major, he received his BA from Harvard (after taking a year off to work as a copy editor at Grove in New York). Within a few years, Andrew and Billy got their diplomas from NYU and Brown, respectively; John studied at Brown too. At six feet six, Billy was the tallest, eclipsing his father; but they all reached at least six feet. "They were unbelievably good-looking guys—smoking," recalled a schoolmate.

Even as Gordon's operatic treatment of Sir John Falstaff continued to gestate, images of the rotund, comical knight began appearing across the Bay Area.

First came PlumpJack Wine & Spirits, a storefront that opened in 1992 on Fillmore Street in Cow Hollow. It was the brainchild of Gavin Newsom and Billy Getty, along with his brothers. They'd all developed an appreciation for good wine thanks to their fathers, both passionate oenophiles. On summer trips to the Palio in Siena, teenage Gavin, for one, had perked his ears as the elders waxed rhapsodic about the new Super Tuscans, whose names tripped off the tongue—Sassicaia, Tignanello, Solaia. Now he and the boys decided to shake up the conservative wine world with a new type of shop— with whimsical design elements, a youthful but informed vibe, and cut-rate prices. PlumpJack was an immediate hit.

A total of $174,000 in seed money had been cobbled together from a dozen or so friends and relatives, including Matthew Pelosi (Ron and Barbara's son) and several Gettys: Gordon (who kicked in $15,000); cousins Christopher, Ariadne, and Mark; and brother Andrew, then twenty-four. It was Andrew who asked Gordon if they could name the venture after his opera. The title character's conviviality embodied the spirit they wanted for their business, and of course it was a nice tribute to Gordon. "Boys, I won't sue you," he said.

After his prep school days, John became obsessed with rock music. Living primarily between Los Angeles and London, he taught himself to play the guitar and styled himself like a rock star, complete with long hair and tattoos. Drugs were also part of his lifestyle. According to family friends, he became an addict.

In 1994 he fathered a daughter, Ivy Love Getty, with Alyssa Boothby, a woman with whom he had a short relationship in Los Angeles. Ann and Gordon were ecstatic over the arrival of their first grandchild. She had been born on December 20, Gordon's birthday—surely a good omen; Ann, who never had a daughter, was thrilled to help raise a girl. So Ivy grew up under their watchful eyes in the Getty mansion. "Ann made Ivy central to her life. The relationship meant a great deal to her," says a friend.

At two and a half, Ivy was already mixing with high society. "This is a great bunch—everyone from the chief justice of the California

Supreme Court to Ivy Getty," Denise Hale observed as she surveyed the group of twenty-four who had sat down to a lunch she was hosting in honor of couturier Gianfranco Ferré at her 8,000-acre ranch in Sonoma. (Ivy was wearing a lavender tutu.)

When Ivy was three, Ann founded a Montessori-based school in her capacious basement. It became known as the Playgroup. About two dozen neighborhood children were invited to attend, with never a fee or an application (it was said around town that kids were "tapped," rather like the Skull and Bones secret society at Yale). Seven full-time teachers were on staff, as well as a chef trained at Chez Panisse, who prepared organic lunches.

Peter, with his curly hair and professorial manner, bears the strongest resemblance to his father. He's musical as well. Gordon taught him to play piano at the age of two. With a college classmate, Peter formed a band called the Virgin-Whore Complex. Under the stage name Spats Ransom (a reference to his cousin's kidnapping), he was guitarist and vocalist, as well as the writer of many of the songs on the two albums they produced, *Stay Away from My Mother* and *Succumb*. He also founded a boutique record label, Emperor Norton, named after the eccentric nineteenth-century San Franciscan who proclaimed himself "Emperor of these United States."

By the mid-nineties Peter was living in Los Angeles and dating model and actress Lauren Hutton. Then he met Jacqueline "Jacqui" de la Fontaine, a stylish bohemian with wide brown eyes. She had a young daughter, Gia, from her relationship with Gian-Carlo Coppola, son of director Francis Ford Coppola. In 1986, when Jacqui was pregnant with her, twenty-two-year-old Gian-Carlo was killed in a speedboat accident. Peter moved into Jacqui's Spanish-style bungalow at the top of the Hollywood Hills, where he helped raise Gia.

Andrew, who was described by friends as "jolly," made an attempt at acting. In 1991 he starred in *Rex Justice*, a twenty-five-minute parody of the criminal justice system directed by his best friend, Chris Vietor, an heir to the Jell-O fortune (some of their pals, including

Gavin Newsom, had bit parts). Despite his sturdy six-foot-three build and fair-haired good looks, the consensus was that Andrew was no thespian. "I never want to act again," he said. Nonetheless, his parents hosted a lavish Academy Awards–themed premiere party, complete with red carpet, at Bimbo's, a hot nightclub. Most of the 450 guests were in their early twenties, but the Pelosis came, as did the *Hollywood Reporter*'s George Christy. Andrew subsequently moved to Los Angeles, where he enrolled at USC film school, with aspirations to write screenplays and direct. He moved into an eight-bedroom house in the Hollywood Hills.

Billy, the only son left in San Francisco, began dating Vanessa Jarman, a tall blonde with flawless looks and keen determination. They had known each other since sixth grade. A UCLA graduate, she was working as an artists' representative. At the time, Billy was on the midst of a three-year project to design what would be San Francisco's ultimate bachelor pad, a twenty-fifth-floor penthouse in Russian Hill with breathtaking views. Working with Modesto-based Leavitt/Weaver—the firm that had designed the PlumpJack store—he gutted the 5,500-square-foot space, installing hand-tinted concrete-slab floors and floor-to-ceiling windows that opened onto a wraparound terrace. The central elevator bank was encased in rough rock, which was then covered in 24K gold leaf—resembling a golden cave. The rest of the apartment was virtually transparent, aside from the movable fiberglass shoji screens. Along with kinetic furniture and black-and-white photography, there was ancient Hellenistic statuary in marble and bronze. When Ann saw it, she approved. It was "radical," she declared.

Simultaneously, Billy was busy expanding the business. In the city, he and Gavin opened a PlumpJack Cafe and acquired the venerable Balboa Cafe. In Napa Valley, they purchased a vineyard, where a Cabernet Sauvignon and other varieties of wine would be produced. Near Lake Tahoe, they opened the PlumpJack Squaw Valley Inn.

More would come, but that was the portfolio in the spring of 1996, when Billy, twenty-five, and Gavin, twenty-eight, sat down for an interview with a young journalist (me). With his long hair in a pony-tail, lanky Billy exuded a laid-back coolness. Gavin, six feet three, had already perfected his slick mane and smooth swagger.

"We wanted to develop a younger generation of wine enthusiasts and avoid the snobbery that is wine," said Newsom. Added Billy, "We went to every wine store in the Bay Area. We walked in in our baseball caps and jeans. Everyone told us, 'We don't sell beer, that's the corner store, boys.' We were disrespected."

They were just cocky enough to still be likable. And who could quibble with their mission to demystify the wine-buying process and offer terrific bottles at affordable prices? At the time, the shop sold two hundred wines with price tags $10 or under.

Gordon also spoke to me. "I offered no more input than any other daddy," he explained. "I said, 'I'll lend you money as long as you work hard. Because even if you lose, you'll learn something.'

"It's a lot of fun to see the entrepreneurial spirit bubbling up in the Getty clan again," he added with glee.

As it happened, a political spirit gurgled up from the same premises—from a mop sink, to be exact. When the young men were applying for their permits, city inspectors put the brakes on things because the space did not have all the requisite plumbing fixtures. "I was like, 'The whole store is carpeted. Why the hell do we need a mop sink?'" recalled Newsom. He became one of those "mad as hell and not going to take it anymore guys" as he attempted to take on city hall. Mayor Willie Brown, as lore has it, said, "I'm sick of this guy complaining." Thinking it would be better if Newsom were working for the city rather than against it, he appointed him to his first political position, on the Parking and Traffic Commission in 1996.

According to Billy, Ann was "very enthusiastic" about their new business. "But she's all over me for everything else," he added.

Ann herself was not available for comment then because she was in Ethiopia, where she was probably on her hands and knees with a shovel.

The Gettys had left New York behind. They sold the apartment at 820 Fifth Avenue to Warner Bros. boss Terry Semel in 1996, but in the previous few years they'd hardly turned on the lights. "I think they slept in it but five nights," said another resident. After all that, New York just wasn't for them.

Ann now preferred the Middle Awash paleoanthropological research area, deep inside the Afar Depression of Ethiopia, where fossil and artifact discoveries were producing the longest single record of human ancestors on earth.

She earned a place on the Middle Awash team after taking paleoanthropology courses at Berkeley from Professor Tim White, a leading fossil finder. She could offer some team members a lift, too. In 1986, Gordon and Ann had acquired a Boeing 727, which was put to such frequent use, like a family station wagon, it became known around San Francisco as the Jetty. In the early 1990s it underwent a complete overhaul, and emerged as one of the most luxurious private rides in the skies.

The floor was made to resemble the stones in a temple near Bangkok, inlays of forty exotic woods were used throughout, and the gold-leaf passageway that separates the two bedrooms was hung with six maps of the heavens created by Andreas Cellarius in the seventeenth century.

"We saw some excellent reproductions of these plates and we suggested to the client that they might be used here," project designer Craig Leavitt of Leavitt/Weaver told *Architectural Digest* when the jet was featured anonymously. "They're beautiful, we'll get the real ones," responded the client, who was identified only as "a student of paleoanthropology."

Gordon, also still fascinated with the origins of man, was providing generous financial backing to the Institute of Human Origins (IHO), a Berkeley-based organization led by Donald Johanson, the charismatic fossil hunter (and former mentor of White) who in 1974 had discovered the 3.2 million–year-old Lucy. She reigned as the oldest known human ancestor until 1992, when White and his team found *Ardipithecus ramidus*, a 4.4 million–year-old.

Then Gordon and Ann fell out with Johanson. They felt he was busier promoting himself than the science. Gordon, who had been underwriting half of the IHO's $2 million annual budget, withdrew his support, and the Gettys threw their backing behind the Berkeley Geochronology Center, a new group. Within the fossil world, it became a fracas of considerable proportion, the subject of much chatter. Paleoanthropology sounds not so different from politics or high society.

At Christmastime 1998, Billy and Vanessa announced their engagement. Naturally, Ann went into high gear planning the festivities for the first wedding in her family, which was scheduled for June. She also took a considerable interest in the bride's gown. She picked up the phone and called her friend Oscar de la Renta in New York. "I want you to dress Vanessa," she told him, according to Boaz Mazor, a longtime de la Renta executive. "I want her to be the most beautiful bride ever, I want her to look unbelievable."

"Oscar dropped everything. He called in all his assistants, the office was turned upside down," Mazor continued. "Then we got a call to cancel everything."

Vanessa decided to go with Narciso Rodriguez. For her, the new young star designer agreed to make his first wedding dress since the one that had launched him to stardom—Carolyn Bessette's, for her wedding to John Kennedy Jr. in 1996.

"Ann was livid! Furious!" says Mazor.

Yet when Vanessa made her entrance to the Renaissance-themed ceremony at a ranch in Napa Valley, riding sidesaddle on a speckled horse at sunset, pretty much everyone had to agree that she chose right. Her form-fitting matte satin gown with crystal-embroidered layers glistened.

The June 1999 ceremony was officiated by Judge Newsom. Gavin was best man and Gordon sang a Welsh song for the 165 guests. Among them were Gettys from far and wide, as well as a new assistant district attorney in town, a thirty-four-year-old up-and-comer named Kamala Harris—Vanessa's new friend. Two years later, Harris threw the shower before the birth of Vanessa and Billy's first child, Nicholas. Brother Alexander arrived in 2003. When Veronica Louise was born in 2008, Kamala was asked to be her godmother.

Vanessa and Kamala's friendship had been fostered by Denise Hale—Nicholas's godmother. Habitually bejeweled and chinchilla-draped, the Serbian-born social lioness is San Francisco's ultimate power broker, some say. "When I was ten years old in Belgrade, my grandmother sat me down and explained life," Hale once told me, in her Slavic accent. "She said, 'Don't waste your energy fighting your enemies. Just go to river and wait for the body of your enemy to pass by. And, my child, they always will.'"

Two months after the wedding in Napa, the Gettys were guests of their friend Kenneth Rainin, a medical products magnate, aboard his two-hundred-foot motor yacht *Rasselas*, named after Samuel Johnson's character, an "Abissinian" prince who traveled throughout ancient Arabia in search of bliss. (A pattern emerges: rich men, the names of their boats, and the search for happiness.)

Ann had certainly earned a holiday; that spring, she had staged yet another elaborate wedding at the Getty Mansion, for actor Don Johnson and Kelley Phleger, whose Chanel couture gown was a gift from Ann on a Jetty-propelled trip to Paris.

While floating somewhere on the Mediterranean, Gordon received a call from his lawyer, a call he knew would come one day. At some point, the media was bound to expose the existence of his other family, in Los Angeles. For years, a very small circle of San Franciscans, including Ann and his sons, had been aware of the situation, but it had so far remained a secret.

"It was the *San Jose* paper that broke the story," one society stalwart said to me, his voice dripping with derision. "The San Francisco papers would have never dared."

On August 20, 1999, the *San Jose Mercury News* went there:

BILLIONAIRE GORDON GETTY'S SECRET
FAMILY OF 4 REVEALED

S.F. SOCIALITE HAS THREE DAUGHTERS,
INHERITANCE BEING NEGOTIATED

According to a family friend, Gordon asked Ann if she wanted to debark from the *Rasselas* and fly home. "No, we're going on with the trip," she said.

Anticipating this day, Gordon's lawyer had a prepared statement from him. Now it was released: "Nicolette, Kendalle, and Alexandra are my children. Their mother, Cynthia Beck, and I, love them very much. The most important concern is that the children's needs be addressed with a minimum of disruption, and this will be our first priority. The Getty family has been fully supportive throughout this situation, and for that, I am very grateful."

Nicolette, then fourteen, Kendalle, age ten, and Alexandra, who was eight, had been brought up with the surname Beck. (Doing the math, Nicolette was presumably born in 1985, the year that began with Ann setting sail down the Nile.) In April 1999, a lawyer working on their behalf had filed documents in Los Angeles Superior Court requesting that their names be changed to Getty, which was what tipped off a *San Jose Mercury News* reporter.

"She is a nice lady and lives in the LA area," was all Gordon's attorney divulged about Cynthia after the story broke. The press, as well as the Sherlock Holmeses of high society, endeavored to learn details of Getty's other family, but few real facts ever emerged, in the papers or on the cocktail-party circuit. "No one we know knows her," a Beverly Hills doyenne declared to me, which was a common refrain.

According to another close Getty family friend, Gordon had revealed his secret first to his third-born son: "Gordon drove over to see John in Berkeley. 'You know, I have three daughters,' he said."

Understandably stunned, John kept the news to himself initially. Until one day when Gordon, Ann, and the four boys were all aloft on the Jetty. As a family discussion grew heated, John blurted it out: *"Dad has another family."* According to this family friend, Ann sat in her seat "stone-faced."

"She was upset when she found out, but they came to an understanding, and she was permissive about letting Gordon visit the girls," said another friend.

According to most accounts from the Getty social circle, Gordon ended the affair when the news of it exploded, though one of their intimates claims it continued. In any event, Gordon did introduce his Los Angeles family to his San Francisco family, in hopes of establishing cordial relations, which by and large happened. But not overnight. "There was a hiccup," says a childhood friend of the boys. Money was an issue. Gordon made it clear that his daughters and sons would be inheriting equal shares of his estate. "The boys weren't liking it—that everything suddenly had been diluted by about half," this source says. But in time everyone became amicable. And even with the addition of the three heirs, Gordon's children will, by most estimates, eventually receive hundreds of millions each.

Nonetheless, the revelation was society's equivalent of the San Francisco earthquake. This time, many awaited the aftershocks with glee. But exactly two months after the deluge of headlines around the world following the *Mercury News* scoop, here was the report in the *Chronicle*'s Social Scene column: "Dinner, anyone? Ann and Gordon Getty have been giving some simply MAHvelous dinner parties lately, such as the one they and Jo Schuman gave Sunday for author Dominick Dunne." The same week, the article reported, the Gettys also hosted suppers for pianists Katia and Marielle Labèque and for the writers in town for the National Kidney Foundation's Authors' Lunch.

The next month, much of San Francisco society assembled inside the Getty mansion, when Ann hosted a reception after the funeral of Pat Steger, who for twenty-five years had written the thrice-weekly Social Scene column for the *Chronicle*. In a town where "Society" still really mattered, Steger ranked high. A graduate of the Hamlin School for Girls, she reported diligently (usually clad in a mink coat) on the comings and goings of the Bay Area elite—Ann above all. Around town, it was believed that Steger was aware of Gordon's other family, but that this was one scoop she chose not to break.

Nor did anyone else in San Francisco's press corps. (Dan Reed, the *San Jose Mercury News*'s award-winning investigative reporter who did break the story, was, according to a colleague, a "Falstaffian" figure, with a "six foot four, 330-pound frame, uncombed beard, and untucked shirts.") After Steger's funeral mass at St. Ignatius, which was filled with 13,200 Ecuadorian white roses, Ann welcomed everybody to the house for vodka and cheese puffs, Pat's staples. "I always enjoyed her columns, but she was also a great personal friend," Ann commented to the *Chronicle*. "She came many times for dinners which were private. . . . She respected that and didn't write about it. I thought she was a wonderful person."

With her highly trained staff—and the near-constant services of Stanlee R. Gatti, the Bay Area's premiere event designer—it was nothing for Ann to throw a dinner for sixty, and sometimes many more. The Getty mansion functioned like an embassy, and a concert hall (Placido Domingo, Anna Netrebko, Jessye Norman, and other greats sang in the music room or the courtyard, usually after a dinner). When an important dignitary, cultural luminary, or royal came to town, more often than not Ann would host a formal event in their honor.

But sometimes she was absent. Upon arrival, guests would be informed that Mrs. Getty was indisposed or traveling; they would be hosted instead by Charlotte Mailliard Shultz, the state of California's chief of protocol and wife of former secretary of state George Shultz. On occasion, however, Ann just didn't feel like attending these formal functions. Shortly before sixty guests were due to arrive in black tie for a dinner in honor of celebrated art historian Rosamond Bernier, for example, Ann had her secretary call her friend Boaz Mazor; he was instructed to use a side door to the house that night, and meet his hostess upstairs. "We had the most marvelous, cozy dinner in Ann's bedroom while everyone was downstairs. She was wearing gray flannel pants and a brown sweater," he recalled. "'*I can't stand those dinners,*' Ann said."

On Sundays around this time, Ann took to hosting informal suppers in the kitchen for her family and their close friends, many of whom happened to be heavyweights in their fields, such as conductor Michael Tilson Thomas, Senator Feinstein, Mayor Brown, and Berkeley professor Alex Pines. When Kamala Harris was added to the list for Sunday Supper, she had really arrived.

Nearly every Sunday Supper (it became such a thing, it was uppercased) included Ann's best friend, Jo Schuman Silver. Around 2005, when Ann was redecorating Silver's apartment, she and Gordon installed her in one of their guest rooms, which features eighteenth-century Syro-Turkish paneling—hand-painted, gilded, and ornamented with semiprecious stones; Ann bought it at auction in London. The opulent mother-of-pearl and wood-inlaid bed is decorated with rare Qajar *verre églomisé.*

A five-foot, platinum-haired, Chanel-clad bundle of energy, the Brooklyn-born Jo arrived in San Francisco in 1977 with her second husband, a garment business owner. He died in 1985, by which time she had become soul mates with Steve Silver, who in 1974 had created *Beach Blanket Babylon*, a camp musical review, at the Savoy Tivoli theater. With a parade of performers in gaudy costumes and wigs, it spoofed celebrities and political culture and became a San Francisco institution.

In the early nineties, Steve contracted HIV. He and Jo married in 1994; he died the following year, and she took the reins of *BBB*. Having grown up in a show business–oriented family (music producer Clive Davis is a cousin), she took to producing naturally, and became a San Francisco icon herself—as well as the godmother of Ivy Getty. Whether or not it was a factor of being busy with the show, Schuman Silver stayed on in the sumptuous Turkish room. "Why would I ever leave?" she once asked rhetorically.

Ann and Gordon's marriage continued to sail. "They were made for each other," an old friend of theirs observed. "It has a lot to do with them loving the same things—music, wine, beautiful things. They're each eccentrics—they both have a certain madness."

13

New Vintages

In October 2000, Peter and Jacqui were married at the Coppola winery in Napa Valley. (Francis Ford Coppola walked her down the aisle.) Beforehand, Ann took Jacqui on the Jetty to Paris for fittings at the haute couture houses, at which the free-spirited Jacqui wore sneakers and a down jacket. Ann picked up the reported $600,000 tab for Jacqui's new wardrobe, including her Balmain wedding dress, which alone cost $100,000.

Jacqui's own natural style was embraced in Hollywood, where she became a stylist and costume designer. Her clients (who were often friends too) ranged from the Beastie Boys to Demi Moore. "I really trust her taste," Moore told *Harper's Bazaar*.

A year after Peter and Jacqui's nuptials, Ann orchestrated a wedding for the ages, when Gavin Newsom married Kimberly Guilfoyle, a prosecutor in the San Francisco District Attorney's Office (and a onetime girlfriend of Billy's). The couple met at a Democratic state fund raiser held at PlumpJack. Nearly every inch of the Italianate St. Ignatius Church was covered in garlands of gardenias for the evening service. The veil of her crystal-encrusted Vera Wang gown was anchored by an Edwardian diamond *trembleuse* (trembling) tiara lent by Ann. A lavish banquet followed at the Getty mansion for some five hundred guests, ranging from writer Danielle Steel to Mark Getty, a groomsman. But one couple was conspicuously absent: Billy and Vanessa.

Billy and Gavin's friendship had ruptured shortly after his wedding in Napa. Around town, there was speculation about the cause of the rift, but neither man has ever publicly commented. In the aftermath of the falling-out, Billy stepped away from PlumpJack. Gordon bought out his stake in the business. He and Ann remained devoted to Gavin; Gordon has said he considers him like a son. "Gavin is Fortinbras to the Hamlet of Billy," one San Franciscan wryly observed.

(Over the years, Newsom's political opponents have tried to weaponize his connections to the Gettys, portraying him as a child of privilege. But while the Gettys have contributed generously to his campaigns, other San Francisco families have given as much, if not more. In 2018, the *Los Angeles Times* reported that eighteen Gettys had contributed $516,925 to his nine campaigns, including his gubernatorial run that year; during the same span, members of the Pritzker dynasty had given him $608,000, while several other leading Bay Area families had given hundreds of thousands as well.)

In California government, a major changing of the guard was at hand. On January 8, 2004, Newsom was sworn in as San Francisco's youngest mayor in more than a century; Harris became the state's first Black district attorney. (Vanessa served on the finance committee of Harris's campaign.)

The politicians came up together, but Gavin's rise was meteoric. After issuing marriage licenses to same-sex couples, the charismatic thirty-six-year-old leaped onto the national stage as his approval ratings soared to an unheard-of 78 percent. One day he would make a strong run for the White House, it was commonly assumed around San Francisco, and certainly inside the Gettys' house.

For decades, Gordon and Ann had been intimate friends with senators and governors; but who would emerge in the family closest to the highest powers in the land? Those who knew Vanessa only from her appearances at society galas—her statuesque figure clad in glamorous gowns—might end up surprised.

In January 2005, Newsom and Guilfoyle (who had a frosty relationship with Harris when the two women worked together in the DA's office) announced their separation. "It was a bad match, but happily there were no children involved," Judge Newsom said after their divorce became official in 2006, when Guilfoyle joined Fox News in New York. Two years later, Gavin's wedding to actress and Stanford graduate Jennifer Siebel, on a meadow at her parents' ranch in Montana, was a down-home affair—even if many of the two hundred guests were movers and shakers of California politics and business who arrived by private plane. Within eight years, the couple had four children—Montana, Hunter, Brooklynn, and Dutch.

In Hollywood, Peter and Jacqui's house became one the coolest spots in town. The likes of Leonardo DiCaprio, the Olsen twins, Nicolas Ghesquière, Ashton Kutcher, and Demi Moore could be found hanging out in the couple's living room. And that was just a Tuesday. Her celebrity-packed parties—particularly her annual Halloween bash held amidst the tombstones of Hollywood Forever Cemetery—were major events.

Three years after their wedding, Ann paid $7 million for a landmark mansion in Cow Hollow for the couple, though they were not looking for a San Francisco residence at the time. "She really wanted Peter back in San Francisco, and she would not stop," says a friend. Ann embarked on a massive renovation of the Italianate Victorian mansion, built in 1876 by a music impresario named Leander Sherman. When she acquired it, it was a luxury hotel, Sherman House.

Before it ultimately became a home for Peter, Sherman House was a good project for Ann's fledgling career. After all those years of absorbing lessons from her father-in-law, Sister Parish, and various curators, she launched herself as a design professional. In the mid-1990s, she had quietly opened Ann Getty & Associates, an interior decorating firm, but the work didn't really come to the public's attention until 2003 when, simultaneously, she launched Ann Getty Home, a collection of custom furniture and reproductions of important historical pieces, and unveiled the renovation of one of the most extravagant homes in America—her own.

She and Gordon had bought the mansion next door. By dint of considerable engineering, it was eventually seamlessly joined to the Gettys' original house. Utilizing all her know-how, Ann completely reimagined her home of thirty years. Even as it was "completed," work continued: the Gettys bought the next house over. By the time the three properties were joined—which gave the couple some 30,000 square feet—she had created one of the most palatial private residences in America. "We're building all the way to Oakland, at this rate," a friend of Gordon's recalls him saying in jest.

"We joked that now that the children are gone, we needed a bigger house," Ann quipped.

In the fall of 2003, I visited the house to interview Ann about her burgeoning design career. We chatted in the dining room, which was lined with chinoiserie panels made in 1720 for the Elector of Saxony, as a butler served a lunch of chicken salad. (Alas, Francis Bullimore was no longer on duty. The revered majordomo died of a heart ailment in 1996 at age eighty-two, at the Getty residence. The Gettys had looked after him at home well after he reached retirement age, as they did with other staff members, including the boys' nanny. According to his obituary in the *San Francisco Examiner,* Bullimore was survived by a sister in Norfolk, England, "and his cherished schnauzer, Nietzsche.")

Gordon was occupied that morning composing music in his study downstairs, but he popped into the dining room for a moment. Looking very much the absent-minded professor, he offered an optimistic prediction of his wife's professional prospects. "New businesses usually fail, especially the fun ones, but I think this one has a definite chance of succeeding," he said as he took the opportunity to engage in some good-natured self-promotion, presenting me with a copy of his new CD, a recording of *Joan and the Bells*, a cantata portraying the trial and execution of Joan of Arc.

Ann, dressed in her daytime uniform of jeans and an immaculate white shirt, cut a commanding figure, standing at five feet ten with flowing red hair.

Stately as the Getty mansion was, there were unexpected touches, like the trampoline set up in the vast marble-lined interior court-yard, and coloring books strewn about the walnut-paneled library: although their classrooms were belowstairs, the schoolchildren had the run of the house.

Paintings by Canaletto, Degas, Matisse, Bonnard, and Mary Cassatt adorned the walls, and museum-quality furniture abounded, including true showstoppers such as a pair of *coffres de mariage* signed by master cabinetmaker André-Charles Boulle. Many items were made originally for England's stateliest homes, such as Badminton, Houghton Hall, and Spencer House, by such masters as Thomas Chippendale, Giles Grendey, and James Linnell.

"There's stuff in there any museum would kill for," an eminent antiques dealer later told me. An auction house expert said, "Ann took the cake for extravagance. She always went for the rarest, the most important things. But then she would hang things in a won-derfully irreverent way. She put a Degas in her bathroom. Well, I'd do it if I could. Though I don't know if I approve of her sawing up Coromandel screens."

With chinoiserie as her theme, Getty transformed her newly enlarged residence into a spectacular Aladdin's cave of treasures, exotic and layered.

"I like things on things," she said, explaining her design philoso-phy as well as the evolution of her house.

Since her formative years with Mrs. Parish, Ann's taste had grown bolder. She reached a point where she was ready to replace Parish-Hadley's signature yellow walls and chintzes with her own vision—though she still remembered Sister fondly: "She scared me, of course. She would march you through things and watch to see if you got it. . . . I couldn't make my mind up about anything. Finally she told me I had to make decisions—and I did."

When she began her own decorating business, Ann faced inevitable skepticism. "There may be the perception that I'm spoiled, have no sense of the price of things, that I just wouldn't understand a budget. . . . I can clear that up very easily," she said. "I can convince them that I work hard, have a good team, and can listen."

In addition to her originality, Ann had access to rare sources. (The Jetty helped.) In Myanmar, she discovered a textile made from hairs of the lotus flower, harvested after the rainy season. Monks traditionally stitched together their robes from the cloth, which is woven only in small pieces. "I thought it was just fabulous, because it is always cool to the touch," she said.

In a cavernous former army barrack in San Francisco's Presidio, Getty opened her atelier, stocked with acres of rare textiles, passementerie, porcelains, objets d'art, carpets, and antiques. Her staff included three full-time upholsterers/seamstresses. "[It's] like Santa's workshop," said one of Getty's clients, frozen-food heiress Alexis Swanson Traina. "There's nothing she can't do."

For Alexis and her husband, tech entrepreneur (and later US ambassador to Austria) Trevor Traina, Getty brought exoticism and fantasy to a sedate brick 1905 mansion the couple purchased. The walls of the library, for example, were covered with thousands of peacock feathers. "It's magic," Trevor said.

While Ann Getty also completed jobs for other prominent San Franciscans, including socialite Adrianna Pope Sullivan and philanthropist Terry Gross, her client roster included many family names. For Peter, she did succeed in bringing Sherman House back to its nineteenth-century glory days, and then some—even if he might initially have been reluctant to move in. In 2003, just after it was acquired, she had her work cut out for her. Peter was flying up from

Los Angeles that afternoon for a design meeting. "He should be here any minute, or he's a dead man," she remarked to me during our interview.

For John, she refurbished another historic house in Berkeley— Temple of the Wings, a stunning villa in the Aesthetic movement style that was designed in 1914 by architect Bernard Maybeck. John didn't seem to occupy it very much, however; he was mostly in London or Los Angeles.

She also gave Andrew some help with his house in the Hollywood Hills. But Billy and Vanessa went their own way, décor-wise. She "has her own ideas," Ann explained. After his wedding, Billy sold his Russian Hill penthouse (for $15 million, a new record price for an SF co-op), and the couple bought a five-story stucco mansion in Pacific Heights built in 1912.

Ann made attempts to decorate for Gavin too. But, just weeks before he was elected mayor, she was having little success. "He doesn't want furniture. His idea is just a park bench in the middle of the living room," she complained.

One Getty friend told me that Ann also helped decorate a house for Gordon's former mistress. "Cynthia liked Ann's taste. She asked for her help."

In Los Angeles, as the aughts progressed, Peter and Jacqui were veering apart. Invitations to her fabulous, movie star–filled parties were coveted by everyone except her introverted husband, it seemed. "Peter would hang out in the garage, smoke weed, and knit. He didn't want anything to do with the parties," recalled a friend. An avid knitter, Peter enjoyed creating brightly colored and quite lengthy scarves. "They were incredibly gorgeous—works of art."

By 2009, Peter had repatriated to San Francisco, where he settled into Sherman House. That summer, he and Billy wrote a blog on SFGate, the *Chronicle*'s website, entitled "What the Butler Didn't

See." In it, as they wrote in their inaugural post, they planned to explain "what's it like being rich."

They recalled the disconnect they felt as children when they visited friends' homes, where the furniture was comfortable, could be horsed around on, and "looked like it had been built within our lifetimes."

"Our furniture, on the other hand, looked like people had died in it, and half of it you couldn't even touch. . . . When it was finally impressed upon us that we came from a wealthy family, one of our thoughts was that perhaps we could now finally afford some proper furniture." And while their friends got to put up posters of rock bands and Farrah Fawcett, they had to stare at "scary" oil paintings.

The backlash was swift, and went viral. "Shut the fuck up. Shut the fuck up with your idle life," wrote *Gawker*, in the first of several online screeds.

Peter had to contend with more press the following year, when his divorce battle became public. As Jacqui sought a financial settlement, she made allegations in court involving Peter and drugs, abusive behavior, and pornography. Those allegations soon surfaced on the internet, including, of course, on *Gawker* ("You may remember Peter Getty as the obnoxious and self-consciously privileged San Francisco columnist. . . .").

Peter and Jacqui, who had no children together, eventually came to an agreement. Reportedly, he no longer keeps in touch with Jacqui or Gia. Jacqui remains close with Peter's relatives in Los Angeles.

"Gettys don't go for bitterness—not after everything they've been through," observed a family friend.

I returned to the Getty mansion for another interview in 2012, by which time Ann had completed an impressive body of design work. A selection of residences she had decorated appeared that October in a lavishly illustrated book, *Ann Getty Interior Style*, written by Diane Dorrans Saeks and published by Rizzoli.

When Saeks approached her with the idea of doing a book, Getty was reluctant. "I didn't feel right promoting myself," she told me. Fortuitously, just before our interview, an advance copy had arrived, which was resting on a George II carved parcel-gilt and ebonized stool in front of us. "I'm pleased with it," she announced as she paged through it. "I'm glad I did it. Because I think it's a nice record." (*Ann Getty Interior Style*, which went into a second printing, has become a collector's item; some rare-book dealers have charged as much as $2,000 for a copy.)

In our conversations, Ann also spoke fondly of her late father-in-law. "It's not fair!" she said about his misanthropic reputation. "He was funny and fun to be with."

Most people have a "very inaccurate impression" of him, she added. "He was sensitive and very intelligent. . . . He was careful with money, and not self-indulgent at all. His parents were very strict, and he continued to live as he had lived when he was a boy, quite simply, like a monk."

He suggested she start collecting fine French furniture. "My means were not so great" at the time, she recalled. "So, I started with English lacquer. When I bought my first piece, he said it looked like a soap box. . . . He was really quite expert."

The first of the next generation of Gettys made her debut in July 2013. In front of six hundred guests at the St. Francis Hotel, Gordon, in white tie, presented Ivy Love Getty at the 49th San Francisco Debutante Ball. That fall, she enrolled at Loyola Marymount University, where she studied studio arts and graphic design.

As always, the Gettys' December gala holiday party provided a grand finale to the year. Though it primarily fetes Gordon's birthday, it also celebrates Ivy's. In 2013, she turned nineteen, and it was his eightieth, which called for a particularly splendid affair.

For days before the event, their block ("Billionaires Row") was closed to traffic so an elaborate tent could be erected. Large as the Getty residence is, they needed extra room for the six hundred guests, all in long gowns, furs, jewels, and black tie. Lavish decorations abounded—"it was so opulent, you couldn't believe it," said one attendee—but the installation in the marble courtyard was poignant: an homage to Emily Dickinson and her poem "The White Election," the inspiration for Gordon's breakthrough composition. A portrait of Dickinson painted by Ann was on display.

In addition to the reigning powers of California politics and society, the guest list included many of Gordon's old cohorts from St. Ignatius, the Leakey Foundation, and the music world.

Foremost, it was a stunning gathering of Gettys—nearly every one of them, from every branch of the family, from around the world. After being depicted for so long as such a fragmented and fractious clan, here was a very different picture. All three of the Georgettes, for example, as well as their cousin Tara—now long free of his guardian ad litem—warmly embraced the uncle they had long ago sued.

Various ex-wives and widows—still in the bosom of the clan—mingled too, including Lady Victoria, Sir Paul's widow; Gloria, George's first wife; and Karin, Ronald's widow. Front and center was Teddy, looking fabulous at age one hundred. She held court on an antique silk-moiré divan, accompanied by her daughter, Gigi Gaston. ("He was the most amazing man I ever met in my life," Teddy said of her first husband shortly before she died in 2017 at 103, in Los Angeles.)

Gordon's daughters, the cause of so much shock when their existence was revealed, chatted genially with Ann—stunning in a yellow Carolina Herrera ball gown—and with their half brothers.

"We're a genuinely close family," Balthazar told *Chronicle* correspondent Catherine Bigelow (Pat Steger's former assistant, and successor on the society beat). "We're here to honor Gordon, who's such a wonderful uncle to all of us. And definitely one of the great characters of all time."

"In a freaky way, they really *are* tight-knit," another attendee at the party observed later. "No one else in the world knows what it's like to be them except them—that's part of their bond."

It was certainly a family that embraced many different personalities and styles. With her dark hair in dreadlocks, Nicolette, Gordon's eldest daughter, wore a beige woolen dress, black tights, and biker-style boots; Kendalle, in a black satin cocktail dress, topped her platinum hair with a small 1930s-style hat. Alexandra wasn't spotted (she spent a number of years in Japan), but at other Getty family parties she has appeared wearing elegant gowns, with long straight red hair and red lipstick highlighting her fair complexion.

Vanessa chose a stunning red satin strapless gown, one of the looks that doubtless led *Vanity Fair* to name her to the International Best-Dressed List in 2014. The only Bay Area resident chosen, she was in company with the Duchess of Cambridge and Cate Blanchett, among others. By this time, Ann had pulled back from the social scene, making her daughter-in-law her natural successor—especially when boosted by Denise Hale, who frequently announced that Vanessa was the next queen of San Francisco.

While Vanessa enjoyed socializing, her husband preferred golfing or staying home, much like his father and his brothers. "They all have a reclusive bent," said a childhood friend about the Getty men. "They are all quite happy to be alone at home."

In Los Angeles, John settled down somewhat, and created a couple of striking homes for himself. In the 2010s he bought two houses that had been designed in the 1920s by A. F. Leicht, an admired architect known for his eccentric style. One of them, dubbed the Castle, combined art deco, Spanish, and Assyrian styles. (Its previous residents included Bob Dylan and later Flea of the Red Hot Chili Peppers.)

Deploying a sharp eye for design that pleased his mother, he became a connoisseur of the Aesthetic movement, neo-Gothic, and Victorian periods. Among the important pieces that he acquired was the "Industry and Idleness" cabinet, designed circa 1860 by revered English architect William Burges. Massive yet delicately detailed, the polychrome and giltwood cabinet features fancifully decorated paneled doors and enameled tiles. In the 1960s, Christopher Gibbs acquired it for the Cheyne Walk house of John's uncle Paul. In 2004, after his death, it was among a small group of Sir Paul's furnishings auctioned at Christie's in London. According to a news report, it was purchased by an anonymous telephone buyer for £274,050. Lord Andrew Lloyd Webber was the underbidder.

John also amassed an outstanding collection of rare guitars—including a '63 Fender Jazz Bass, a '64 Gibson Hummingbird, a '69 Zemaitis twelve-string, and a '72 Fender Telecaster with a rosewood fingerboard—reflecting his passion for music, a source of pride for Gordon.

John's circle of friends included many musicians, some of whom he also jammed with, such as Tom Petty and Led Zeppelin's Jimmy Page; in Los Angeles, he was also close to his cousins and to his former sister-in-law, Jacqui. Yet he remained under the radar. Never photographed at parties, he was not a boldface name, unlike his relatives in San Francisco.

In his forties, he finally embraced parenthood. Ivy, then a teenager, enjoyed stays with him in Los Angeles and London. "We became extremely close and he jumped at finally playing the role of the father he always wanted to be and became this almost strict protective father," she later wrote. "He loved being my father and he was always so proud."

Though Ivy was primarily raised by Ann and Gordon, with a big assist from Jo Schuman Silver, Ivy's mother was involved too; Alyssa (who became a jewelry designer) and John stayed in touch and on good terms.

One of Ivy's happiest visits with her father was on his birthday in Los Angeles. They had dinner at Nobu Malibu, and then paid a visit to the grave site of his grandfather and uncles George and Timothy at the Getty Villa. "We had a beautiful and sentimental time. He was surrounded by his best friends and me," she recalled.

He was a cool dad. A dandy, his wardrobe included suits custom-made for him by Glen Palmer, an Englishman who moved to LA in 1975 and became the tailor to rock gods such as Rod Stewart, Tom Petty, Ronnie Wood, and the members of Fleetwood Mac (Palmer created the Renaissance-style garments they wore on the cover of *Rumours*).

Andrew Getty, also in Los Angeles, became increasingly secluded inside his house in the Hollywood Hills. He labored, in fits and starts, over one movie, as producer, director, and screenwriter. Purportedly, it was inspired by nightmares he had as a child.

In the film, *The Evil Within*, a young man named Dennis suffers from debilitating nightmares. A demon haunts Dennis through his own reflection in an antique, full-length mirror, and convinces him that committing murder is the only way to free himself.

Andrew reportedly invested about $6 million of his own money in the film. While his income from the family trust was ample, it could only stretch so far. To make ends meet, there were weeks when he ate only cereal, according to a staffer on the film. A good deal of his budget went into animatronic robots for the film, which Andrew built himself. (He studied engineering at NYU.)

But, said a friend, "He had been struggling with addictions." On March 31, 2015, Andrew, age forty-seven, was found dead on the floor of his bathroom. While there was a toxic level of meth in his system, the coroner determined that his death was caused by gastro-intestinal hemorrhage.

"It was heartbreaking," said the friend. "He was not a bad person but something bad happened to him."

Two years after Andrew's death, *The Evil Within* was released on

VOD and DVD. "A passion project built on a foundation of uncommon artistic commitment . . . [it stands] today as a testament to its creator's singular mad ambition," a critic wrote in the *Guardian*.

The afternoon of December 15, 2016, in the faux-marbled, three-story music room of Sherman House, Peter married Shannon Bavaro, a technology advisor. They had been dating a few years, and had a year-old daughter, Ava. Newly elected US senator Kamala Harris officiated. Before the ceremony, she offered advice to the bride. "She said to be in the moment, remember why I was there, and to embrace the love and the joy. She is so wise," Bavaro recalled afterward. Their son, Dexter, was born about a year later.

That evening, Gordon and Ann hosted a dinner dance at home for two hundred friends, ranging from Peter's old Virgin-Whore Complex bandmates to the Pelosis. The bride wore Vera Wang. "That's it. That's the one," Ann had said as soon as they saw the gown in Wang's New York showroom.

At long last, Gordon's musical compositions were receiving good reviews, particularly for two one-act operas he'd written. *Usher House*, based on Edgar Allan Poe's horror story, premiered in Cardiff with the Welsh National Opera in 2014, before going to San Francisco. *The Canterville Ghost*, based on the humorous Oscar Wilde story, premiered at Germany's Leipzig Opera in 2015. In 2018, both gothic tales were united under a bill dubbed *Scare Pair*, and staged at venues in LA and New York. *Los Angeles Times* critic Richard S. Ginell called *Canterville* "engaging" and "unexpectedly delightful."

As written by Wilde in 1887, "Canterville" begins as a rich American family, the Otises, move into Canterville Chase, an English country house, despite warnings that it is haunted. Indeed, its resident ghost, Sir Simon de Canterville, rises up to terrorize. But he is no match for these pragmatic Americans, particularly the couple's rather obnoxious twin boys, who torment the ghost. Getty added some contemporary satirical elements, such as the family using consumer products and litigation to solve their problems. Where does Gordon get these ideas?

He answered some questions in an hourlong documentary directed by Peter Rosen, *Gordon Getty: There Will Be Music,* which PBS stations broadcast in 2017. "If you are a composer, melodies are going on in your noggin all the time," he explained about his creative process. He also discussed his two-decade-long writer's block and how he overcame it: "I felt I couldn't be taken seriously, maybe even by myself, unless I could write something a little grander and more complicated . . . and then finally it dawned on me, that it isn't true—I could become even less complicated."

On an afternoon in November 2018, I was invited to lunch at Balboa Cafe with Gordon Peter Getty, to talk about wine.

The sky above Cow Hollow, like the entire city, had an alarming orange cast, the result of the devastating Camp Fire burning to the north. Before Gordon arrived, there was a commotion on Fillmore Street: a car halted suddenly, and the driver honked and gawked at California's new governor-elect crossing the street. "You'd be a good Bruce Wayne!" she yelled. Gavin Newsom did look pretty movie star–like as he strolled into the restaurant.

His inauguration as California's fortieth governor was just weeks away, but the opportunity to have a taste of the PlumpJack 2016 Cabernet Sauvignon Reserve, which would not be released until the following autumn, had apparently drawn him to Balboa today.

Then Getty arrived. With unruly hair, he was clad in a plaid shirt, rumpled khakis, and a maroon parka shell, which he never took off. A few weeks shy of his eighty-fifth birthday, he had strikingly luminous blue eyes. His father was known for his blue eyes.

Gordon and Gavin exchanged a warm hug. But they quickly got down to business.

"I've only tasted this in the barrel," said Newsom, eyeing the 2016.

"This is a helluva wine," commented Gordon as soon as he took a sip, after which the two of them exchanged comments on the structure and expressiveness of the vintage.

(Wine authority Robert Parker awarded the Cab a rare "100" score. "Hits the ground running with the most stunning perfume of crushed black cherries . . . ," he wrote in his rave, in which he also gushed over how the "rich, decadent palate is beautifully lifted with fantastic freshness." His conclusion: "If 'PlumpJack awesome' isn't a phrase to the describe the ultimate in deliciousness, it should be.")

Getty's lunch was a hamburger, served rare, with no bun. For about seventeen years, he has followed a strict paleo-style diet, abstaining from starches and sugar. "It's not a diet, it's a religion," he said.

The octogenarian did seem full of beans. When another guest at the table, PlumpJack's general manager John Conover, noted that the PlumpJack 2016 Cabernet Sauvignon Reserve was still five years away from its optimal drinking time, Gordon scoffed. "I'm the Roy Moore of wines—I like 'em young," he said boisterously.

His spriteliness somehow brought to mind all those Gettys who are in line for massive windfalls when he leaves this earth. Per the terms set in 1934, the Getty family trusts terminate at the end of the last "measuring" life of J. Paul Getty's sons. Gordon's surviving children and their cousins will presumably each be collecting hundreds of millions.

"Gordon has tried to be as nice and as generous as possible to everyone in the family, because he doesn't want them rooting for him to die," someone once involved in managing Getty family finances said.

Getty's enthusiasm for the wine business certainly remained robust. As PlumpJack's wines developed a cult-like following, the

PlumpJack Group continued to grow. Along with more shops, restaurants, and hotels, two other Napa vineyards were acquired— Odette and Cade. When Newsom became mayor, he sold his shares in PlumpJack's San Francisco enterprises to Gordon Getty; he bought them back when he became lieutenant governor. Then, when he was elected governor, Newsom placed his stake in the companies in a blind trust run by a family friend. Since 2009, operations have been overseen by the group's president, Hilary Newsom Callan, Gavin's sister. (She and her husband, Jeff, have two daughters, Talitha and Siena.)

Gordon, the majority owner, ultimately calls the shots. "My idea is to make the best wine I can make . . . to see if I can make as good a wine as anyone in the world," he said.

A fine glass of wine is also literally a distillation of his belief that biology and economics are intertwined. "Believe it!" he said. "Natural selection and market selection are the same thing."

A few years ago, Getty roiled the wine world when he became the first owner of a luxury brand to seal some of his bottles with screw caps—that type of enclosure known to consumers of Boone's Farm Apple Wine and jugs of the ilk.

While cork has been the material of choice to seal wines since the early seventeenth century, about one in ten bottles suffers from cork taint and oxygen seepage. Even so, high-end winemakers always scoffed at the idea of screw caps.

"I thought it would be better for quality, but everybody was afraid to do it," said Gordon. "I said, 'I'm not.' I thought, it's a no-brainer— under the right circumstances. I said, 'Just make sure UC Davis [with its respected Department of Viticulture and Enology] is guiding us through every step of the process, and that we only do it with our very best, most expensive wine.' And never more than fifty percent, so you could compare to cork over time."

News of his initiative flummoxed the trade. "There was a lot of harrumphing that we had no respect for tradition," Getty recalled. "Wine is a very conservative business."

Brisk sales and more rave reviews vindicated him. The 2012 Odette Reserve Cab and the 2013 PlumpJack Reserve Cabernet Sauvignon were the first screw-tops ever to get perfect scores from Parker. And other prestigious winemakers have followed Getty's lead.

"Even if we failed, we would have gotten bragging rights as innovators, for doing something everybody else was afraid to do," he said. "I'm a risk taker . . . so was my father. It worked out pretty good for him.

"It's all true about him being a tightwad," he added. "But he was a dear. I was the apple of his eye."

Nonetheless, after eight decades, it appeared that Gordon had finally escaped his father's shadow: "Critics used to write about me as 'the son of.' Not anymore. Now my work is taken more on its own merits," he said, bringing the conversation around to music.

His considerable body of compositions, including operas, choral and orchestral works, piano pieces, and songs, has been performed worldwide, at such venues as New York's Carnegie Hall, London's Royal Festival Hall, Vienna's Brahms-Saal, Moscow's Bolshoi Theatre, and Beijing's National Centre for the Performing Arts. The Pentatone label has released about a dozen recordings of his works, which are published by his company, Rork Music.

In the end, music provided his escape from "the curse."

"You can gag on that silver spoon," he said. "Having too much money is dangerous, especially for children. More than you need is a curse. . . . [but] if you have ideals, and that ideal is something bigger than you—music is something bigger than me, it's a mountain I'm trying to climb—then you might escape the curse. There are other Gettys who have dodged it, others have been clobbered."

14

Passing the Baton

Less than a month after that lunch, on December 12, 2018, Bill Newsom died at home, of unspecified causes at age eighty-four.

The same day, Kendalle posted on her Instagram account a portrait she had painted in oil of Gordon eight years earlier. "Today, my father, depicted here as The Emperor tarot card, lost his very best friend in the world," she wrote. (In the tarot deck, the Emperor is the father figure.) "They'd known each other since they were about 12. . . . I loved Bill, and I still do. Today hurts so badly and I'm so tired of having feelings."

She didn't use the Getty surname on any of her social media accounts. She was "Kendalle Aubra" on Twitter and Instagram, where her account was called "Freudian.slit." When she was photographed in 2010 at a charity benefit in San Francisco, she was identified as "Kendalle Fiasco." Like her sisters, she grew up in Los Angeles with their mother. After living in Brooklyn for several years in the mid-2010s, she returned to LA, where she lives with her boyfriend, Johnny Latu, a musician.

She has close relationships with her father and other Getty relatives. In March 2019, she flew with Gordon, Ivy, Balthazar, and his family to Africa, where she assisted Phinda staff on their missions dehorning black rhinos. On Instagram, she posted photos and detailed the laborious procedure, which involves tranquilizing an animal with a dart, blindfolding it, and inserting plugs in its ears, prior to the cutting. Kendalle took a particular shine to one rhino. "They sprayed her horn nubs with a purple antibacterial spray that I got excited about, and they let me spray her toenails with it and add a heart to her side! I named her Fiona. She's six years old," she wrote.

One post drew a snarky comment, accusing Kendalle (who serves on the advisory board of the Africa Foundation, along with her sister Nicolette and Alexander, Mark's eldest son) of wasting jet fuel. Kendalle wrote an informed reply. She rattled off a long list of facts and statistics detailing the foundation's efforts on behalf of wildlife conservation and human rights before concluding, "How about you ask questions before you judge and stop wasting so much hate?"

While many San Franciscans have greeted Kendalle and her sisters at the Gettys' large parties, few saw them outside of those events or knew much about the young women or their creative and political endeavors.

An activist since the age of thirteen, Kendalle founded the Angry Feminist Pin-Up Calendar in 2018 to aid survivors of abuse and violence. Net proceeds are donated to organizations including Planned Parenthood and the Battered Women's Justice Project.

In the calendar, she upends traditional pin-up tropes "to empower femme-identified people of all shapes, colors, sizes, and backgrounds," as she wrote. For her own turn as Miss March, her theme was inspired by some strong characters, she explained, though she didn't mention that she was related to one of them: "We paid homage to one of my all-time favorite films, #Barbarella (of course) from that fierce scene where #TalithaGetty, uncredited, offers Barbarella a hit of 'Essence of Man.' Thank you, 1968, for so many incredible films," she wrote.

Kendalle's most prominent tattoo, running down her right arm, is a depiction of Barbarella. A nose ring and frequently changing hair coloring (green, oftentimes) are among her other features.

In 2020, after long being intrigued by talk of the so-called gay agenda, she published The Gay Agenda—a weekly planner meant to be, in her words, "fabulous" as well as "radical and fierce . . . something to reinforce and reunite the LGBTQi+ with my kind of feminism—intersectional feminism, of course—to join our political avant-gardes together in the battle for cultural progressivism."

Kendalle is also an active member of the Poetry Brothel, a roving, risqué literary burlesque whose patron saint is Oscar Wilde, where she recites her poetry under the stage name Ophelia Up. Inspired by turn-of-the-century brothels in New Orleans, Paris, and Buenos Aires, the Poetry Brothel, according to its site, "strives to promote empowered sexuality practices and radically open artistic expression."

On Twitter, Kendalle described herself as "Artist, Activist, Cotton Candy Barbarella." On other platforms, she called herself "a contemporary flapper, a pre-apocalyptic Tank Girl," and "a retrofuturist weened on riot grrrl and Edgar Allan Poe." According to the introduction she wrote for a blog, "I'm a bit of a cultural bastard, which has enabled me to look at pop culture in a disentangled, disengaged way. For this I am incredibly thankful."

Her elder sister, Nicolette Beck, has lived in San Francisco's Mission District for the past decade with her husband, Michael Hays, a musician and performance artist. In recent years, they became distressed watching the fabric of the neighborhood change as gentrification made the area unaffordable to many longtime residents and businesses. In 2020 they founded a nonprofit, Bigote de Gato, which will function as a theater, a school, an arts incubator, and a community center. Class subjects will include mime, improv, clown theater, and puppetry. They intend to form a bilingual theater troupe from their student body—creating a path for anyone to become a performer. "We believe that by facilitating creative expression in more people, we can help heal our city and perhaps our world," Nicolette explained.

Alexandra, the youngest, lived in Japan for some years, where she studied art and modeled. Her bio: "Freethinking person. Vegan. I paint and box for fun." Working in watercolors, pen and ink, and digital, she is producing figurative portraits, anatomical studies, and manga art. She is the youngest of J. Paul Getty's nineteen grandchildren—born some thirty-nine years after Anne G. Earhart, the eldest. On social media she identifies herself as Alice Sarah Beck, but she generally goes by her middle name, Sarah, making her the namesake of the family matriarch.

Considering how their existences became widely known—with their petition in court to change their surname to Getty—it is notable that none of Gordon's daughters, by this point, chose to use the name.

While the young women came into view in public forums, their mother remained virtually unknown. Even after one of the most bizarre police raids in Los Angeles history.

On May 8, 2019, the LAPD swarmed an eight-thousand-square-foot mansion in Bel-Air. They seized about a thousand firearms—a shocking arsenal that included AR15-style rifles and submachine guns—and arrested a resident of the house, Girard Damian Saenz, age fifty-seven.

"I had never seen so many weapons in my career of thirty-one years," one of the LAPD officers commented.

After pleading not guilty to sixty-four felony counts—for which he could face forty-eight years in prison—Saenz was released from custody after posting a $100,000 bond. At a preliminary hearing in February 2020 three of the charges were dropped. More than eighteen months later there had been no further action in the case, according to the website of the Superior Court of California, County of Los Angeles.

The most shocking part: Cynthia Beck was identified as the owner of the home, and, according to some reports, the "longtime companion" of Saenz as well as the former mistress of Gordon. She was not present in the house at the time of the raid, nor charged with any crimes. No other information about her has appeared in the media.

Notwithstanding that Beverly Hills doyenne's pronouncement that "no one we know knows her," Cynthia's father was wealthy and accomplished. He was also one of Gordon's fellow board members at the Leakey Foundation.

Born in 1926, Robert M. Beck was brought up by a single mother in Dust Bowl–era Nebraska. He served as a navy radarman in the Pacific during World War II, then studied physics on a GI Bill scholarship at UCLA, before he emerged as one of the pioneers of computing. After working for Northrop and Packard Bell, he joined the founding group of Scientific Data Systems. In 1967, having earned a fortune, he retired from the business. He and his wife, Helene, Cynthia's mother, raised cattle on their ranch in Montana; on their farm in Southern California, they grew persimmons, kumquats, and other exotic fruits, following Rudolf Steiner's strict biodynamic precepts. Beck also provided significant support to the search for the origins of man. A $1 million challenge gift that he made to the two-year-old Leakey Foundation in 1970 was instrumental in getting the organization off the ground. He died in 2014 after a long struggle with Parkinson's.

Three weeks after the drama of the police raid in Bel-Air, Ann and Gordon hosted a $28,000-a-couple fund raiser for Kamala Harris's presidential bid at home in San Francisco. An enjoyable summer followed. The couple took the Jetty to Croatia for the annual family meeting (a change of pace: the event is traditionally held in Italy). From there, they flew with Billy, Vanessa, and their three children to Argentina, to watch the total solar eclipse.

Ivy was particularly active. Having obtained her BFA from Loyola Marymount, she was drawing and painting, as well as walking red carpets, clad in extravagant looks by Alexander McQueen, Gucci, and other designers. At the star-studded amfAR Gala Cannes at the Hôtel du Cap, she wowed in a dramatic floral creation by Australian designer Toni Maticevski; with her soft blond tresses, she conjured Bardot. After the Côte d'Azur, she ventured through the Season in London and the couture shows in Paris (where she saw her cousin August's show at the Ritz), before flying back to California for the wedding of August's sibling, Nats, to Gigi Gorgeous. "Welcome to the family @gigigorgeous," Ivy declared in an IG post from "#nigiwedding" in Montecito.

For the Gettys, as well as for legions of San Franciscans, there was a bittersweet finale to 2019. It was the end of the line for *Beach Blanket Babylon*. Forty-five years on, it claimed to be the world's longest-running musical revue; with its seemingly never-ending parade of over-the-top costumes, wigs, and laughs, it had become one of the town's most beloved institutions, part of the fabric of the city.

While Jo Schuman Silver, at seventy-four, was still crackling with energy—and still ensconced in one of Ann and Gordon's guest rooms—she felt it was time to end the show. At its farewell performance on New Year's Eve, Club Fugazi (to which it had transferred in 1974) was packed with the powers that be, including Speaker Pelosi, Senator Dianne Feinstein, and Governor Newsom (who said he was first taken to the show by his grandfather). There was a palpable feeling that a chapter in the life of the city was closing. But a new one seemed to be beginning. When the curtain rose, Ivy Love Getty, resplendent in a red and gold sequined gown and a red sequined top hat, shimmied confidently to center stage.

Two weeks later, at the San Francisco Ballet's opening-night gala, she descended the long marble staircase under the rotunda of the ornate Beaux Arts–style City Hall wearing an ice-blue satin ball gown that Oscar de la Renta had made for her grandmother thirty years before, paired with gold opera-length gloves and a shimmering headband holding her hair in an elevated ballet bun updo. She was accompanied by her boyfriend of two years, Tobias "Toby" Engel, a twenty-eight-year-old English/Austrian photographer whose dark floppy hair recalled Timothée Chalamet.

"A full-on Cinderella moment," gulped one onlooker (although this Cinderella skipped the cinders part).

"The feeling was, the baton was being passed," observed Tony Bravo, the *Chronicle*'s young arts and culture columnist.

A month later, the Gettys, like everyone, had their future plans upended by Covid-19. The much-anticipated world premiere of Gordon's new opera, *Goodbye, Mr. Chips*, slated to open the Festival Napa Valley in the summer, was postponed. Going virtual, Billy (by now a fervent health and fitness enthusiast) and Vanessa helped the Biden/Harris ticket rake in over $8 million on one Zoom fund raiser alone, along with high-powered cohosts from Hollywood such as Jeffrey Katzenberg, Ryan Murphy, and J. J. Abrams. Ivy took to Instagram, clad in skimpy leopard-print spandex, to implore her growing following to elect Joe and Kamala, by showing off a voter-themed handbag and mask (courtesy of Hilary Newsom). Meanwhile, Gordon donated $1 million to the Lincoln Project, reportedly making him the largest contributor to the organization.

In the most bizarre election cycle in memory, some airtime was devoted to pondering Kimberly Guilfoyle's path from Gavin Newsom to recent beau Donald Trump Jr. "I think I got it right this time," she told Breitbart. "Life's interesting," Newsom said diplomatically, when BuzzFeed brought up the topic with him.

At the Democratic National Convention, when Harris accepted her historic nomination for vice president, she acknowledged people she considers family: "Family is my best friend, my nieces, and my godchildren."

Not everything in 2020 was political or virtual. Ivy (now represented as a digital influencer by the Ford Models agency) and Toby managed to slip onto Capri, where he proposed in the Italian moonlight on September 1. "A very magical evening," she captioned a shot she posted of her ring finger sparkling with her sapphire engagement ring, which prompted an avalanche of comments. "Congrats duuude welcome to the wifey club ♥♥♥" read the one from cousin Nats.

From Capri, Ivy FaceTimed her adored grandmother to share the news. "Monga," as Ivy called her, naturally commenced planning for the wedding, scheduled for November 2021.

But joy was soon replaced by grief and shock. On September 13 Ann Gilbert Getty, by all appearances still vigorous at seventy-nine, suffered a heart attack after she sat down for Sunday Supper at home, with her husband and Jo. She was rushed to the hospital, where she died the following morning.

"Devastated," "unmoored," "shut-down" were words that a friend used to describe Gordon several weeks later.

Ivy, also shattered by the loss, posted a stream of tributes to her grandmother, as did many family members, including Gordon's daughters. "She was an inspirational, spunky, strong, beautiful woman. The world grieves her loss," remarked Sarah.

"R.I.P. goddess," Kendalle wrote.

Had it not been for the pandemic, there would doubtless have been an epic funeral and other public events to mourn Ann's death and celebrate her life. San Francisco was shaken by the passing of this woman who had loomed so large for half a century. "The whole city is quite saddened. People saw a world disappear. So many looked up to her," said Martin Chapman, curator of European decorative arts at the Fine Arts Museums of San Francisco.

Of the San Francisco–reared Gettys, John Gilbert Getty was the least well known. He succeeded in evading the public eye. To most Getty-watchers, he was an absent, enigmatic figure.

When his body was found in San Antonio, Texas, on Friday, November 20, 2020, his family was plunged into mourning again. Even as the circumstances of his death were initially unknown and mysterious, a picture of his life began to develop. He had battled addictions and troubles, but he had also been able to lead, by many measures, quite a rewarding life before he died at fifty-two.

Information began to filter out the next day, as John's relatives and friends shared their disbelief and grief on social media. Among the first was John's childhood friend Chris Vietor, who posted photos from a Getty family trip to Africa in 1984. Gisela Getty wrote a remembrance of John from the days when she was married to his elder cousin, Paul III: "I still see you, as this beautiful boy sitting in my kitchen in S.F. with great curiosity about life. You always came to see your cousins Anna, Balthazar in a time that was difficult for me. I will always hold you very dear in my heart. Highest Namaskar."

"I will miss laughing with you and talking to you for hours and hours about everything and nothing. . . . We had such a colorful life and you often helped me to remember moments I had forgotten," wrote his cousin Aileen.

Jacqui posted a photo of John in a white three-piece Glen Palmer suit. "I am saddened by the loss of my once upon a time brother in law," she wrote.

It took seventy-two hours for word of his death to drop on a media site: TMZ reported on Monday that his body had been discovered unresponsive in a hotel room and that no foul play was suspected, while the cause of death was pending an autopsy. A family spokesman provided a statement: "With a heavy heart, Gordon Getty announces the death of his son, John Gilbert Getty. . . . John was a talented musician who loved rock and roll. He will be deeply missed."

Around the world, the predictable deluge of "Tragic Dynasty" headlines rolled. The reports beneath them carried very little information; they largely rehashed previous drug-related deaths of other Gettys, perpetuating the image of the entire family as messed up and dysfunctional.

A week later, London's *Daily Mail* revealed that John's body had been found in his room at the Hotel Emma, a luxury property. The room was neat; John was sitting upright on the bed, propped by pillows, with his legs crossed—the lotus position used in meditation. His eyes were open, his glasses were in his left hand, and his laptop was open in front of him. Ultimately, the Bexar County Medical Examiner's Office reported that Getty died of "cardiomyopathy and chronic obstructive pulmonary disease [COPD, an inflammatory lung disease] complicated by fentanyl toxicity." The manner of the death was accidental, the office determined.

Getty was in San Antonio because he was preparing to move there. He had become enamored of the city.

Two weeks before his death, he had phoned an old friend in Los Angeles. "He sounded in really good spirits. He said he wanted to have dinner soon," she told me.

"He was magical . . . so handsome, so charismatic, with a heart of gold," she added. "He was incredibly smart. *People* smart. He could see through any situation that was bullshit. He had a really pure soul. He was unbelievably empathetic."

In a stream of posts in the days after his death, Ivy illuminated aspects of her father's character: "He never tried to ignore me he called me all the time as a kid—it was me that was always hesitant because I was so used to female figures running my life, but I instantly let that all go when I became a teenager and felt like we related so much. . . ."

She also expressed pride in being "the only consistent woman in my father's life." He never married, perhaps because she was "a complete bitch" to all of his girlfriends. "I was scared if he found someone else he would stop being a father to me," Ivy recounted. He "lived and breathed music" and "understood fashion like no other. He used to keep a whole walk-in closet of vintage Pucci women's clothing just because he liked it."

In her post, Kendalle reflected on her late sibling, and her own situation: "Two days ago, for the second time in my life, one of my brothers died. John, we were never close but I find myself very affected by this loss anyway. You were hard on me. I guess you felt that it was your duty. It's been scary being the bastard daughter of our father and his mistress in a family that is so notorious. I hid my truth, but never because I hated you guys. I'm sorry. I promise to take care of your daughter from here on out. . . ."

The next day, she changed her name on her IG bio. She was now Kendalle Getty.

Under the brilliant sunshine of Labor Day 2021, as the pandemic appeared to be finally in retreat, Kendalle kicked off a season of new beginnings and closure for the Gordon Gettys. On vacation in Greece with her boyfriend Johnny Latu, she climbed to the Acropolis, where on bended knee, he proposed.

The following week, the grandees of San Francisco emerged from isolation and assembled at the Conservatory of Music to memorialize Ann on the first anniversary of her death. It was what was left of San Francisco society, anyway. *"Old, old,"* said one attendee of the crowd. But there was one bright face among them. On the day that only weeks earlier some prognosticators predicted might be *his* political funeral—the California gubernatorial recall election—Gavin Newsom was beaming. At 11 a.m. that morning, as the service began, he was clearly confident of the resounding victory he would have that night, which renewed talk of a presidential run, and an old rivalry ("Are Newsom and Harris on a Collision Course?" asked a *Los Angeles Times* headline).

That fall, other momentous events unfolded. Capping three days of celebrations that began with a ball at the Palace of Fine Arts, where Earth, Wind & Fire performed, Ivy Love Getty and Tobias Alexander Engel were joined in holy matrimony under the stately dome of San Francisco City Hall. When the ceremony began at 6 p.m. on Saturday, November 6, Nancy Pelosi, the officiant, was resplendent in a gold Giorgio Armani pantsuit. Just before midnight the previous evening, the Speaker of the House, under the rotunda of the US Capitol, had signed the historic $1.8 trillion Bipartisan Infrastructure Framework. "I hightailed it out of there for Ivy, who I've known since she was a baby," Pelosi told the crowd. Ivy's spectacular gown, rumored to have cost $500,000, featured four layers—the outermost one resembling fragments of a mirror—behind which trailed a sixteen-foot embroidered veil. It was the handiwork of one of her grandmother's favorite designers, John Galliano, who also dressed the bridal party, including maid of honor Anya Taylor-Joy, the bright new star. At the gala dinner that followed at the Getty mansion, Pelosi stayed past midnight, mixing with hundreds of Ivy's and Tobias's young friends and relatives. (The Los Angeles contingent included August, Nats, Gigi, and Kendalle, as well as Balthazar, with his daughter Violet and her girlfriend.) "It was all so inclusive—you could let your freak flag fly," commented one guest. The baton had officially been passed to the new generation.

But the senior most member of the dynasty wasn't done. Days later, *Goodbye, Mr. Chips*, Gordon Getty's fourth opera, received its world premiere. While Covid had indeed derailed plans for the fully staged live performances that had been scheduled for Festival Napa Valley, the eighty-seven-year-old composer took the opportunity to reimagine his opera for film. Over the course of the pandemic, a large cast, orchestra, and chorus were recorded separately, then filmed on sets in San Francisco and New York. As critic A.A. Cristi observed in BroadwayWorld, the new medium allowed for "seamless storytelling," giving Gordon the opportunity to more fluidly present his musical adaptation of the beloved 1934 novella of the same name, the tale of an emotionally repressed and disheveled English schoolmaster who blossoms over the course of his long career, in the face of some profound losses along the way.

If Gordon Getty were ever to write an opera based on his own family, it would be loaded with extraordinary characters, and require many acts.

Conclusion

From Los Angeles, San Francisco, Baja California, and Kodiak Island to London, Rome, Cape Town, and Bangkok, Gettys have left their marks on fields including art, music, marine and wildlife conservation, climate change, media, intellectual property, politics, LGBTQ rights, gender transitioning, fashion, interior design, high society, film, wine, books, yachting, horse racing, holistic living, and finance.

Yet in the public imagination, they are often still thought of as "the tragic dynasty."

While misfortune has continued to befall some Gettys—sometimes in cinematic fashion—the family has proven remarkably durable. Of the seventy-six individuals who appeared in *Fortune*'s inaugural 1957 rich list, direct descendants of just three of them made it onto the 2020 Forbes 400: Ray Lee Hunt, youngest son of Texas wildcatter H. L. Hunt; Bennett Dorrance and Mary Alice Dorrance Malone, grandchildren of John T. Dorrance, inventor of the Campbell Soup formula; and Gordon Getty.

Other than suggesting that oil and soup have been the most lucrative commodities over the last six decades, this statistic serves as evidence that fortunes are fleeting. And it demonstrates that, while some people born to privilege compound their good fortune, others squander their assets.

In addition to mere wealth, a dynasty has to be judged by what the founder and his heirs have contributed to society. The cohesiveness of the family—or lack thereof—is also a yardstick. Compared to their peers, the Gettys stack up well. H. L. Hunt used his fortune to support and fuse together far-right political extremism and Christian evangelism—begetting movements that spawned the Tea Party, Trumpism, and other toxins—while his descendants have not made particularly significant charitable or cultural contributions. John T. Dorrance's progeny—who, in contrast to the Gettys, never sold their company—lead decorous but dull lives of leisure. "You would never describe *any* of them as cosmopolitan," said one of their Philadelphia neighbors.

In an interview conducted shortly before her death in 2020, an heiress to the Anglo-Irish Guinness brewing fortune offered her opinion that the public doesn't want to know about a dynastic family's positive contributions—which is why such families remain press-shy. "If you are a member of any of these families, you really don't want to talk—because the press always uses the wrong bit . . . they are not interested in the goody-goody bits. Because the public is not interested in the goody-goody bits. That's the problem, always," said Lindy, the Marchioness of Dufferin and Ava—a daughter of Loel Guinness and a niece of Lady Ursula d'Abo, J. Paul Getty's last mistress.

"What the public wants to read about is the dramas . . . the money. . . . ," she scoffed. "When you talk about these things, you're compounding the sadnesses of the families. That's the snag."

Americans, on the whole, venerate wealth, and are voracious viewers of ostentatious displays of it; but picturing a person who is rich and happy is less appealing. "The idea that people who are reputedly wealthy must be miserable seems to gladden countless hearts," J. Paul Getty himself observed in his final memoir. "After a time, a person who is wealthy grows a tough impervious skin. It is a protective carapace essential for survival."

As his son Gordon noted, some Gettys have been "clobbered."

Given the unlimited opportunities for indulgence that their fortune afforded them, it's perhaps surprising that more of them didn't meet a tragic fate. ("I am shocked that any of them have survived," as one of their friends said.)

Why did some founder and some flourish?

In the interviews William Newsom gave in 2008 and 2009 to the Regional Oral History Office at UC Berkeley's Bancroft Library, he made these observations:

"I have learned that simply giving a person a lot of money and saying, 'Here, have a good time,' is a mistake.

"The only people I've ever seen who are satisfied with life are people who achieve something beyond mere wealth.

"Paul's children are doing well, but it wasn't money that made them do well. It was something else they had inside them. Aileen has become a very passionate worker in the AIDS field. Tara, the youngest, is in Africa now running a business. Mark Getty has done remarkably well with Getty Images."

In addition to being unconventional, the Gettys have been, and continue to be, curious and progressive people—in their thinking, in their politics, even in their consideration of gender.

"Pretty much since we came out of the womb, we've been who we are," as Nats Getty explained. "And no one was going to tell us otherwise."

Afterword

On the morning of October 14, 2022, a pair of young women walked into Room 43 of London's National Gallery. Each opened a can of Heinz cream of tomato soup and hurled the liquid at one of the museum's most beloved paintings, Vincent van Gogh's *Sunflowers* (1888).

A shocking act of vandalism, it seemed at first. But as news of the incident ricocheted around the world and a video of it went viral, it emerged that the "perpetrators" were climate activists who belonged to a grassroots organization called Just Stop Oil—three words in large block letters on their white T-shirts as they began shouting. "What is worth more, art or life?" yelled one of them.

That the protestors knew a layer of glass would protect the priceless painting was a fact some media outlets didn't report; but many of the headlines soon blared about the "Oil Heiress" who had helped bankroll the operation.

The California-based Climate Emergency Fund, which Aileen Getty had cofounded in 2019, had indeed provided Just Stop Oil with hundreds of thousands of dollars to fund its disruptive climate activism. (Though Getty has no direct control over their actions.)

As part of its "October uprising," Just Stop Oil had also blocked roads and oil terminals across England, and spray-painted both Scotland Yard and Harrods. These demonstrations garnered little press. The soup toss, on the other hand, hit a nerve, drawing massive global attention. Arguably, the involvement of a member of one of the world's richest, most storied families—whose fortune derived from fossil fuels—boosted that coverage. It was also an indication that, in addition to money, the Gettys still have gumption, a trait that tends to wither in old-money families.

Some of the commentary on Aileen was vitriolic, in response to which CEF posted a statement of concern: "Seeing a lot of hate for our cofounder Aileen Getty." At home in Los Angeles, she wrote an opinion piece which was published in the *Guardian*. "While some have ridiculed the activists . . . I am proud of the bigger conversation they have started," she wrote. "The unfortunate truth is that our planet has no protective glass covering."

Bold as some of her choices might be, she is shy, and private. In the weeks after the incident, she declined scores of interview requests. But she agreed to share some of her thoughts with me in an email. "The targeting of a beloved symbol of our culture felt threatening and destructive for many people," she wrote. "The climate activists themselves acknowledge that it looked like a crazy and destructive act." But desperate times call for desperate measures, she believes. There won't be a future if governments and corporations don't transition to renewable energy soon.

"My hope is that we, as a society, can shift the conversation away from the soup on the plastic covering of a painting and accept these actions from brave climate activists for what they are—an alarm that jolts us out of the status quo and focuses us on the real emergency at hand: we are killing life on this planet," Aileen adds. "We can have a fossil fuel powered economy, or we can have thriving life on planet earth. We can't have both."

Even as some reports portrayed her as a desecrator of art and the National Gallery, none of the press recollected that her father had virtually saved the institution in 1985, with his fifty-million-pound gift. The protestors likely entered the building from Trafalgar Square through the Getty Entrance, adorned with a bronze bust of Sir Paul. After his death the family patronage has continued. Aileen's brother Mark served as chairman for a decade, and his daughter-in-law, Sabine, currently cochairs its "Young Ambassadors" program. On Aileen's personal Instagram page, she faced a little flak from some family members just after the soup incident. "But why are they taking it out on art?" asked her cousin Kendalle from California. "Vincent van Gogh lived in poverty and loved nature. Why outrageously deface his work?" wrote Domitilla, Mark's former wife, from Italy.

It bears remembering that, like a number of her relatives, Aileen battled drug addiction for many years. Unlike some of them, she survived. I asked her how she managed it. "I found that the same ills that are the root cause of an unlivable planet are the cause of my addictions—the inability to connect deeply and honestly with myself and others, including Mother Earth," she responded. "Addiction represented my smallness, the terror with which I anticipated each moment, my inability to successfully integrate into society, my very poor education and lack of preparation. I realize now that my coping mechanisms were primitive. The mechanisms driving that narrative are not built to create fulfillment."

She's had to contend, too, with being HIV positive since the mid-1980s. (*USA Today* reported in 1991 that she had "from six months to a year to live.") In addition to being a survivor, she's a grandmother today, at sixty-five. "I'm head over heels in love with her," she told me, referring to five-year-old Georgia, the daughter of her son Andrew Wilding and his wife, Alexandra. Under his stage name, Kowloon, Andrew has been releasing tracks from his planned sophomore album, which he performed for family and friends in September 2022, at Resident DTLA, a lively bar in downtown Los Angeles. "I don't set out with a theme or concept," he explained about his song-writing process. "It's a bit like carving a sculpture from a block of marble and revealing what's inside."

More than most families, the Gettys have seen myths created about them. Some are true; the others I tried to dispel. As best I could, I tried to keep it factual and chronological, which can sometimes be less than scintillating, and run counter to perceptions and myths. A few of the reviewers of the book, particularly in Britain, were reluctant to accept the idea that J. Paul Getty wasn't quite so mean or that most of his descendants weren't such wastrels.

After *Growing Up Getty* was published in July 2022, I received emails, DMs, and text messages from around the world. Some came from members of the Getty family. I thought their notes displayed a good degree of self-awareness. "I am struck by how . . . you shone a light on everyone . . . What was interesting to me is that no one was left in anyone's shadow," wrote one granddaughter. "I am intrigued by your choice to pivot from the tragic and dramatic and indulgent lifestyles to humans adapting in the best way they know how to the world they are so privileged to live in with means they are so lucky to have."

"I thought it was a very balanced portrayal of my grandfather," wrote one of the grandsons. "Nobody is perfect, but I think this time he had a fair trial. . . . Of course, it's difficult for people to have sympathy and invariably they will come to the same conclusion of a rich, spoilt, overindulged family. They aren't entirely wrong, but sadly I have seen real-life problems with several members of the family, and happily many have been overcome."

On Instagram and Facebook, I received a series of DMs from members of a very specific group—former staff members in Ann and Gordon's San Francisco mansion. Far from being disgruntled ex-servants, they expressed real fondness for their former employers, and marveled over having been part of such an extraordinary world. "I have wonderful memories and lots of stories! I am British, as were most of the staff, except Alfonso the chef," wrote a woman who worked there for twenty years. "I was there when Ivy was delivered to the front door!"

"It's complicated, but they loved me, and I loved them back," wrote a gentleman employed in the house for twelve years. "Oh John. My favorite. I well up thinking of him. Most like his mother. SO creative. SO disruptive. SO impulsive. SO loving (so in need for love) . . . It still hurts." But this writer wasn't entirely rosy: "Andrew was a total prick . . . Peter is most like gpg [Gordon Peter Getty]. Obtuse."

For many in San Francisco, and beyond, the sudden death of Ann Getty was a turning point of sorts. As curator Martin Chapman put it, "People saw a world disappear."

On October 14, 2022, the very day the soup was flung in London, the trophies of that world—1,500 superlative works of fine and decorative arts from the Getty mansion—went on display at Christie's in New York, a few days before they went on the block. Five months earlier, the auction house had made the startling announcement that virtually the entire contents of Ann and Gordon's mansion would be sold in a series of landmark auctions, the proceeds of which would benefit the Ann and Gordon Getty Foundation for the Arts, devoted to the support of arts and science organizations.

The speed at which the collection was to be dispersed surprised many. Why did Gordon, at eighty-eight, want to go through the upheaval? Where would he go? Word subsequently traveled that he would be moving into the third and smallest of the trio of houses he and Ann had assembled on Broadway, which would be redecorated for him (and hung with copies of some of the paintings sent to Christie's). The art and antiques were Ann's thing, not Gordon's. Before she died, both of them had extensive discussions with Christie's and Sotheby's to solicit proposals for a philanthropic sale that would showcase the collection to a global audience. In the trade, there had been gossip for years about which firm would win the fierce battle to sell the collection. When deputy chairman of Christie's Americas Jonathan Rendell read a eulogy written by Charles Cator, deputy chairman of Christie's International, at Ann's memorial service, it was a clue as to which house had been victorious.

In the months before the sale, Christie's experts shouldered the herculean task of cataloging the 1,500 works, while the marketing department began a lavish worldwide sales and publicity campaign. (In a prelude, in June, the auction house raked in almost $6 million when it offered twelve spectacular jewels that had been created for Ann by renowned jewelry artist Joel Arthur Rosenthal, known as JAR.)

Over the course of a week in October 2022, it took ten separate auctions (four live and six online) to sell it all. During that time, elaborate installations in Christie's Rockefeller Center sales rooms re-created the looks of various areas in the Getty mansion—including the Turkish Room, with its fourteenth-century Egyptian panel inlaid with alabaster, red porphyry, and mother-of-pearl; Ann's bedroom, with its regal canopied gold and blue bed, made by Thomas Chippendale for Harewood House circa 1770; and the dining room, featuring twelve German panels painted for Augustus the Strong, circa 1720.

I walked through the installations one morning with the gentleman formerly employed in the Getty household who had written to me. He recognized every object, lovingly picking up some and pointing out secret compartments or mechanisms. "Nobody will live like this again," he said. "It's too bad they couldn't have kept one room intact and installed it in a museum, like the Salon Doré in the Legion of Honor in San Francisco. It's behind a velvet rope, but it gives you a glimpse of how those people lived in the eighteenth century. If they had done the same thing with, say, the Gettys' dining room, a hundred years from now visitors could see their lifestyle—the opulence and wealth. But maybe they wouldn't believe it."

When it was all over, the Ann & Gordon Getty Collection fetched in excess of $150 million, placing it in value, Christie's announced, behind only two previous blockbusters, The Collection of Yves Saint Laurent and Pierre Bergé and The Collection of Peggy and David Rockefeller. As expected, the big-ticket items soared: Mary Cassatt's *Young Lady in a Loge Gazing to Right* sold for $7,489,000, setting a new record for the artist; the German panels, estimated at $200,000, realized $2,280,000; a pair of Qing Dynasty cloisonné and enamel censors in the form of cranes fetched $1,620,000, more than twenty times its estimate. At the same time, the smaller items went for many multiples of their estimates—a set of Victorian salt cellars and sweet-meat dishes commanded $28,000, and a Tiffany silver cabbage tureen brought in the same amount.

In the wake of the auction, San Franciscans have been avidly wondering what will become of the Getty mansion, such a local landmark. At the same time, the fate of the dynasty's original seat, Sutton Place, became the subject of speculation when the UK government sanctioned Alisher Usmanov, the sixty-eight-year-old Russian metals magnate, who acquired the estate in 2005. "Sanctioning Usmanov . . . sends a clear message that we will hit oligarchs and individuals closely associated with the Putin regime and his barbarous war," said Liz Truss, then the foreign secretary.

Meanwhile, at Wormsley, the cricket pitch and the opera pavilion began to draw visitors again once pandemic restrictions were lifted. But the house itself has been quiet. According to friends, Mark has become ever more reclusive, and has opted to spend most of the year in Italy with his wife, Caterina, their young daughter, Sol, and Caterina's teenage son, Achille. In addition to their palazzo in Rome, they have acquired one in Siena, where Mark can be close to his beloved Palio, which in the summer of 2022 resumed in all its glory following a two-year pause. No winner for Mark this time. "COVID forced me to skip a generation of horses and therefore they are all young and inexperienced," he explained. Nonetheless, he was proud of

Arestetulesu, his six-year-old Sardinian, who ran in the August race. "He did well for his first Palio." The race occurred just one day after a significant milestone for Getty Images, where Mark remains chairman of the board. On August 15, leaders of the company rang the opening bell at the NYSE, to celebrate the completion of their combination with CC Neuberger Principal Holdings, a publicly traded special purpose acquisition company. "We believe our return to the public markets will enable us to invest aggressively in the products and services that will allow us to meet the needs of everyone," Mark commented on the occasion.

Arguably, Mark's cousin Anne Earhart eschews the spotlight more than any other member of the family. But last summer she received more awards. At The Ranch in Laguna Beach, she was named Environmentalist of the Year by Waterman's, the environmental arm of the Surf Industry Members Association. At the Rainbow Room in New York, her foundation, Marisla, was the honoree at the annual gala held by Oceana, the global ocean advocacy group. Anne's daughter Sara Lowell, Marisla's marine conservation director, accepted the award.

The style setters in the family have been on the rise, too. A warehouse in Downtown LA's Arts District was the setting for Nats's first-ever runway show for his company, Strike Oil, which has been gaining visibility thanks to such customers as Machine Gun Kelly, who has been spotted wearing the "Horny Hoody," the "Cracked Sweatpants," and other items. "The Future Is Past" was the title he chose for the collection. "The collection is an ode to time and space, the here, the now, what was, and what will be again," he stated. "It's my way of exploring different versions of myself."

He spoke about his decision to come out as transgender in early 2021. "As intense and horrible as COVID was, it gave me the time and space to finally be quiet with myself and to really reflect because I didn't have a thousand distractions . . . I was like, 'Holy shit! Okay! I think I'm ready.'"

Along with his spouse, Nats attended the annual Getty Family Meeting, which as convened at a resort on the Adriatic. "Strap in, Croatia," newcomer Gigi announced on Instagram shortly before the couple landed in Dubrovnik. By all accounts, she was welcomed with open arms by the extended family.

Ivy, named to the International Best-Dressed List, made her debut appearance at the Metropolitan Museum's Costume Institute Gala, wearing a custom Oscar de la Renta gown crafted from vintage lace that belonged to her grandmother Ann. Along with her husband, Toby, Ivy relocated to Manhattan, moving into an apartment in NoHo. At about the same time, her uncle Peter and his wife, Shannon, along with their two young children, became New Yorkers, too. (They bought an Upper East Side townhouse once owned by Ghislaine Maxwell.)

According to friends, Billy has been spending much of his time in Hawaii, while Vanessa has continued to appear at glamorous events around the world. When John was found dead in a hotel room in San Antonio, he was in Texas looking for a new house.

There'd been an exodus from San Francisco, then. Why? In the texts of lawsuits filed in the spring of 2022, possible reasons can be gleaned. (It's not because everybody finally tired of the fog.)

In March, Gordon Getty's middle daughter Kendalle filed a complaint in the District Court of the State of Nevada against a former investment advisor named Marlena Sonn. Sonn, Kendalle alleged, had breached her fiduciary duties. Two months later, in the United States District Court for the Eastern District of New York, Sonn filed a countersuit against Kendalle as well as her sister Sarah, and Robert I. Liberman, CEO of Vallejo Investments, Inc., the Gettys' San Francisco family office.

In its fifty-page complaint, Sonn v. Getty et al touches on significant issues for the Getty family—ones relating to the structures of their immense family trusts, and the tax bills they might face when Gordon dies and the fortune is distributed. Under California's "throwback" rule, trust income is subject to considerable taxation if the beneficiary is a California resident around the time of a "major income event," which the death of Gordon will certainly be.

As we have seen, the story of the Getty trusts is long and complicated. The original Sarah C. Getty Trust, written in 1934 in California, was partitioned into four separate trusts, one for each branch of the family, in the 1980s.

According to Sonn's suit, "In or around 1995, the administration of the Gordon P. Getty Trust and several other successor trusts . . . was transferred from California to Nevada, as part of a deliberate strategy to avoid paying California state taxes on income trust. In order to effectuate this strategy, each of the individual beneficiaries was assigned a corporate trustee, i.e., a Nevada-based corporation formed in their name, for the purposes of residing in and serving as trustee from the State of Nevada in their stead, so that each beneficiary could continue living in California . . ." In Kendalle's original complaint against Sonn, however, it is stated clearly that "Plaintiff Getty is currently a resident of the State of California."

As Sonn's suit further alleges, Gordon's trust was partitioned again in 2004, into two separate trusts—the Orpheus Trust and the Pleiades Trust. Upon Gordon's death, his sons will be the beneficiaries of the former; his daughter will benefit from the latter. (In Greek mythology, Orpheus was a musician and poet who journeyed to Hades in an attempt to bring his wife back from the dead; the Pleiades were the daughters of Atlas, the titan who held up the sky.)

Which brings us to how these suits arose. In 2013, Kendalle and Sarah hired Sonn to manage their financial portfolios, with an emphasis toward making "socially responsible" investments. Sonn claims she began to raise "objections and concerns about the legality of the California tax avoidance scheme." According to her suit, the sisters initially shared these concerns—but eventually fell in line with the family "status quo," at which point they terminated Sonn's services.

According to her website, Sonn is president of Amazonia Wealth Management. "She specializes in working with progressive, Ultra High Net Worth millennials, women, inheritors, and family offices to align their wealth with their values." The office address listed on the website is a WeWork location in Brooklyn. Sonn's complaint contains several paragraphs describing a complicated relationship with Kendalle: "She also regularly turned to Ms. Sonn for advice on interpersonal relationships . . . Ms. Sonn was there for Kendalle in times of need, to . . . help her navigate her personal troubles or perceived emergencies."

As Sonn seeks a financial settlement for the compensation she says she is owed, her lawsuit makes potentially incendiary allegations: "Ms. Sonn had reasonable cause to believe that Defendants were engaged in a scheme or conspiracy to avoid paying hundreds of million in taxes to the State of California . . ." Given the size of this potential tax hit, one can infer that the Pleiades Trust's assets alone are in the billions.

Over the summer, Kendalle and Sonn's lawsuits were consolidated and transferred to the United States District Court for the District of Nevada. At last report, the judge had stayed the cases pending a settlement conference that was scheduled for early 2023. Aside from a column published in June 2022 in the *Los Angeles Times*, the litigation has not been reported on.

In 2022, Kendalle, an artist who lives between Los Angeles and New York, established a new website for herself: whoiskendallegetty .com. On it, she lists the "various pseudonyms" she previously went by (including "Kendalle Fiasco"), then reveals herself officially: "Kendalle is the daughter of Gordon Getty, the son of Getty Oil Company founder J. Paul Getty."

Given her complicated upbringing, it wasn't an easy decision to "come out" as a Getty and use the surname. "The early days were terrifying," Kendalle told me. "I didn't know what to expect."

But she's glad she did it: "I feel substantially more free now, finally not bearing the burden of secrecy. It's been overall a positive change . . . I've also noticed an increased sense of pride, associating by name with a family of mavericks, artists, philanthropists, and geniuses."

Sure, there have been troubles in the family, too, Kendalle acknowledges. But that's okay: "Obviously we aren't perfect. Perfection is for math tests."

She adores her father. "He is a very loving, deeply eccentric, truly brilliant, and very funny man who always chooses to see the good in people," she says.

Kendalle has a damaged relationship with her mother, however—which is a subject Kendalle, who earned an MFA at New York University, is processing as she prepares her first solo exhibition, which she plans to unveil in 2023. "The Hostile Home" will be a surrealistic, multiroom installation that combines sculpture, video, and audio works. "It is an abstract recreation of my mother's home, which I was raised in," she explains. Items such as a kitchen chair with nails poking up through the seat, a sofa upholstered in sandpaper, and plates of rancid food will express, Kendalle says, "the pervasive sense of feeling unwelcome" she felt in the house. "I wish to externalize internal conflict," she adds.

However much she might be taxed, Kendalle, like her relatives, is still going to be exceedingly rich when Gordon Peter Getty leaves this earth. Given the wherewithal to do whatever they want, what will each of them do? Only one thing seems for sure—it won't be dull.

Acknowledgments

My *Growing Up Getty* journey commenced when I visited the Getty Research Institute, in Los Angeles, where I became absorbed in J. Paul Getty's diaries and correspondence. My acknowledgments begin, then, with sincere thanks to the dedicated and learned GRI staff who helped me access and navigate through this wealth of material.

I didn't realize it at the time, but my research for this book had begun decades before. In my magazine career—at *Vanity Fair* and *W*, and as a contributor to *Town & Country* and *Sotheby's* magazine— my travels sometimes took me to such extraordinary places as Outer Broadway in San Francisco and Wormsley Manor in Buckinghamshire. I had the very good fortune to interview a number of Gettys and learn about some of their endeavors and passions. Then there were the many fascinating people in the orbit of this dynasty who I profiled and stayed in touch with (Christopher Gibbs and Gillian Wilson, to name just a couple favorites). Among them, the gravitational pull toward this charismatic and often elusive clan was palpable.

On a visit to Rome, Carlo Scimone and Margherita Rostworowski so graciously welcomed me into their home, where he shared his extraordinary memories and photographs with me.

In the course of my reporting for this book, many of the people I spoke to preferred to remain anonymous. Public as some Gettys are, most of them remain resolutely private. I am especially indebted to the family members who did speak to me and engage with me in various ways for this book.

At Gallery Books, my heartfelt thanks to the miraculous, meticulous, and always supportive editorial director, Aimee Bell. In her office, associate editor Max Meltzer was a tireless force for good sense. Under the same roof (virtual though it was during the making of this book) my gratitude extends from Simon & Schuster president Jonathan Karp to the entire Gallery Books team, including publisher Jennifer Bergstrom, deputy publisher Jennifer Long, director of publicity and marketing Sally Marvin, executive publicist Jennifer Robinson, managing editor Caroline Pallotta, and senior production editor Samantha Hoback.

At Aevitas Creative Management, my sincere thanks go to David Kuhn and Nate Muscato and their team.

In my research, I benefited hugely from the heroic work of Abby Field Gerry. Thanks also to Dale Brauner. When it was time to search for photos, Mark Jacobson and Cole Giordano sorted through myriad Getty images.

Many of the twentieth century's most celebrated photographers including Slim Aarons and Horst focused their lenses on Gettys; some of their iconic portraits are reproduced in this volume. I am extremely grateful to be able to also publish superb photographs by Jonathan Becker, Simon Watson, Dafydd Jones, and Firooz Zahedi.

While writing in Covid-era Manhattan, communications from far-flung sources enlivened the solitary days. An especially helpful and generous email arrived one morning from Robina Lund, who wrote from her home in Aberdeenshire (after Jenny Morrison, features writer for the Scottish *Sunday Mail* and *Daily Record*, graciously helped me locate her). Robina succinctly explained how some of the key myths surrounding the Gettys had been created and perpetuated—payphone included.

Bibliography

General References

Argyll, Margaret Campbell. *Forget Not: The Autobiography of Margaret, Duchess of Argyll.* London: W. H. Allen, 1975.

Bedford, Nicole Russell. *Nicole Nobody: The Autobiography of the Duchess of Bedford.* Garden City, NY: Doubleday, 1975.

d'Abo, Lady Ursula. *The Girl with the Widow's Peak: The Memoirs.* Dorset, England: Dorset Press, 2014.

de Chair, Somerset. *Getty on Getty: A Man in a Billion.* London: Cassel, 1989.

Fredericksen, Burton B. *The Burdens of Wealth: Paul Getty and His Museum.* Bloomington, IN: Archway, 2015.

Gaston, Theodora Getty. *Alone Together: My Life with J. Paul Getty.* New York: Ecco/HarperCollins, 2013.

Getty, Gordon. *Logic and Economics: Free Growth and Other Surprises.* Gold River, CA: Authority Publishing, 2018.

Getty, J. Paul. *As I See It: The Autobiography of J. Paul Getty.* New York: Prentice-Hall, 1976.

———. Diaries 1938–1976. Getty Research Institute, Los Angeles.

———. *How to Be Rich.* New York: Playboy Press, 1965.

———. *The Joys of Collecting.* New York: Hawthorn Books, 1965.

———. *My Life and Fortunes: The Autobiography of One of the World's Wealthiest Men.* New York: Duell, Sloan and Pearce, 1963.

Hewins, Ralph. *The Richest American: J. Paul Getty.* New York: E. P. Dutton, 1960.

Lund, Robina. *The Getty I Knew: An Intimate Biography.* Kansas City, MO: Sheed Andrews and McMeel, 1977.

Newsom, William. "Politics, Law, and Human Rights." Interviewed by Martin Meeker, 2008–2009. Regional Oral History Office, Bancroft Library, University of California, Berkeley, 2009.

Pearson, John. *All the Money in the World: The Outrageous Fortune and Misfortunes of the Heirs of J. Paul Getty.* London: William Collins, 2017. (Originally published as *Painfully Rich.*)

Reginato, James. "Boulle Fighter: The Getty's Decorative Arts Curator Unveils Her Spectacular Galleries." *W*, October 1997.

———. *Great Houses, Modern Aristocrats*. New York: Rizzoli, 2016.

Rosen, Peter, dir. *Gordon Getty: There Will Be Music*. New York: Peter Rosen Productions, 2015.

Shulman, David, dir. *Gettys: The World's Richest Art Dynasty*. London: BBC Studios Documentary Unit, 2018.

Smith, Richard Austin. "The Fifty-Million-Dollar Man." *Fortune*, November 1957.

Spence, Lyndsy. *The Grit in the Pearl: The Scandalous Life of Margaret, Duchess of Argyll*. Stroud, Gloucestershire: History Press, 2019.

CHAPTER ONE: SUTTON PLACE

Billington, Joy. "What Does All That Money Buy." *Cincinnati Enquirer*, October 26, 1975.

Cooney, Kevin. "The Seven Sisters." *New York Times*, October 19, 1975.

Dupre, John. "Mrs. Paul Getty the Sixth?" *Australian Women's Weekly*, November 5, 1975.

Eakin, Hugh. "Self-Portrait of the Oilman as Collector." *New York Times*, December 24, 2010.

Evan, Peter. "Jean Paul Getty (the Richest Man in the World) Talks about Women." *Cosmopolitan*, September 1968.

Farnsworth, Clyde H. "Surrey Estate of Getty Empire: 'Richest Man' Label Irks Getty." *New York Times*, July 30, 1964.

Fontevecchia, Augustino. "The Getty Family: A Cautionary Tale of Oil, Adultery, and Death." *Forbes*, April 23, 2015.

Getty Family Papers. Getty Research Institute, Los Angeles (1987.1A.09-01).

Gold, Jack, prod. *The Solitary Billionaire: J. Paul Getty*. Interview by Alan Whicker. London: BBC, aired February 24, 1963.

Jackson, Debbie. "Throwback Tulsa: Billionaire J. Paul Getty Got His Start in Tulsa." *Tulsa World*, December 10, 2017.

Lenzner, Robert. *The Great Getty: The Life and Loves of J. Paul Getty—Richest Man in the World*. New York: Crown, 1985.

Long, Ralph W. "Buys Pierre Leasehold." *New York Times*, December 19, 1939.

Lubac, Robert. "The Odd Mr. Getty." *Fortune*, March 17, 1986.

Mallory, Carole. *"Alone Together."* The Wrap (website), September 24, 2013.

———. "Theodora (Teddy) Lynch Getty Gaston Talks about the Gettys, Oil, Plastic Surgery and Elephants." *HuffPost* (blog), February 16, 2011.

Marble, Steve. "Teddy Getty Gaston, Who Wrote an Unflinching Memoir about Her Marriage to J. Paul Getty, Dies at 103." *Los Angeles Times*, March 12, 2017.

Marlowe, Lisa. "Chez Getty: Staying in Luxury at Billionaire's Rome Home Turned into a Treasure-Filled Hotel." *New York Times*, December 14, 1997.

Martin-Robinson, John. "From Edwardian Idyll to Meetings with Nehru: The Life of Lady Ursula d'Abo." *Spectator*, July 5, 2014.

Miller, Mike. "Louise Dudley 'Teddy' Lynch, J. Paul Getty's Fifth and Final Wife, Has Died at 103." *People*, March 10, 2017.

Miller, Russell. *The House of Getty*. London: Bloomsbury, 1985.

Newman, Judith. "His Favorite Wife." *New York Times*, August 30, 2013.

Newsweek. "Incredible Billionaire." March 7, 1960.

New York Times. "76 in U.S. Found to Have Fortunes above $75,000,000." October 28, 1957.

Nicholas, Sadie. "Lady Ursula d'Abo—the Beautiful Girl Who Outshone the Queen." *Express* (London), November 8, 2017.

O'Reilly, Jane. "Isn't It Funny What Money Can Do?" *New York Times*, March 30, 1986.

Rork, Ann. Letters. Getty Research Institute, Los Angeles (1987.1A.48-06).

Rozhon, Tracie. "A Rooftop Palazzo with a Split Personality." *New York Times*, January 15, 1998.

Shuster, Alvin. "Getty, 80, Feted on Birthday." *New York Times*, December 16, 1972.

Suzy. "J. Paul Getty: The Absolute Billionaire." *Town & Country*, July 1964.

Telegraph. "Lady Ursula d'Abo, Train Bearer at the 1937 Coronation." November 6, 2017.

Time. "Real Estate: Hate Those Hotels." October 26, 1959.

Vincent, Alice. "'Penny Pincher? I Don't Even Know the Girl': The Surprisingly Prodigious Sexual Appetite of J. Paul Getty." *Telegraph* (UK), September 13, 2018.

Weinraub, Judith. "She Was 'the Top': A Duchess's Memoirs of a Lively Lifetime." *New York Times*, December 7, 1975.

Wilson, Gillian. *Baroque & Régence: Catalogue of the J. Paul Getty Museum Collection*. Los Angeles: J. Paul Getty Museum, 2008.

CHAPTER TWO: THE TRAGIC YEARS

Coll, Steve. *The Taking of Getty Oil*. New York: Atheneum, 1987.

Didion, Joan. *The White Album*. New York: Simon & Schuster, 1979.

Gebhard, David. "Getty Museum: Is It 'Disgusting' and 'Downright Outrageous'?" *Architecture Plus*, September 1974.

Jones, David. "Call Girl Who Nearly Toppled a Government Reveals All." *Daily Mail*, January 26, 2007.

Kotkin, Joel. "The Problems of Having $720 Million." *Washington Post*, February 6, 1977.

MacIntyre, Ben. "The Dirty Duchess of Argyll Was Ahead of Her Time." *Times* (London), February 2, 2019.

Mega, Marcello. "I Was the Secret Lover of the World's Richest Man." *Scottish Mail on Sunday*, September 9, 2017.

Morrison, Jenny. "Oil Tycoon Paul Getty's Lover Says New TV Drama Based on His Life Is Full of Lies." *Daily Record* (Glasgow), September 9, 2018.

Muchnic, Suzanne. "A Getty Chronicle: The Malibu Years." *Los Angeles Times*, July 6, 1997.

New York Times. "Roman Villa Is Recreated on Coast to House Getty Art Collection." January 17, 1974.

O'Neill, Anne-Marie. "Can't Buy Me Love." *People*, April 13, 1998.

People. "For a Dozen Lucky Ladies in J. Paul Getty's Life, the Party Isn't Over Yet." July 19, 1976.

————. "World's Richest Man." March 18, 1974.

Petzinger, Thomas, Jr. *Oil and Honor: The Texaco-Pennzoil Wars*. New York: G. P. Putnam's Sons, 1987.

Potts, Timothy. "20 Years at the Getty Genter: A Getty Museum Perspective." *The Iris* (blog), May 31, 2018. http://blogs.getty.edu.

Reginato, James. "The Luck of the Lambtons." *Vanity Fair*, November 2012.

Roberts, Glenda D. "Interview with Robina Lund, Lawyer and Personal Advisor to Jean Paul Getty 1st." *Emotional Wellbeing* (podcast), Abderdeen: 2018. https://www.mixcloud.com/uxwbob/glenda-d-roberts-interview-with-robina-lund-lawyer-and-personal-adviser-to-jean-paul-getty-1st/.

Warhol, Andy. *The Andy Warhol Diaries*. Edited by Pat Hackett. New York: Warner Books, 1991.

Whitman, Alden. "Paul Getty Dead at 83; Amassed Billions from Oil." *New York Times*, June 6, 1976.

Wilson, Andrew. "Who Framed Margaret of Argyll?" *Tatler*, March 2014.

Wilson, William. "A Preview of Pompeii-on-the-Pacific." *Los Angeles Times*, January 6, 1974.

Wong, Amelia. "The Never-Boring Life of J. Paul Getty, World's Richest Man." *The Iris* (blog), October 18, 2016. http://blogs.getty.edu.

CHAPTER THREE: THE GEORGETTES

Adams, John H. *A Force for Nature: The Story of NRDC and Its Fight to Save Our Planet*. San Francisco: Chronicle Books, 2010.

Associated Press. "FPPC Seeks Getty Fine." *Sacramento Bee*, October 17, 2003.

————. "Getty Heiress Settles Campaign Finance Suit." *Los Angeles Times*, March 31, 2004.

————. "Getty Son Sued for Divorce on Cruelty Grounds." *San Bernardino County Sun*, August 2, 1967.

————. "Nature Conservancy's Mystery Donor Is Southern California Oil Heiress." *Napa Valley Register*, May 11, 2002.

Astre, K. "Highland: Thailand's Marijuana Awakening." *Cannabis Now*, June 8, 2017. cannabisnow.com.

Batti, Renee. "The Art of Change: Noel Perry's Art and Education Efforts Are Aimed at Creating a Better Future." *Almanac News* (San Mateo County), May 25, 2005.

Bennett, Laurie. "Getty Oil Heir Quietly Supports Democrats." *Forbes*, July 30, 2012.

Blair, James. "Conservation and Community in Laguna San Ignacio." *ICFND.org*, May 3, 2018.

Bluth, Alexa A. "Oil Heiress Settles Case on Ballot Donations." *Sacramento Bee*, March 31, 2004.

Boots, Michelle Theriault. "Alaska's Biggest Ever Commercial Seaweed Harvest Is Happening Right Now." *Anchorage Daily News*, May 19, 2019.

Brazil, Ben. "Orange County Philanthropist Helped Save Crucial Mexican Lagoon Used by Gray Whales for Breeding." *Los Angeles Times*, October 11, 2019.

Carnegie Medal of Philanthropy. "Announcing the 2019 Carnegie Medal of

Philanthropy Recipients" (press release). http://www.Medalofphilanthropy
.org/anne-g-earhart.

Cecco, Leyland. "Meet the 'Star Ingredient' Changing Fortunes in Alaska's
Waters: Seaweed." *Guardian*, June 11, 2019.

Christine, Bill. "Dame Fortune Continues to Smile on Riordan." *Los Angeles Times*,
March 27, 1986.

Clinton, Mary Jane. Talk of the Times. *Times* (San Mateo, CA), September 9, 1969.

———. Talk of the Times. *Times* (San Mateo, CA), January 26, 1972.

Conroy, Sarah Booth. "The Founding Force of Wilhelmina Holladay." *Washington
Post*, February 15, 1987.

Corkery, P. J. "Cube Me." *San Francisco Examiner*, July 8, 2002.

Daly, Kate. "Water World: Woodside Resident Curates 'California: The Art of
Water' at the Cantor." *Almanac News* (San Mateo County), November 2016.

Darling, Juanita. "Ecologists Fear Baja Salt Mine Would Threaten Gray Whales."
Los Angeles Times, March 6, 1995.

Dedina, Serge. "In Memory of Don Pachico." Wildcoast (website), undated post.

———. *Saving the Gray Whale*. Tuscon: University of Arizona Press, 2000.

de Waal-Montgomery, Michael. "Coconuts Is a Local News Startup Fast Becoming the Patch of Southeast Asia." *Venture Beat*, January 4, 2016.

Dillow, Gordon. "Getting Close Up and Personal with Whales." *Los Angeles Times*,
April 3, 1994.

Earhart, Nico. "Coming to Fruition." *The Wind-Blown Golfer* (blog), April 24, 2019.
https://www.thewind-blowngolfer.com.

Encyclopedia.com. "Mitsubishi Oil Co., Ltd." March 13, 2020.

Evey, Stuart. *ESPN: Creating an Empire*. Chicago: Triumph Books, 2004.

Farmed Seafood. "Healthy, Sustainable, and All-Around Virtuous: Blue Evolution
Seaweed." May 7, 2018. https://farmed-seafood.com.

Fatsis, Stefan. "At $5.2 Billion, Metromedia's Kluge Tops Forbes' Richest Ameri-
can List." *Salinas Californian*, October 11, 1989.

Fox, Christy. "Gettys on Their Honeymoon." *Los Angeles Times*, May 21, 1971.

Frater, Patrick. "Netflix Buys 'Highland' Thai Marijuana Documentary." *Variety*,
May 24, 2017.

Ganguly, Shicani. "Olazul: Small Aquaculture Is Beautiful." Triple Pundit (website), December 27, 2012. https://TriplePundit.com.

Gates, Bob. "Jackie Getty: Turf Globetrotter." *Los Angeles Times*, September 7,
1975.

Gorlick, Adam. "Stanford Historian, Venture Capitalist Energizes Votes over
Political Reform." *Stanford Report*, May 24, 2010.

Halper, Evan. "Political Donors Shielded by Loophole." *Los Angeles Times*, September 30, 2002.

Hicks, Cordell. "Just Wed Gettys Will Take Europe Cruise." *Los Angeles Times*,
June 30, 1951.

Hicks, Robin. "Q&A with Coconuts Media Founder Byron Perry." Mumbrella
(website), July 2015.

Holladay, Wilhelmina Cole. *A Museum of Their Own*. New York: Abbeville Press, 2008.

Bibliography

———. "Oral History Interview with Wilhelmina Holladay." Interviewed by Krystyna Wasserman. Archives of American Art, Smithsonian Institution, Washington, DC, 2005.

Jacobs, Jody. "The Next Best Thing to Walking on Water." *Los Angeles Times*, October 16, 1974.

———. "A Tribute to Jimmy Durante." *Los Angeles Times*, November 15, 1976.

Jones, Jack. "J. Paul Getty Eulogized at Services." *Los Angeles Times*, June 11, 1976.

Kennedy, Robert F., Jr. "Poisoning a Sanctuary for the Sake of Salt." *Los Angeles Times*, August 5, 1998.

Knoerle, Jane. "California Dreaming: Woodside Woman Stages Major Exhibit of California Images at Stanford Art Museum." *Almanac News* (San Mateo County), May 19, 1999.

Lawrence, Steve. "State Watchdog Asks Court to Fine Heiress." *Napa Valley Register*, October 17, 2003.

Lenzner, Robert. "Splitting Up Getty's $4 Billion." *Boston Globe*, October 21, 1984.

Los Angeles Times. "Gloria Alice Gordon Betrothal Announced." March 13, 1951.

———. "Mexico Deep-Sixes Plan for Baja Lagoon Saltworks." March 3, 2000.

MacNiven, Jamis. "Beau Perry's Premium Oceanic." *Buck's Stories* (blog), September 7, 2014.

Moran, Dan. "Fair Political Practices Panel Accuses Getty Heiress of 'Campaign Money Laundering.'" *Los Angeles Times*, October 17, 2003.

Moran, Sheila. "Getty Heir Part of Racing Scene." *Los Angeles Times*, March 17, 1977.

Multiplier (website). "An Interview with Beau Perry, Founder and Former Director, Olazul." September 7, 2013. https://multiplier.org.

New York Times. "George F. Getty 2nd, Oldest Son of Oil Billionaire, Dies on Coast." June 7, 1973.

———. "Japan Fighting Her Biggest Oil Spill." December 25, 1974.

Palmer, Barbara. "Children in 19th-Century Art Reflect Nation's Fears." *Stanford Report*, March 1, 2006.

Perlman, Jeffrey A. "Tollway Foes Find Ally in Foundation." *Los Angeles Times*, December 27, 1992.

Perry, Claire. *The Great American Hall of Wonders: Art, Science, and Invention in the Nineteenth Century*. London: D. Giles Ltd., with the Smithsonian American Art Museum, 2011.

———. *Pacific Arcadia: Images of California, 1600–1915*. New York: Oxford University Press, 1999.

———. *Young America: Childhood in 19th-Century Art and Culture*. New Haven: Yale University Press, 2006.

Princeton Alumni Weekly. "Class of '46 Notes." May 9, 1952.

Rao, Amrita. "Claire Perry: Art as an American Wonder." *Stanford Daily*, October 24, 2011.

Rogers, Patrick. "The Man Behind the Mission." NRDC (website), April 19, 2016. https://www.NRDC.org.

———. "Saving the Breeding Grounds of the Pacific Gray Whale." NRDC (website), May 12, 2016. https://www.NRDC.org.

Roosevelt, Margot. "Prop 23 Battle Marks New Era in Environmental Politics." *Los Angeles Times*, November 4, 2010.

Rubenstein, Steve. "Getty Campaign Gifts Questioned: Water, Park Bond Measures Allegedly Favored by Heiress." *San Francisco Chronicle*, October 17, 2003.

Sandomir, Richard. "Stuart Evey, a Founding Force at ESPN, Is Dead at 84." *New York Times*, December 12, 2017.

San Francisco Chronicle. "Getty Heir Agrees to Pay $135,000 Fine." March 31, 2004.

Schiller, Ben. "Farming Gets a New Crop—Seaweed." *Fast Company*, October 23, 2014.

Schreibman, Jack. "Elite Meet to Weep over Last Trader Vic's Lunch." *Napa Valley Register*, March 24, 1990.

Shamdasani, Pavan. "Local Content Delivered Fast Is the Secret of Success for Byron Perry's Coconuts Websites." *South China Morning Post*, December 13, 2014.

Shiver, Jube, Jr. "Gettys Resolve Dispute over Trust: Agreement Reached on Provision for Unborn Heirs." *New York Times*, May 31, 1985.

Silva, Horacio. "Family Ties." *New York Times*, September 25, 2001.

Smith, James F. "Activists Break New Ground to Help Shake Off Saltworks Project." *Los Angeles Times*, April 23, 2000.

Solina, Samie. "Seaweed Farming Could Make Waves in the Future." KTUU (Alaska), July 2, 2019. https://www. KTUU.com.

Soon, Alan. "Coconuts, a Fast-Growing, Cities-Focused Network of Sites in Asia, Takes a Hard Right into Paid Memberships." Nieman Lab (website), April 2018. https://www.niemanlab.org.

Suh, Rhea. "Laguna San Ignacio: A Living Testament to NRDC's Work." NRDC (website), March 2018. https://www.NRDC.org.

Suzy. "Charles—Prince of a Host for World Colleges." *New York Daily News*, June 13, 1984.

United Press International. "Getty's Son Dies; Wounds Are Found." *Sacramento Bee*, June 7, 1973.

———. "Rites Today for J. Paul Getty's Eldest Son." *San Francisco Examiner*, June 9, 1973.

Welch, Laine. "Dutch Harbor Stays in Top among U.S. Fishing Ports." *Anchorage Daily News*, Februrary 25, 2020.

———. "Fish Factor: Alaskan Interest in Growing Keeps Growing." *Cordova Times*, June 5, 2021.

Williams, Tate. "A Growing Pool-Funding Effort to Support Environmental Defenders." *Inside Philanthropy*, July 17, 2018.

———. "The Oil Company Heiress Devoting Her Wealth to Oceans." *Inside Philanthropy*, May 23, 2014.

———. "Three Things to Know about Marisla's Beto Bedolfe." *Inside Philanthropy*, May 29, 2014.

Woody, Todd. "Koch Brothers Jump into Prop 23 Fight." Grist (website), September 2, 2010. https://grist.org.

———. "No on Prop 23 Campaign Rakes in Cash as Enviro Justice Advocates Join the Fight." Grist (website), September 28, 2010. https://grist.org.

Chapter Four: The Ronald Line

Associated Press. "Getty Son Bankruptcy." *New York Times*, December 18, 1992.

———. "Getty's Son, J. Ronald, Turns Interest to Movies." *San Antonio Express*, February 4, 1971.

Barraclough, Leo. "Johnny Kenton, Debs Paterson Receive Pia Pressure Awards." *Variety*, April 3, 2016.

Charleston, Libby-Jane. "Meet the Miller Sisters." 9Honey (website), April 2021. https://honey.nine.com.au.

Colacello, Bob. "A Royal Family Affair." *Vanity Fair*, February 2008.

Croffey, Amy. "Stars and Socialites Swoop on Zimmermann's Miami Launch." *Sun-Herald* (Sydney), July 30, 2017.

Gao, Alice Longyu. "22-Year-Old Isabel Getty on Working with Dolce & Gabbana and Overcoming Tradition: New Face, Fresh Style." *Billboard*, March 28, 2017.

Harrison, Annabel. "Isabel Getty, Sabrina Percy & Amber Le Bon's Artworks for Royal Ascot." Luxury London (website), June 19, 2019. https://luxurylondon.co.uk.

Hello!. "Christina Getty Weds Arin Maercks in a Picture Perfect Florida Ceremony." January 21, 2002.

Holden, Adam. "A Moment with Constantia Glen's Alexander Waibel." *Berry Bros. & Rudd Wine Blog*, February 12, 2021. https://blog.bbr.com.

Lawrence, James. "Grape Expectations: A Tour of South Africa's Vineyards." Luxury London (website), May 7, 2019. https://luxurylondon.co.uk.

Lawrence, Vanessa. "High Note." *W*, November 2017.

Madrid, Graham Keeley. "Euro Royals Go Wild in the Cotswolds." *Times* (London), July 5, 2017.

Maule, Henry. "The Billionaire Who Got Blackballed." *Daily News* (New York), May 22, 1966.

Money-Coutts, Sophia. "Meet Isabel Getty!" *Tatler*, September 28, 2016.

New York Post. "Thanking Lenny." February 8, 2016.

Norwich, William. "Sister Act." *Vogue*, July 1995.

O'Donaghue, Clare. *Constantia Glen: A Timeless History*. Rondebosch, South Africa: Quivertree, 2018.

Page, Bruce. "The Spoils of Sutton Place: Will Getty's Will Be Done?" *New York*, December 18, 1976.

Perès, Daniel. "Sister Act." *W*, May 1997.

Powell, Rosalind. "Princess Olympia of Greece Puts on a Stylish Show to Toast Two Landmark Royal Birthdays." *Hello!*, July 2017.

Salvat, Maryanne. "Getty's Fabulous Getty." *Miami Socialholic*, August 30, 2012.

Shakespeare, Sebastian. "The New Marie-Antoinette!" *Daily Mail*, July 6, 2017.

Steuer, Joseph. "The Marvelous Miller Girls." *W*, December 1992.

Suzy. "Inside the Glamorous Royal Wedding and All the Glittering Parties." *W*, August 1995.

Tatler. "High Summer." September 2019.

Thomas, Kevin. "Getty Son Rigging for a Movie Gusher." *Los Angeles Times*, June 11, 1970.

Thorpe, Sophie. "The Power of Restraint." *Berry Bros. & Rudd Wine Blog*, November 8, 2014. https://blog.bbr.com.

United Press International. "Billionaire's Son Weds in German Church Service." *Green Bay Press-Gazette*, October 25, 1964.

———. "Jean-Ronald Getty Weds German Girl." *New York Times*, October 24, 1964.

Wallace, Lisa. "Constantia Views: Two Families Share a Winemaker, a Winery and a Love of Bordeaux Wines." *House & Garden*, September 29, 2016.

CHAPTER FIVE: PAUL JR.

Barber, Lynn. "J. Paul Getty: Money Talks." *Sydney Morning Herald*, August 29, 1987.

BBC News. "Profile: Sir John Paul Getty II." June 13, 2001.

Beaton, Cecil. *Beaton in the Sixties: The Cecil Beaton Diaries as They Were Written*. London: Weidenfeld & Nicolson, 2003.

Bosworth, Patricia. *Jane Fonda: The Private Life of a Public Woman*. Houghton Mifflin Harcourt, 2011.

Cash, William. "The New Gettys." *Evening Standard* (London), October 10, 2003.

Drake, Alicia. *The Beautiful Fall: Fashion, Genius, and Glorious Excess in 1970s Paris*. New York: Little, Brown, 2006.

Dunne, Dominick. "Fatal Charm Part Two." *Vanity Fair*, September 1985.

Edmonds, Frances. "Cricket: A Love as Boundless as His Wealth." *Independent* (London), May 16, 1993.

Faithfull, Marianne. *Faithfull*. New York: Little, Brown, 1994.

Fitzgerald, Olda. "England's Getty Center." *Architectural Digest*, March 1998.

Fletcher, H. George, ed. *The Wormsley Library: A Personal Selection by Sir Paul Getty, K.B.E.* London: Maggs Bros. with the Pierpont Morgan Library, 1999.

Gaignault, Fabrice. *Égéries Sixties*. Paris: Fayard, 2006.

Gale, Laurence. "Wormsley Cricket Ground—a Lasting Legacy." Pitchcare (website), July 31, 2015. https://www.pitchare.com.

Haden-Guest, Anthony. "Light Shines on a Dark Star." *Financial Times*, May 25, 2020.

Hambly, Vivienne. "Beautiful Music." *The English Garden*, May 2019.

Hamilton, Alan. "Getty: Proud to Be British." *Times* (London), March 11, 1998.

Hicks, India. "Victoria Getty." India Hicks (website), February 15, 2015.

Hopkins, John. *The Tangier Diaries 1962–1979*. New York: Cadmus Editions, 1997.

Howard, Paul. *I Read the News Today, Oh Boy: The Short and Gilded Life of Tara Browne, the Man Who Inspired the Beatles' Greatest Song*. London: Picador, 2016.

Hughes, Simon. "Simon Hughes Meets John Paul Getty." ESPN, September 12, 1998. https://www.espn.com.

Johns, Glyn. *Sound Man: A Life of Recording Hits with the Rolling Stones*. New York: Plume, 2015.

Kavanagh, Julie. *Nureyev: The Life*. New York: Pantheon Books, 2007.

Levy, Shawn. *Dolce Vita Confidential: Fellini, Loren, Pucci, Paparazzi, and the Swinging High Life of 1950s Rome*. New York: W. W. Norton, 2016.

———. *Ready, Steady, Go!: Swinging London and the Invention of Cool*. New York: HarperCollins, 2002.

McEvoy, Marian. *Bill Willis*. Marrakech: Jardin Majorelle, 2011.

Medford, Sarah. "Palais Intrigue." *Wall Street Journal*, September 12, 2017.

New York Times. "Talitha Pol, Wife of Paul Getty Jr." July 14, 1971.

Petkanas, Christopher. "Fabulous Dead People: Decorator Bill Willis." *New York Times*, May 14, 2010.

Reginato, James. "The Prince of Pimlico: In Matters of Art and Décor, London Antiques Dealer Christopher Gibbs Rules Britannia." *W*, November 1998.

Richards, Keith. *Life*. New York: Little, Brown, 2010.

Rocca, Fiammetta. "Paul Getty's New Life." *Vanity Fair*, August 1994.

Runtagh, Jordan. "Beatles' 'Sgt. Pepper' at 50: The Doomed Socialite Behind 'A Day in the Life.'" *Rolling Stone*, May 31, 2017.

Saxon, Wolfgang. "J. Paul Getty Jr., Philanthropist, Dies at 70." *New York Times*, April 18, 2003.

Smith, Roberta. "Library Treasures, Bound for Eternity." *New York Times*, January 29, 1999.

Telegraph (UK). "Prince Dado Ruspoli." January 15, 2015.

———. "Sir Paul Getty." March 4, 2003.

Times (London). "Sir Paul Getty." September 10, 2003.

Tuohy, William. "Bestowing a Look at Britain's Benefactor." *Los Angeles Times*, August 19, 1994.

———. "Court Deals a Blow to Getty Quest for 'Graces.'" *Los Angeles Times*, October 28, 1994.

Vogue. "Moroccan Wake-Up: Mr. and Mrs. Paul Getty Junior Have Shaken to Life a Deserted House in Marrakech, Made It Imaginative, Rare—with a Little Mystery." January 1970.

Vreeland, Diana, ed. *Yves Saint Laurent*. New York: Metropolitan Museum of Art, 1983.

Vyner, Harriet. *Groovy Bob: The Life and Times of Robert Fraser*. London: Faber and Faber, 1999.

Wallace, William. "John Paul Getty Jr., 70; Oil Heir Evolved from Excess, Tragedy into Patron of British Culture." *Los Angeles Times*, April 18, 2003.

Yaeger, Lynn. "The Mysterious Allure of Talitha Getty's Bohemian Marrakech Style." *Vogue*, August 2015.

Chapter Six: Mark

Ashworth, Jon. "Gettys Focus Cash on UK Prospects." *Times* (London), April 4, 1994.

Asome, Carolyn. "Home! Bright Young Things." *Times* (London), June 23, 2018.

Bagley, Christopher. "Jewelry Designer Sabine Getty Rocks the Boat." *W*, May 2016.

BBC News. "Artist's Cold Call Cuts Off Phone." April 7, 2006.

———. "Mass Honours Sir Paul Getty's Life." September 9, 2003.

Beckerman, Josh. "Getty Family to Regain Majority Stake of Getty Images." *Wall Street Journal*, September 4, 2018.

Bigelow, Catherine. "Getty-a-Go-Go." SFGate (website), August 16, 2013. https://www.sfgate.com.

Blackhurst, Chris. "The MT Interview: Mark Getty." *Management Today*, August 31, 2010.

Caracciolo, Marella. "Up at the Villa." *W*, April 2005.

Carleton, Will. "Mark Getty's Son Photographer Alexander Getty Features Work in New Exhibition." *Photo Archive News*, December 23, 2014.

Carlson, Erin. "The Wardrobe on Tatum Getty." *Nob Hill Gazette*, June 5, 2018.

Chaffin, Joshua. "Getty Images in $2.4bn Buy Out." *Financial Times*, February 25, 2008.

Cook, John. "Getty Images Moving from Nasdaq to NYSE." *Seattle Post-Intelligencer*, October 29, 2009.

Corcoran, Jason. "How I Made It: Mark Getty, Chairman of Getty Images." *Sunday Times* (London), February 2, 2003.

di Robilant, Andrea. "The Most Dangerous Horse Race in the World." *Town & Country*, June 2016.

Economist. "Blood and Oil." March 2, 2000.

Ellsworth-Jones, Will. *Banksy: The Man Behind the Wall*. New York: St. Martin's Press, 2012.

Elwick-Bates, Emma. "Memphis Beat." *Vogue*, December 2016.

Evening Standard. "Banksy and Bono Dial £20m for Aids." February 15, 2008.

Feitelberg, Rosemary. "Nats Getty Talks 'Strike Oil' Fashion, Activism, Ridley Scott, Artistic Escapades." *WWD*, October 17, 2018.

Forbes. "Looking for a Gusher in . . . File Photos?" October 13, 1997.

Garrahan, Matthew. "Getty Chief Jonathan Klein to Refocus on Chairman's Role." *Financial Times*, March 13, 2015.

———. "Getty Images Back in the Family as Carlyle Group Sells Out." *Financial Times*, September 4, 2018.

Getty, Mark. *Like Wildfire Blazing*. London: Adelphi, 2018.

Getty, Sabine. "Original G." *Tatler*, September 2019.

Gillman, Ollie. "Princess Beatrice Attends Joseph Getty and Sabine Ghanem's Rome Wedding." *Daily Mail*, May 30, 2015.

Henderson, Violet. "Diamond Life." *Vogue UK*, March 2015.

Hurley, James. ". . . And the Award for Best Picture Goes to Getty Images (More Often than Not)." *Times* (London), March 29, 2019.

Kennedy, Maev. "Getty Heir's £10M Gift to National Gallery." *Guardian*, July 12, 2001.

Khan, Nura. "Inside Sabine and Joseph Getty's Rehearsal Dinner." *Vogue UK*, December 30, 2016.

Lerman, Rachel. "Corbis Sale to Chinese Company May Be Boon to Getty." *Seattle Times*, January 22, 2016.

Lewis, Jane. "Mark Getty: 'I'm One of Those People Everyone Hates.'" *Money Week*, April 8, 2019.

Macon, Alexandra. "Ivy Getty Wears John Galliano for Maison Margiela to Walk Down the Aisle at City Hall in San Francisco." Vogue.com, November 7, 2021.

Magnaghi, Brooke. "Fashion It-Girl Sabine Ghanem Dishes on Her Personal Style and Impossibly Chic Wardrobe." *HuffPost*, November 4, 2015.

Masters, Sam. "How Mark Getty Grew from the Child Seen in *All the Money in the World* to Be One of Britain's Richest Men." *Independent* (London), January 3, 2018.

Murphy, David. "Seven Gettys Sign Up for Irish Passports." *Independent* (London), September 30, 1999.

Nikkhah, Roya. "Garsington Opera: Behind the Getty Gates." *Telegraph* (UK), May 29, 2011.

Nisse, Jason. "Getty Family Takes Stake in UK Acquisition Venture." *Independent* (London), January 9, 1994.

Peretz, Evgenia. "Postcards from Paradise." *Vanity Fair*, December 2003.

Pithers, Ellie. "Life in Full Color." *Vogue UK*, March 2018.

Reguly, Eric. "Getty Snaps Up Supplier of Images in £100m Deal." *Times* (London), September 17, 1997.

Roberts, Paul. "It's Crunch Time for Seattle-Based Photo Giant Getty Images, and for Photographers." *Seattle Times*, December 1, 2019.

Studeman, Kristin Tice. "Getty's Images." *W*, December 18, 2014.

Tatler. "How to Win at the Social Season." May 21, 2019.

———. "The Social Power Index." August 2019.

Tharp, Paul. "Fund Grabs Getty." *New York Post*, February 26, 2008.

Tregaskes, Chandler. "They've Got It: The Evolution of the It Boy." *Tatler*, October 2020.

von Thurn und Taxis, Elisabeth. "Sabine Ghanem's Fairy-Tale Wedding to Joseph Getty at a Castle in Rome." *Vogue*, July 29, 2015.

Wintle, Angela. "Businessman and Author Mark Getty on His Passion for Italy and His Family's English Country Estates." *Sunday Times* (London), July 1, 2018.

Zhang, Michael. "Getty Images to be Fully Controlled by the Getty Family Once Again." PetaPixel (website), September 5, 2018. https://petapixel.com.

Chapter Seven: Aileen

Arnold, Amanda. "Jane Fonda's 82nd Birthday Party Was Wild." *The Cut* (*New York Magazine* blog), December 23, 2019. https://www.thecut.com.

Beck, Marilyn. "New—Naughty—Nicole in the Works." *Province* (Vancouver), August 18, 1994.

Bigelow, Catherine. "Gettys Gamble Big at Annual AIDS Research Fundraiser." *San Francisco Chronicle*, November 26, 2019.

Brolley, Brittany. "Elizabeth Taylor's Grandchildren Grew Up to Be Gorgeous." The List (website), July 13, 2018. https://www.thelist.com.

Collins, Nancy. "Liz's AIDS Odyssey." *Vanity Fair*, November 1992.

Economist. "How the Anarchists of Extinction Rebellion Got So Well Organized." October 10, 2019.

Firozi, Paulina. "Cash, Banners and Bullhorns: Big Philanthropists Throw Weight behind Disruptive Climate Activists." *Washington Post*, July 12, 2019.

Gardner, Chris. "Elizabeth Taylor's AIDS Foundation to Host Inaugural Fundraising Gala on Fox Lot." *Hollywood Reporter*, February 12, 2020.

Gliatto, Tom. "Hanging In." *People*, April 6, 1992.

Greenfield, Robert. *Timothy Leary: A Biography*. New York: Harcourt, 2006.

Harder, Amy. "Climate-Change Funders Shift Focus amid Pandemic and Election." Axios (website), May 14, 2020.

Bibliography

Hello!. "Elizabeth Taylor and Her Beloved Former Daughter-in-Law Aileen Getty." August 14, 1993.

Hook, Leslie. "Donations Pour In as Extinction Rebellion Goes Global." *Financial Times*, October 11, 2019.

Jenkins, David. "Meet the Man behind the World's Coolest Festival." *Tatler*, November 2016.

Jewell, Bryony. "Getty Oil Heiress Donates £500,000 to Fund Backing Protesters Extinction Rebellion." *Daily Mail*, September 6, 2019.

Knight, Sam. "Does Extinction Rebellion Have the Solution to the Climate Crisis?" *New Yorker*, July 21, 2018.

Lewis, Judith. "Aileen Getty Comes Clean." *Poz*, May 1996.

Matthews, Damion. "Gwyneth Paltrow Cochaired a Black-Tie Poker Party for amfAR at the Getty Mansion in San Francisco." *Vogue* online, November 18, 2019.

Needle, Chad. "Positive Connection." *A&U*, December 2015.

Neilson, Trevor. "Introducing the Climate Emergency Fund." Medium (website), July 11, 2019.

Ochs, Alyssa. "A Newcomer with a Famous Name Steps Up for HIV/AIDS Funding in the American South." *Inside Philanthropy*, March 4, 2018.

Oumano, Elana. "Dark Victory." *San Francisco Examiner*, January 10, 1993.

Patchen, Tyler. "Alabama AIDS Initiatives Earn Grants from Elton John AIDS Foundation and Others." *Birmingham Business Journal*, April 27, 2018.

People. "Heiress Aileen Getty Becomes Elizabeth Taylor's Almost Daughter-in-Law." March 17, 1980.

"Q&A Piano Man—Director," undated. ispirazzjoni.com.

Reginato, James. "The Elton John AIDS Foundation Pulled Out All the Stops at Its Fall Gala." *Vanity Fair* online, November 8, 2017, https://www.vanityfair.com/style/2017/11/elton-john-aids-foundation-gala.

Reynolds, Daniel. "Project Angel Food Honors Aileen Getty with Elizabeth Taylor Leadership Award." HIVPlusMag (website), September 10, 2014. https://www.hivplusmag.com.

Ruspoli, Tao, dir. *Just Say Know*. Los Angeles: LAFCO, 2002.

Schwartz, John. "Meet the Millionaires Helping to Pay for Climate Protests." *New York Times*, September 29, 2019.

Sessums, Kevin. "The Gettys' Painful Legacy." *Vanity Fair*, March 1992.

Snow, Shauna. "A Getty against Establishment." *Los Angeles Times*, May 29, 1990.

South China Morning Post. "Drug Addict Getty Heiress Has AIDS." January 13, 1988.

SubmitHub. "Kowloon," undated. https://www.submithub.com.

Weaver, Hilary. "Jane Fonda Was Arrested for a Fifth Time at a Climate Change Protest the Day before Her Birthday." *Elle*, December 21, 2019.

Webster, Ben. "Getty's Oil Cash Goes to Extinction Rebellion." *Times* (London), September 7, 2019.

———. "Philanthropist Aileen Getty Has a Long History of Giving Cash to Good Causes." *Times* (London), September 6, 2019.

West, Kevin. "Celluloid Prince." *W*, April 2009.

Williams, Jeanne. "AIDS Grips Liz's Ex-Daughter-in-Law." *USA Today*, November 14, 1991.

Williams, Paige. "A Journal of Reclamation Reaches a Peak in Spain." *New York Times*, August 10, 2006.

Williamson, Elizabeth. "Fonda Brings Hollywood to Capital for Protests." *New York Times*, December 21, 2019.

Wyllie, Julie. "Aileen Getty and Rory Kennedy Lead New Climate Fund to Support Activists and Protestors." *Chronicle of Philanthropy*, July 12, 2019.

Yarbrough, Jeff. "The Passion of Elizabeth Taylor." *Advocate*, October 15, 1996.

CHAPTER EIGHT: ARIADNE

Abramian, Alexandria. "Heir Time." *LA Confidential*, February 2015.

Allende, Mayte. "August Getty RTW Spring 2018." *WWD*, September 2017.

Bala, Divya. "From American Dynasty to Parisian Couture: *Vogue* Speaks to Designer August Getty." *Vogue Australia*, July 2, 2019. vogue.com.au.

Barnes, Brooks. "GLAAD's Bold New Campaign: An L.G.B.T. Constitutional Amendment." *New York Times*, June 29, 2019.

———. "Growing Up Getty." *New York Times*, June 23, 2018.

Carter, Lee. "August Start." *W*, October 2014.

Channel Q (internet radio). "Let's Go There: August Getty." April 15, 2019. https://www.google.com/url?sa=t&rct=j&q=&esrc=s&source=web&cd=&ved=2ahUKEwiZqfP6vZDxAhWtFlkFHds0AREQFjABegQIBhAD&url=https%3A%2F%2Fwww.audacy.com%2Fwearechannelq%2Fblogs%2Flets-go-there-w-shira-ryan%2Faugust-getty&usg=AOvVaw3v0xAurA2bSc4tji7OzWR3.

Chikhoune, Ryma. "Gigi Gorgeous Releases Own Cosmetics Line with Ipsy." *WWD*, October 2019.

Cox, Rich. "The Gayest Davos in History Still Isn't Gay Enough." Reuters, January 20, 2020.

Deeny, Godfrey. "August Getty Plans to Bring Glamour Back to the Paris Couture." Fashion Network (website), November 12, 2018. https://us.fashionnetwork.com.

Diaz, Gil. "Ariadne Getty: A Visionary With a Heart of Gold." LGBT News Now (website), November 2, 2021.

Directo-Meston, Danielle. "Inside Rising Designer August Getty's Surrealist Show at Universal Studios." Racked Los Angeles (website), November 12, 2015. https://la.racked.com.

Eytan, Declan. "Meet the 24-Year-Old Heir to the Getty Family Fortune, Who Is Banking on Ball Gowns as Big Business." *Forbes*, July 27, 2018.

Ferraro, Rich. "GLAAD and Ariadne Getty Foundation Host LGBTQ Panel during the World Economic Forum Annual Meeting in Davos and Call for Action." GLAAD blog, January 24, 2019. https://www.glaad.org/blog.

Foreman, Katya. "August Getty Atelier Spring Couture 2019." *WWD*, January 24, 2019.

Garcia, Michelle. "Buying Art in the Age of Instagram." *Out*, April 25, 2019.

Ginsberg, Steve. "Ready Getty Go." *WWD*, December 1, 1987.

GLAAD (website). "The Ariadne Getty Foundation Pledges $15 million to GLAAD." February 1, 2018. https://www.google.com/url?sa=t&rct=j&q=&esrc=s&source =video&cd=&ved=2ahUKEwih36H8vJDxAhUPbc0KHWGsCwgQtwIw AXoECAkQAw&url=https%3A%2F%2Fwww.glaad.org%2Fblog%2Fariadne -getty-foundation-pledges-15m-glaad-and-brings-lgbtq-inclusion-world-stage -world&usg=AOvVaw0fzVKcu-9WwnZtCfThZwip.

Goldsmith, Belinda. "How Gigi Gorgeous and the Gettys Are Pushing LGBT+ at Davos." Reuters, January 25, 2020.

Gorgeous, Gigi. *He Said, She Said: Lessons, Stories, and Mistakes from My Transgender Journey*. New York: Harmony Books, 2019.

———. "The Proposal: Nats & Gigi." YouTube video, March 8, 2018. https:// www.google.com/url?sa=t&rct=j&q=&esrc=s&source=web&cd=&ved =2ahUKEwjl6YbugJHxAhUvGFkFHeIiBS0QwqsBMAB6BAgUEAE &url=https%3A%2F%2Fwww.youtube.com%2Fwatch%3Fv%3DVxTyFSNe JBQ&usg=AOvVaw12EWlurKZUK9G5WnTzfIbs.

Gorgeous, Gigi, and Mimi. "All the Money in the World with Nats Getty." *Queer-ified with Gigi Gorgeous and Mimi* (podcast). June 2021. https://podcasts.apple .com/us/podcast/queerified-with-gigi-gorgeous-mimi/id1568356118?i= 1000525701562.

Guerrero, Desirée. "Gorgeous & Getty." *Advocate*, April/May 2019.

Hallemann, Caroline. "Ariadne Getty Gives $1 Million to GLAAD." *Town & Country*, December 20, 2017.

———. "A Member of the Getty Family Speaks Out about *All the Money in the World*." *Town & Country*, December 20, 2017.

Heath, Ryan. "Queer Davos Peeks Through." Politico (website), January 25, 2019.

Howard, Justin. "Framing a Getty." *Black Chalk*, December 2015.

Jackson, Corinn. "David LaChapelle and August Getty Created a Dystopian Model Wasteland at Universal Studios." Fashionista (website), November 12, 2015.

Janklow, Angela. "Getty Goil." *Vanity Fair*, March 1988.

Johns, Merryn. "Rainbow Rebel." *Curve*, Spring 2019.

Journal News (White Plains, New York). "Cher Shares Home with Getty Heiress." February 19, 1988.

Keveney, Bill. "Getty Lawyer Says FX's 'Trust' Portrays Family in 'Defamatory, Wildly Sensationalized' Way." *USA Today*, March 16, 2018.

Kopple, Barbara, dir. *This Is Everything: Gigi Gorgeous*. New York: Sander/Moses Productions, 2017.

Lathan, Corinna. "What Davos Taught Me about Supporting My Transgender Child." World Economic Forum (website), February 16, 2018.

Lawson, Richard. "Introducing Gigi Gorgeous, Who Needs No Introduction." *Vanity Fair* online, February 9, 2017, https://www.vanityfair.com/hollywood /2017/02/gigi-gorgeous-this-is-everything-sundance-interview.

London, Lela. "Oil Heir Nats Getty Debuts Lifestyle Fashion Brand with the Help of YouTuber Gigi Gorgeous." *Forbes*, February 6, 2019.

Lopez, Julyssa. "Gigi Gorgeous Had a Stunning Beach-Front Wedding." *Brides*, September 24, 2019.

Los Angeles LGBT Center. "Honoree Ariadne Getty—49th Anniversary Gala Vanguard Awards." YouTube video. Los Angeles: September 24, 2018. https://www.google.com/url?sa=t&rct=j&q=&esrc=s&source=web&cd=&ved=2ahUKEwiYmfmpu5DxAhV0FVkFHdMaBDAQtwIwBHoECAUQAw&url=https%3A%2F%2Fwww.youtube.com%2Fwatch%3Fv%3DXP6PcWDzQQk&usg=AOvVaw1ZrCDYQxKAhM45LZMbwmzC.

Magsaysay, Melissa. "Fashioning New Perspectives: August Getty, Gigi Gorgeous & Nats Getty." *LALA*, Summer 2019.

Malkin, Mark. "Ariadne Getty Honored as *Variety*'s Philanthropist of the Year." *Variety*, July 31, 2019.

McKenzie, Lesley. "Artist & Activist Nats Getty Debuts Lifestyle Brand Strike Oil." *Hollywood Reporter*, January 15, 2019.

Megarry, Daniel. "August Getty." *Gay Times*, February 2019.

Moore, Booth. "Ariadne Getty, August Getty, Nats Getty and Gigi Gorgeous Celebrate LGBTQ Advocacy." *WWD*, July 31, 2019.

Musto, Michael. "August Getty Wears His Colors Out, Loud and Proud." *Los Angeles Blade*, June 23, 2020.

Ocamb, Karen. "Ari Getty and a Camelot of Her Own Creation." *Los Angeles Blade*, January 29, 2021.

———. "Nats Getty Unmasked." *Los Angeles Blade*, June 25, 2020.

Ohland, Gloria. "Photo Finish." *LA Weekly*, June 25, 1987.

Politico (website). "Rainbow Wave." January 21, 2020.

Preston, Devon. "The Skin I'm In." *Inked*, June 2021.

Quinn, Dave. "Get a First Look at the Cover of Gigi Gorgeous' Memoir as She Reveals 'Emotional' Writing Process." *People*, October 16, 2018.

Reginato, James. "Outrageous Fortune: This Is Not Your Mother's Getty Family." *Town & Country*, February 2020.

Salessy, Heloise. "A Look at the 500,000-Swarovski-Encrusted 'Million Dollar Dress.'" *Vogue France*, November 2018.

Sessums, Kevin. "'Define Yourself': Ariadne Getty on Family, Philanthropy and Queer Activism." *Washington Blade*, October 20, 2019.

Sheeler, Jason. "How August Getty Navigated the Fashion Industry as a Member of One of America's Wealthiest Families." *Telegraph* (UK), February 14, 2020.

Sloan, Elizabeth. "Gigi Gorgeous & Nats Getty: 5 Fast Facts." Heavy (website), July 13, 2019. https://heavy.com.

Stratis, Niko. "Nats Getty on Becoming His Authentic Self." *Paper*, June 16, 2021.

Tempesta, Erica. "Transgender YouTube Star Gigi Gorgeous Reveals She Backed Out of Sex Reassignment Surgery." *Daily Mail*, March 3, 2019.

Tran, Khanh. "David LaChapelle and August Getty Meld Art and Fashion in Hollywood." *WWD*, November 12, 2015.

United Press International. "Getty Heir Converts Snap into Art Form." *Scrantonian Tribune*, February 21, 1988.

Varian, Ethan. "Fixture in Her YouTube Videos, and Now in Her Life." *New York Times*, July 28, 2019.

Wagmeister, Elizabeth. "Gigi Gorgeous and Nats Getty on Meeting, Marrying and the Importance of Representation." *Variety*, June 4, 2020.

West, Melanie Grayer. "A Gift for City Tourists." *Wall Street Journal*, May 24, 2011.

WWD. "August Getty RTW Spring 2015." September 2014.

Wynne, Alex. "August Getty Atelier Couture Fall 2019." *WWD*, July 8, 2019.

———. "August Getty Atelier Couture Spring 2020." *WWD*, January 22, 2020.

———. "August Getty Atelier Sets Paris Presentation during Couture." *WWD*, October 1, 2018.

Chapter Nine: Paul III

Abramovitch, Seth. "Balthazar Getty on Growing Up Getty." *Hollywood Reporter*, February 9, 2021.

Brunner, Jeryl. "Talking Money with a Getty." *Forbes*, December 14, 2018.

Creeden, Molly. "A Clothes Collection Inspired by the Bauhaus." *T (New York Times)*, August 9, 2019.

Croft, Claudia. "Design: Rosetta Getty." *Sunday Times* (London), May 3, 2015.

Delray, Dean. "Balthazar Getty, Actor/Musician, Artist." *Let There Be Talk*. (podcast), May 4, 2020. https://www.google.com/url?sa=t&rct=j&q=&esrc=s&source=web&cd=&ved=2ahUKEwjV48eFzZDxAhWiUt8KHc3v AI0QtwIwBXoECAcQAw&url=https%3A%2F%2Fwww.youtube.com %2Fwatch%3Fv%3DbcFrSvspT64&usg=AOvVawlJmrQCvrh9wgpUs -G2uk-J.

Directo-Meston, Danielle. "Balthazar Getty on His New L.A. Store, Monk Punk Fashion Line and Music." *Hollywood Reporter*, June 13, 2019.

Edwardes, Charlotte. "Balthazar Getty: I'm Finally OK with Being a Getty." *Evening Standard*, July 18, 2016.

Egan, Maura. "Dynasty's Child." *New York Times*, September 23, 2001.

Fleetwood, Amelia. "Breath of Fresh Air." *Santa Barbara*, March 2019.

Gerstein, Josh. "Anna Getty May Have Renounced U.S. Citizenship." *Politico* (website), February 2, 2012.

Getty, Anna. *Anna Getty's Easy Green Organic: Cook Well—Eat Well—Live Well*. San Francisco: Chronicle Books, 2010.

Goldstein, Melissa. "Higher Ground." *C*, January 2016.

Greener Living Today. "Anna Getty Interview with *Greener Living Today*." May 2009.

Haldeman, Peter. "Ojai's Golden Hour." *New York Times*, July 11, 2015.

Hilton, Perez. "Balthazar Getty Turns to Kabbalah to Save Marriage." December 14, 2009. https://perezhilton.com (blog).

KTLA 5. "Balt Getty on New Single 'Money.'" *KTLA LA Morning News*, December 14, 2018. https://www.google.com/url?sa=t&rct=j&q=&esrc=s&source =web&cd=&ved=2ahUKEwiQ5NqUzpDxAhWmY98KHdDICbkQwqs BMAF6BAgIEAE&url=https%3A%2F%2Fwww.youtube.com%2Fwatch %3Fv%3DT44vh6E493w&usg=AOvVawllPC5wCvyt5fQ35t4swyl8.

Lawler, Danielle. "Head over Hills." *Tatler*, April 2020.

Lennon, Christine. "A Fashionable Life: Rosetta and Balthazar Getty." *Harper's Bazaar*, September 2010.

Macalister-Smith, Tilly. "Free-Style." *Telegraph* (UK), August 1, 2015.

McCully, Martha. "Fashion House." *California*, May 2018.

Moore, Booth. "Rosetta Getty RTW Spring 2020." *WWD*, September 8, 2019.

O'Sullivan, Eleanor. "Mutual Admiration Abounds off the Set." *Asbury Park Press*, March 19, 1990.

Price, Jason. "Solardrive: Balthazar Getty and His Collaborators Discuss His New Project." Icon vs. Icon (website), May 8, 2013. https://www.iconvsicon.com.

Ruffer, Zoe. "Rosetta Getty Takes Spring Break on a South African Safari." *Vogue* online, May 9, 2019.

Scott, Danny. "A Life in the Day of Balthazar Getty, Member of a Troubled Dynasty." *Times* (London), August 28, 2016.

Singer, Maya. "A Weekend under the Tuscan Sun with Rosetta Getty." *Vogue*, July 3, 2018.

Spargo, Chris. "All the Money in the World: Billionaire Heirs Rosetta and Balthazar Getty Treat Guests to Horse Races, Dinner under the Stars, and Fireworks at Their Fourth of July Party in Tuscany." *Daily Mail*, July 5, 2018.

Sykes, Plum. "The Power of a Name: Dynasty." *Vogue*, March 2001.

Turro, Alessandra. "Rosetta Getty, Farfetch Celebrate Fourth of July in Tuscany." *WWD*, July 6, 2015.

Warner, Kara. "How Balthazar Getty 'Struggled' with Billionaire Family's Dark Legacy—and Survived Scandal." *People*, January 4, 2018.

Wong, Amelia. "Not-Your-Average Visitor's Take on the Getty." *The Iris* (blog), December 15, 2016. http://blogs.getty.edu.

WWD. "Very Marry." August 14, 2003.

CHAPTER TEN: TARA

Arden, Isabella. "Bits & People." *Palm Beach Daily News*, November 23, 1986.

Ashton, Paul. "SuperYacht World Hall of Fame: *Talitha*." *SuperYacht World*, July 1, 2016.

Bigelow, Catherine. "Getty Hosts the Africa Foundation." SFGate (website), November 24, 2015. https://www.sfgate.com.

Brooks, Phillip. "Sails Now On." Sail the World (website), January 12, 2017. https://sailtheworld.info.

Campbell, Stewart. "Treasure Hunter: Yacht Owner Tara Getty on His Epic Round-the-World Adventure." *Boat International*, May 5, 2016.

Carroll, Jerry. "Getty's Rocky Marriage." *San Francisco Chronicle*, February 24, 1986.

Cunliffe, Tom. *Blue Bird: Seven Decades at Sea*. West Sussex, UK: Kos Picture Source, 2010.

Departures. "Tara Getty: Africa Foundation." September 2013.

Eden, Richard. "Talitha Getty Lives On." *Telegraph* (UK), August 9, 2008.

Elkann, Alain. "Gisela Getty." Interview, August 19, 2018. https://www.alainelkanninterviews.com.

Eszterhas, Joe. "Exclusive Interview with Paul Getty." *Rolling Stone*, May 9, 1974.

Fortescue, Sam. "Second Wind." *Boat International*, September 2020.

Bibliography

Getty, Tara. "Life on a South African Game Reserve." *Evening Standard*, September 11, 2009.

Haldeman, Peter. "Phinda Getty House." *Architectural Digest*, February 2008.

Hossenally, Rooksana. "The Corsica Classic Regatta Celebrates Its 10th Anniversary This August Despite the Coronavirus." *Forbes*, August 15, 2020.

Houston, Dan. "Griff's First Win." *Classic Boat*, October 2012.

Johnson, Laurie. "2 Getty Kidnappers Sentenced in Italy." *New York Times*, July 30, 1976.

Kellett, Francisca. "Safari School." *Financial Times*, February 19, 2019.

Lyons, Madeleine. "John Paul Getty's Home Sells for Close to €2.45m." *Irish Times*, October 20, 2012.

Manners, Dorothy. "Gossips Keep Eye on 'Pool.'" *San Francisco Examiner*, August 22, 1968.

McNeil, Donald G. "Company Draws Rich Eco-Tourists to Africa." *New York Times*, June 25, 1997.

Miami Herald. "J. Paul Getty III Marries Ex-Model." September 14, 1974.

Orlando Sentinel. "Court Names Protector for Getty's Grandson." March 26, 1975.

Parker, Jennifer Leigh. "Want to Stop Poaching? Build a Smart Park." *Forbes*, December 2019.

Ross, Rory. "Jon Bannenberg, the Godfather of Modern Yacht Design." *Vanity Fair*, August 2018.

Rozzo, Mark. "The Virtually Unknown Saga of Gisela Getty and Jutta Winkelmann, It Girls on a Bumpy Ride." *Vanity Fair*, April 2018.

San Francisco Examiner. "Reclusive Getty." June 5, 1987.

———. "Rich Kid with a Silly Name." September 22, 1968.

Seal, Mark. "The Good Life Aquatic." *Vanity Fair*, May 2005.

———. "Too Big to Sail?" *Vanity Fair*, November 2010.

Taki. "Coming Soon: My Engagement to Kristin Scott Thomas." *Spectator*, June 21, 2014.

———. "A Very Exclusive Club." *Quest*, September 2014.

———. "High Life." *Spectator*, June 15, 2013.

Tang, David. "Take a Bow." *Financial Times*, August 16, 2017.

Telegraph (UK). "Bush Barons." March 25, 2006.

———. "A Grandson Makes Getty Even Richer." August 31, 2001.

Time. "Catching the Kidnappers." January 28, 1974.

Tisdall, Nigel. "The Corsica Classic." *Telegraph* (UK), March 20, 2017.

United Press International. "Getty Set to Meet Demands." July 16, 1973.

Varty, Dave. *The Full Circle: To Londolozi and Back Again*. Johannesburg: Penguin, 2008.

Weber, Bruce. "J. Paul Getty III, 54, Dies; Had Ear Cut Off by Captors." *New York Times*, February 7, 2011.

Woo, Elaine. "J. Paul Getty III Dies at 54; Scion of Oil Dynasty." *Los Angeles Times*, March 13, 2014.

WWD. "Getty Up." June 22, 2006.

Chapter Eleven: Pacific Heights

Anderson, Susan Heller. "Only the Flight Is Economy Class." *New York Times,* November 30, 1983.

Associated Press. "Nation's Richest Man Upset by Forbes List." October 1, 1983.

Bernheimer, Martin. "In San Francisco: Premiere of Getty's 'Plump Jack.'" *Los Angeles Times,* June 29, 1987.

Caen, Herb. "Ramblin' Man." *San Francisco Chronicle,* August 1, 1995.

Castro, Janet. "Texaco's Star Falls." *Time,* June 24, 2001.

Cocks, Anna Somers. "The Getty Museum Curator Who Hired the Rolling Stones for 15 Shillings a Head." *Art Newspaper,* January 10, 2020.

Cole, Robert J. "Father Thought He Screwed Up. His Judgement Is Again in Question." *New York Times,* April 24, 1984.

Coll, Steve. "Gettys at Center of Historic Fight." *Washington Post,* April 12, 1987.

Commanday, Robert. "Getty's 'Plump Jack' in Its Gala Debut." *San Francisco Chronicle,* June 29, 1987.

Curtis, Charlotte. "A Dance at the Met." *New York Times,* May 22, 1984.

———. "The Gregarious Ann Getty." *New York Times,* October 8, 1985.

———. "The Reserved Gettys." *New York Times,* May 8, 1984.

———. "Society's New Order Takes Over." *New York Times,* March 18, 1986.

———. "Wall Street's Mystery Man." *New York Times,* March 6, 1984.

Dana, Don. "Dear Friends of the Leakey Foundation." *AnthroQuest, the Newsletter of the Leakey Foundation,* Fall/Winter 2013.

Goodman, Peter. "Gordon P. Getty Emerges as a Composer." *Newsday,* April 18, 1986.

Hayes, Thomas. "Bitter Flareup at Getty over Control of Trust." *New York Times,* November 25, 1983.

———. "Gordon Getty's Goal Realized." *New York Times,* January 10, 1984.

Henken, John. "Gordon Getty Bringing His 'Plump Jack' to L.A." *Los Angeles Times,* March 19, 1988.

Holland, Bernard. "Recital: Mignon Dunn." *New York Times,* December 4, 1983.

Jacobs, Jody. "Leakey Fellows to Host Day," *Los Angeles Times,* May 9, 1975.

Jepson, Barbara. "The World's Wealthiest Composer." *Wall Street Journal,* March 21, 1985.

Lenzner, Robert. "Splitting Up J. Paul Getty's $4 Billion." *Boston Globe,* October 21, 1984.

Loomis, Carol J. "The War between the Gettys." *Fortune,* January 21, 1985.

L. S. B. Foundation News. "D.C. Symposium to Bring Together Famed Scientists 'In Search of Man.'" Fall 1975.

———. "Fourth Annual Leakey Memorial Symposium Scheduled for Nov. 1–2." Summer 1975.

———. "Johanson Reports on Afar at Caltech Lecture Series." Spring 1975.

McCarthy, Brian, and Bunny Williams. *Parish-Hadley: Tree of Life.* New York: Stewart, Tabori & Chang, 2015.

Meenan, Monica. "Christmas with the Gettys." *Town & Country,* December 1979.

Montandon, Pat. "The Big Apple." *San Francisco Examiner*, September 30, 1982.

Morch, Albert. "Man and Fox Set the Tone." *San Francisco Examiner*, December 3, 1973.

Pelosi, Barbara. "Profile: Gordon P. Getty." *L. S. B. Leakey Foundation News*, Spring 1980.

Pelosi, Nancy. *Know Your Power: A Message to America's Daughters*. New York: Random House, 2008.

Pender, Kathleen. "Gordon Getty Gets Down to Business." *San Francisco Chronicle*, February 5, 1987.

———. "S.F. Billionaire under Siege." *San Francisco Chronicle*, March 16, 1987.

San Francisco Examiner. "Dr. Leakey's Spell." May 5, 1972.

———. "Francis Bullimore." April 5, 1996.

Sansweet, Stephen J. "Scion's Struggle." *Wall Street Journal*, January 13, 1984.

Schonberg, Harold C. "The Wealthiest Composer of Our Time." *New York Times*, July 27, 1986.

Shiver, Jube. "Court Rules against Getty Heirs." *Los Angeles Times*, March 19, 1985.

———. "Gettys Resolve Dispute over Trust." *Los Angeles Times*, May 31, 1985.

Suzy. "How a King Made a Convert." *Daily News* (New York), May 11, 1978.

———. "An Ordinary Billionaire's Birthday Bash." *Daily News* (New York), December 4, 1983.

Town & Country. "Dreams of Beauty." April 1983.

Vogue. "House with Heart." October 1977.

Whitefield, Debra. "The Deal: How Getty Ended Up with Texaco." *Los Angeles Times*, January 9, 1986.

CHAPTER TWELVE: THE RICHEST AMERICAN, ONCE AGAIN

Andrews, Susanna. "Arianna Calling." *Vanity Fair*, December 2005.

Begley, Adam. "Ann Getty: Publish or Perish." *New York Times*, October 22, 1989.

Behbehaal, Mandy. "Red Carpet Premiere for Andrew Getty Movie." *San Francisco Examiner*, September 29, 1991.

Borger, Julian. "Getty's Double Life Stuns California High Society." *Guardian*, August 22, 1999.

Brown, Tina. *The Vanity Fair Diaries 1983–1992*. New York: Henry Holt, 2017.

Canedy, Dana. "Alexander Papamarkou, 68, an International Financier." *New York Times*, April 26, 1998.

Cohen, Edie. "Getty's Center." *Interior Design*, June 1998.

Colacello, Bob. "The Rise of Insight." *Vanity Fair*, September 1986.

Corkery, P. J. "Border-Line." *San Francisco Chronicle*, May 8, 2001.

Duka, John. "Alecko Papamarkou: Why the Rich Are Different." *Institutional Investor*, July 1985.

Finz, Stacy. "Getty's Secret Double Life/Second Family in L.A.—3 Daughters." SFGate (website), August 21, 1999. https://www.sfgate.com.

Gibbons, Ann. *The First Human: The Race to Discover Our Earliest Ancestor*. New York: Anchor Books, 2007.

Goodman, Wendy. "Billy Getty's Rise to the Top." *Harper's Bazaar*, March 1998.

Haberman, Douglas. "Billionaire Getty's Double Life." *Daily News* (New York), August 21, 1999.

Hamlin, Jesse. "Publisher Getty Calls It Quits." *San Francisco Chronicle*, March 1, 1990.

Hartlaub, Peter. "Getty's Secret Kids Demand Rights." *San Francisco Examiner*, August 21, 1999.

———. "Getty's Shocking Secret Family: Legal Papers Hint They Want His Name." *San Francisco Examiner*, August 20, 1999.

Hochman, Steve. "A Getty Getting into the Music Business." *San Francisco Chronicle*, October 15, 2000.

Kalb, Jon. *Adventures in the Bone Trade: The Race to Discover Human Ancestors in Ethiopia's Afar Depression*. New York: Copernicus Books, 2000.

Kjaergaard, Peter C. "The Fossil Trade: Paying a Price for Human Origins." *Isis* 103, no. 2 (June 2015).

La Ganga, Maria L. "Gordon Getty's Second Family Was an Open Secret." *Los Angeles Times*, August 30, 1999.

Los Angeles Times. "Engagements: Jarman–Getty." February 7, 1999.

Love, Iris. "Iris Love's Nile Diary." *Vanity Fair*, June 1985.

Mahon, Gigi. "Lord on the Fly." *New York*, February 24, 1986.

Mansfield, Stephanie. "In the Jetstream with Arianna." *Washington Post*, February 1987.

McGlynchey, Kevin. "Philanthropist Ann Light Dies at 79." *Palm Beach Daily News*, January 25, 1988.

McLeod, Beth. "'Frank and Outspoken,' Ann Light Remembered by Relatives, Friends." *Palm Beach Post*, January 31, 1988.

Nolte, Carl. "Kenneth Rainin—Entrepreneur, Donor." SFGate (website), May 6, 2007. https://www.sfgate.com.

Oney, Steve. "The Many Faces of Arianna." *Los Angeles*, October 2004.

Perlez, Jane. "Grove Sold to Ann Getty and British Publisher." *New York Times*, March 5, 1985.

Petit, Charles. "Battle over Old Bones Cools Off." *San Francisco Chronicle*, October 22, 1996.

———. "Berkeley Institute in Battle over Fossils." *San Francisco Chronicle*, April 26, 1995.

———. "Getty Withdraws Backing for 'Origins' Institute in Berkeley." *San Francisco Chronicle*, May 25, 1994.

Reed, Dan. "Billionaire Gordon Getty's Secret Family of 4 Revealed." *San Jose Mercury News*, August 20, 1999.

Reginato, James. "Getty's New Vintage." *W*, March 1996.

———. "Hale Storm." *W*, February 1998.

Reid, Calvin. "Barney Rosset Remembered." *Publishers Weekly*, February 24, 2012.

Reuters. "Getty Name Adopted by His 'Second Family.'" *San Francisco Examiner*, January 29, 2000.

Robins, Cynthia. "Witty Mix of People at Hale Ranch." *San Francisco Examiner*, September 8, 1987.

Rowlands, Penelope. "The Getty Gang." *WWD*, July 11, 1991.

Rubenstein, Steve. "San Francisco Says Goodbye to Pat Steger." *San Francisco Chronicle*, November 19, 1999.

Saeks, Diane Dorran. "On Top of the World: Billy Getty Turns Two Russian Hill Apartments into a Spectacular Penthouse." *San Francisco Chronicle*, March 4, 1999.

San Francisco Chronicle. "A Wealth of Talent." March 1, 1998.

Smith, Randall. "Friendship and Favors Win Wealthy Clients for a New York Broker." *Wall Street Journal*, July 16, 1985.

Steger, Pat. "Billy Getty Pops the Question." *San Francisco Chronicle*, December 29, 1998.

———. "Birthday Bashes and a Getty Blast." *San Francisco Chronicle*, October 14, 1996.

———. "Block Party by the Bay." *WWD*, March 12, 1990.

———. "Dinner Music." *WWD*, July 26, 1990.

———. "Don and Kelly Get Married at the Gettys'." *San Francisco Chronicle*, April 30, 1999.

———. "An Engaging Party Purely for Love. Vanessa and Billy Celebrate at Mom's." *San Francisco Chronicle*, February 17, 1999.

———. "Fairy-Tale Wedding for Getty-Jarman in Napa Valley." *San Francisco Chronicle*, June 21, 1999.

———. "Gavin Bids Bye-Bye to His Roaring 20s: Getty Boys Toss Him a Super Bash for His 30th." *San Francisco Chronicle*, October 13, 1997.

———. "Gettys' Party a Blockbuster." *San Francisco Chronicle*, March 12, 1990.

———. "High-Flying Getty Joins Used-Jet Set." *San Francisco Chronicle*, May 2, 1986.

———. "A Literati Soiree/Dominick Dunne Dines and Signs." *San Francisco Chronicle*, October 1999.

———. "A New Face in Cosmetics Shopping/Sephora Opens with Glitz and a Getty." *San Francisco Chronicle*, December 2, 1998.

———. "PlumpJack's Delicious Anniversary Dinner Was Fine, So Were the Cats." *San Francisco Chronicle*, April 14, 1999.

———. "Uganda and East Bay Highland Flings/It's a Real Social Jungle Out There." *San Francisco Chronicle*, September 9, 1996.

———. "Wedding of Year Is Perfect Match of Oil and Ink." *Palm Beach Daily News*, April 17, 1986.

University of California, Berkeley. "Project History." Middle Awash Project Ethiopia (website), undated. https://middleawash.berkeley.edu.

Varney, Carleton. "Donna Long." *International Opulence*, undated.

Weaver, William. "Flying First Class." *Architectural Digest*, March 1995.

Weidenfeld, George. *Remembering My Good Friends*. New York: HarperCollins, 1994.

Whiting, Sam. "Money Talks." *San Francisco Chronicle*, January 8, 1995.

WWD. "Gettys Are Redecorating 'The Jetty.'" March 2, 1993.

———. "The New Getty." June 24, 1999.

Chapter Thirteen: New Vintages

American Luxury. "Marlon Brando's Home in Hollywood Hills West Purchased by John Gilbert Getty, for $3.9M." November 29, 2018.

Beale, Lauren. "John Gilbert Getty Sells Los Feliz Home for $8.3 Million." *Los Angeles Times*, October 3, 2014.

Bennett, Will. "A Return to True Victorian Values." *Telegraph* (UK), November 29, 2004.

Bernstein, Jacob. "Getty Divorce: Details on Hollywood's Billionaire Scandal." Daily Beast (website), May 25, 2010.

Bigelow, Catherine. "Celebration of Note for Composer Getty's 80th." SFGate (website), December 15, 2013. https://www.sfgate.com.

———. "Design by Getty: Arts Patron Ann Getty Spins Antique Collecting into a Full-Blown Business." *San Francisco Chronicle*, October 26, 2003.

———. "Getty-a-Go-Go." SFGate (website), December 18, 2005. https://www.sfgate.com.

———. "Getty's Intuitive Style." *San Francisco Chronicle*, October 7, 2012.

———. "Gordon Getty's 85th Birthday Soiree, Shared with Granddaughter, a Fairy Tale Come True." SFGate (website), December 22, 2018. https://www.sfgate.com.

———. "Guests of Gettys Aglow." *San Francisco Chronicle*, December 16, 2009.

———. "Peter Getty Seals the Deal on a Long-Ago First Date." SFGate (website), February 16, 2017. https://www.sfgate.com.

———. "S.F. Arts Medallion Awarded to Swig." SFGate (website), October 29, 2012. https://www.sfgate.com.

———. "S.F. Debs Step into a New Era." SFGate (website), July 5, 2013. https://www.sfgate.com.

———. "Swells." SFGate (website), April 18, 2004. https://www.sfgate.com.

———. "Swells." SFGate (website), August 8, 2004. https://www.sfgate.com.

Bing, Jonathan. "Showbiz Has a New Party Line." *Variety*, November 25, 2002.

Bramesco, Charles. "A Millionaire, His Meth Addiction and the Horror Movie 15 Years in the Making." *Guardian*, March 14, 2017.

Butter, Susannah. "His Life Was a Struggle. I Wish I Could Have Protected Him." *Evening Standard*, March 2, 2015.

Byrne, Peter. "How William Newsom's Pipeline into the Getty Fortune Has Put Money—Lots of It—in His Politically Ambitious Son's Pocket." *SF Weekly*, April 2, 2003.

Christiansen, Robert. "Gordon Getty: 'My Dad Thought Music Was Something I Could Do on the Side.'" *Telegraph* (UK), June 2014.

Clark, Andrew. "Yes, We're Doing the Getty Opera." *Financial Times*, October 12, 2012.

Coffey, Brendan. "Tips from Billionaire Gordon Getty." *Bloomberg Markets*, May 2015.

Comiskey, Patrick. "A Wine Guy at City Hall." *Los Angeles Times*, August 3, 2005.

Corkery, P. J. "At the Peak." *San Francisco Examiner*, December 10, 2001.

Feinblatt, Scott. "Gordon Getty's Scare Pair Delivers Shivers and Laughs at Broad Stage." *LA Weekly*, June 26, 2018.

Finnie, Chuck. "Newsom's Portfolio." *San Francisco Chronicle*, February 23, 2003.

Flemming, Jack. "John Gilbert Getty Picks Up a Dramatic Dwelling Designed by A. F. Leicht." *Los Angeles Times*, November 21, 2016.

Friedman, Emily. "Oil Heir Peter Getty Embroiled in Nasty Divorce." ABC News, May 28, 2010. https://abcnews.go.com.

Friend, Tad. "Going Places." *New Yorker*, October 4, 2004.

Getty, Peter, and Billy Getty. *What the Butler Didn't See*, blog on SFGate, June 15, 2009. https://www.sfgate.com.

Ginell, Richard S. "L.A. Opera's 'Scare Pair' at the Broad Stage." *Los Angeles Times*, June 25, 2018.

Gonzales, Sandra. "Former *Mercury News* Reporter Dan Reed Dead at 50." *San Jose Mercury News*, January 8, 2009.

Graff, Amy. "San Francisco's Getty Preschool under Scrutiny." SFGate (website), March 14, 2011. https://www.sfgate.com.

Guthrie, Julian. "Belinda Barbara Newsom Dies at 73." SFGate (website), November 24, 2008. https://www.sfgate.com.

Hamilton, Matt. "Coroner: Getty Heir Had Ulcers, Methamphetamine, Heart Disease." *Los Angeles Times*, June 16, 2015.

Isle, Ray. "California's Governor Blends Politics and Napa." *Food & Wine*, October 2015.

Johnson, Betty. "Niche Fruit Grower Is Also Marketing Director." *San Diego Union-Tribune*, July 20, 2005.

Keeling, Brock. "Reading This Post Will Make You Want to Kill a Getty (Except Vanessa, That Is)." SFist (website), June 16, 2009. https://sfist.com.

Kruse, Michael. "How San Francisco's Wealthiest Families Launched Kamala Harris." Politico (website), August 9, 2019.

Lawrence, Ann. "See and Be Scene." *San Francisco Examiner*, December 11, 2001.

Leitereg, Neal. "John Gilbert Getty of the J. Paul Getty Oil Family Has Sold His Home in Hollywood Hills West for $1.575 Million." *Los Angeles Times*, April 15, 2016.

Macon, Alexandra. "Shannon Bavaro and Peter Getty's Wedding Celebration at the Getty Mansion—the Groom's Parents' Home." *Vogue*, January 30, 2017.

Martin, J. J. "A Fashionable Life: Jacqui Getty." *Harper's Bazaar*, May 1, 2007.

Mather, Kate. "Getty Oil Heir Had Serious Medical Condition, Court Documents Say." *Los Angeles Times*, March 31, 2015.

Matier, Phillip. "Society Pals' Falling Out Affects Newsom, Getty Families." *San Francisco Chronicle*, August 11, 2000.

McNeil, Liz. "How Music Helped Gordon Getty Escape His Family's Famous Curse." *People*, February 9, 2016.

Moffat, Frances. "The Gold Coasters." *Nob Hill Gazette*, September 2010.

Moyer, Justin Wm. "Andrew Getty, 47, Dead in Latest Getty Family Tragedy." *Washington Post*, April 1, 2015.

Naff, Lycia. "Hard-Partying Getty Scion Was on Meth When He Died in His Bathroom of Massive Gastrointestinal Hemorrhage." *Daily Mail,* June 16, 2015.

Nolan, Hamilton. "Rich Getty Heir Wants Blog Fight!" *Gawker* (blog), June 19, 2009. https://www.gawker.com.

———. "Rich Guys Blog, to Make You Mad." *Gawker* (blog), June 16, 2009. https://www.gawker.com.

NRM Streamcast (online network). "*The Evil Within*—Andrew Getty's Original Nightmare." Undated. https://www.nrmstreamcast.com.

Nugget. "Peter Getty's War." *The Daily Nugget* (blog), June 19, 2009.

Reginato, James. "Ann Getty's Exotic Interiors." *Sotheby's,* 2012.

———. "Getty Fabulous." *W,* October 2003.

Reuters. "Andrew Getty Died of Haemorrhage, Ulcer, Bad Heart and Meth—Coroner." *Guardian,* June 17, 2015.

Rich, Nathaniel. "The Fashionable and Philanthropic Force That Is Vanessa Getty." *Vanity Fair,* August 23, 2018.

Ritman, Alex. "Late Getty Heir's Directorial Debut 'The Evil Within' Lands after 15 Years." *Hollywood Reporter,* March 6, 2017.

Rosenblum, Joshua. "Getty: *Plump Jack.*" *Opera News,* September 2013.

Saeks, Diane Dorrans. "Ann Getty Believes Rooms Should Be Witty, Not Fussy." 1stdibs (website), March 3, 2010.

———. *Ann Getty Interior Style.* New York: Rizzoli International, 2012.

———. "Getty Glamour." *Harper's Bazaar,* October 2012.

———. "Gordon Getty Celebrates His 85th Birthday with a Bash at Home." *WWD,* December 17, 2018.

Sernoffsky, Evan. "No Foul Play Suspected in Death of Getty Heir." *San Francisco Chronicle,* April 2, 2015.

7x7. "The Gettys' Blog: Burning Up the Internet." June 16, 2009.

Shadowproof (website). "Sex, Drugs and Violence: Getty Divorce Court Date Today." May 7, 2010. https://shadowproof.com.

Spotswood, Beth. "My Grandmother Would Be Appalled . . ." SFGate (website), June 17, 2009. https://www.sfgate.com.

Stevens, Elizabeth Lesly. "In Gettys' Exclusive Preschool, It's Tough to Fly from Gilded Cage." *New York Times,* March 12, 2011.

Tate, Ryan. "Getty Heir's Humiliating Battle with the Godfather Family." *Gawker* (blog), May 10, 2010.

———. "Nasty Divorce Splits the Coppolas and the Gettys." *Gawker* (blog), March 31, 2010.

———. "Peter Getty: Costumed Layabout Scion." *Gawker* (blog), June 19, 2009.

Thurman, Judith. "A Tale of Two Houses." *Architectural Digest,* March 2003.

Vanity Fair. "The 2014 International Best-Dressed List." September 2014.

Walters, Dan. "Gavin Newsom's Keeping It All in the Family." *Los Angeles Times,* January 6, 2019.

West, Kevin. "In Her Court." *W,* November 2004.

———. "Pacific Heights." *W,* January 2007.

Williams, Kate. "Son of Gordon, Ann Getty Found Dead in L.A. Home." *Los Angeles Times*, April 1, 2015.

WWD. "Freaky Chic," November 4, 2002.

———. "The Price Is Right: Jacqui Getty's Monthly Allowance Request." March 30, 2010.

Yeomans, Jeannine. "Coppolas, Gettys Toast Happy Union." *San Francisco Chronicle*, October 6, 2000.

Zinko, Carolyne. "A Wedding to Remember: Newsom-Guilfoyle Nuptials Talk of the Town." *San Francisco Chronicle*, December 16, 2001.

CHAPTER FOURTEEN: PASSING THE BATON

AnthroQuest. "In Memoriam: Robert M. Beck." Fall/Winter 2014.

Ardehali, Rod. "Man, 58, Who Was Arrested at Bel Air Mansion Where the Feds Found a Huge Cache of Guns Faces 64 Felony Counts and 48 Years in Prison if Found Guilty." *Daily Mail*, July 16, 2019.

Associated Press. "Suspect out of Jail after 1000 Guns Seized from an LA Mansion." May 10, 2019.

Barabak, Mark Z. "Are Newsom and Harris on Collision Course?" *Los Angeles Times*, September 21, 2021.

Beck, Helene. *Jewels from My Grove: Persimmons Kumquats & Blood Oranges—Reflections & Recipes*. San Diego: Chefs Press, 2015.

Beyer, Rebecca. "Judge and Getty Family Advisor." *Stanford*, July 2019.

Bigelow, Catherine. "Miss Bigelow's Babble On by the Bay." Nob Hill Gazette (website), February 18, 2021.

Bravo, Tony. "5 Standout Looks from the 2020 San Francisco Ballet Gala." *San Francisco Chronicle*, January 17, 2020.

———. "Jo Schuman Silver Wants 'Beach Blanket Babylon' Vision to Live On after Show Closes." *San Francisco Chronicle*, December 12, 2019.

Cadelago, Christopher. "This Millionaire Might Be California's Next Governor." *Sacramento Bee*, July 31, 2017.

Criscitiello, Alexa. "Opera by Gordon Getty Out Now from Pentatone." Broadway-World (website), September 9, 2020. https://www.broadwayworld.com.

Cristi, A. A. "Goodbye Mr. Chips By Gordon Getty: An Opera Reimagined For Film to Receive World Premiere." BroadwayWorld (website), October 1, 2021.

Diaz, Alexa. "Man Charged with 64 Felony Counts after 1,000 Guns Seized at Bel-Air Mansion." *Los Angeles Times*, July 16, 2019.

Elinson, Zusha. "Suspect Who Stockpiled More than 1,000 Firearms in Mansion May Face Federal Charges." *Wall Street Journal*, May 14, 2019.

Friend, Tad. "Gavin Newsom, the Next Head of the California Resistance." *New Yorker*, November 5, 2018.

Fry, Hannah. "A Run-Down Mansion, a Getty Connection: The Tale of the Weapons Cache at an L.A. Home." *Los Angeles Times*, May 10, 2019.

Grimes, Kamala. "'Kamala Harris for the People' Holds Fundraiser at Getty Home on 'Billionaires Row' in SF." *California Globe*, June 1, 2019.

Janiak, Lily. "'Beach Blanket Babylon' Says Goodbye with the Performance of a Lifetime." *San Francisco Chronicle,* January 1, 2020.

Justice William Newsom Fund. "Hon. William A. Newsom III Obituary." Undated. https://www.justicewilliamnewsomfund.org.

Kennedy, Dana. "Will Getty Family Curse Claim the Next Generation after the Latest Death?" *New York Post,* November 28, 2020.

Lawrence, Allie. "The Angry Feminist Pin-Up Calendar Is What We Need to Start 2019 Off Right." *Bust* online, December 18, 2018.

Lenthang, Marlene. "Revealed: John Gilbert Getty, 52, Died of a Fentanyl Overdose Coupled with Heart Complications." *Daily Mail,* January 27, 2021.

Levin, Sam. "A Thousand Guns Were Found in an LA Mansion. Then the Mystery Deepened." *Guardian,* May 11, 2019.

L. S. B. Leakey Foundation News. "Robert M. Beck: Rancher, Real Estate Investor, Philanthropist, Vice President, Board of Trustees." Spring/Summer 1977.

Mehta, Seema. "How Eight Elite San Francisco Families Funded Gavin Newsom's Political Ascent." *Los Angeles Times,* September 7, 2018.

Parry, Ryan. "Cops Found John Gilbert Getty Dead with His Eyes and Mouth Open in an 'Indian Style Sitting Pose' in His $500-a-Night San Antonio Hotel Suite." *Daily Mail,* November 30, 2020.

Patten, Dominic. "Kamala Harris' Big Hollywood Virtual Fundraiser Rakes in Big Big Bucks." Deadline (website), September 4, 2020. https://deadline.com.

Ramzi, Lilah. "How the Pandemic Changed Weddings." *Vogue* (website), May 24, 2021, https://www.vogue.com/article/how-the-pandemic-changed-weddings.

Roberts, Sam. "Ann Getty, 79, a Publisher and a Bicoastal Arts Patron." *New York Times,* September 19, 2020.

Ronayne, Kathleen. "William A. Newsom III, California Judge and Environmental Advocate, Dies at 84." *Washington Post,* December 18, 2018.

Ross, Martha. "From Gavin Newsom to Donald Trump Jr." *San Jose Mercury News,* July 16, 2018.

———. "Gavin Newsom Muses on Kimberly Guilfoyle Dating Donald Trump Jr." *San Jose Mercury News,* March 8, 2019.

SFGate (website). "John Gilbert Getty." November 30, 2020. https://www.sfgate.com.

TMZ. "John Gilbert Getty, Heir to Getty Fortune, Dead at 52." November 23, 2020.

Tweedie, James. "Multi-Million Dollar Bel Air Mansion Where the Feds Found Huge Cache of Guns Belongs to Billionaire Getty Scion's Former Mistress with Whom He Had a Secret Family." *Daily Mail,* May 9, 2019.

Wick, Julie. "Essential California: The Ballad of Gavin and Kimberly (and Kamala)." *Los Angeles Times,* August 26, 2020.

Conclusion

Bivens, Terry. "The Dorrance Dynasty Battles Itself." *Philadelphia Enquirer,* March 17, 1991.

Dolan, Kerry A., ed. "The Forbes 400." *Forbes*, October 2020.

Kovach, Gretel C. "Hunt vs. Hunt: The Fight Inside Dallas' Wealthiest Family." *D*, March 2008.

Lombardo, Cara. "A Family Feud Threatens Campbell's Dynasty." *Wall Street Journal*, November 23, 2018.

AFTERWORD

Angeleti, Gabriella. "Getty oil fortune heiress helped fund climate activists who have targeted artworks and museums." *The Art Newspaper*, October 21, 2022.

Agnew, Megan. "Oiling the wheels." *Sunday Times* (London), October 23, 2022.

Catenacci, Thomas. "Big Oil heiress funding 'Just Stop Oil' group that threw soup on Van Gogh painting." Foxnews.com, October 14, 2022.

Gayle, Damien. "Just Stop Oil activists throw soup at Van Gogh's Sunflowers." *Guardian*, October 14, 2022.

Getty, Aileen. "I fund climate activism—and I applaud the Van Gogh protest." *Guardian*, October 22, 2022.

Hammond, George. "Does Alisher Usmanov really own Sutton Place?" *Financial Times*, March 11, 2022.

Hiltzik, Michael. "The Getty oil fortune, a family scandal and an alleged multimillion-dollar tax scam." *Los Angeles Times*, June 21, 2022.

Lodge, Matthew. "Heiress of billionaire Getty oil dynasty donates $1M to Just Stop Oil: Outrage as 'foreign millionaire' bankrolls eco-mob 'disrupting lives of hard-working Britons.'" *Daily Mail*, October 20, 2022.

Tregaskes, Chandler. "Oil heir, activist and fashion designer Nats Getty on finding love and coming out as transgender." *Tatler*, June 2022.

Zhou, Gomi. "Kowloon Blends the Dreamy with Reality in Travel-Inspired Music." Thelunacollective.com, February 7, 2022

"Inside Nats Getty's First Runway Show for Strike Oil." *Paper* magazine, September 6, 2022.

Whoiskendallegetty.com

KPG Investments, Inc., and Kendalle Getty v. Marlena Sonn, No. 3:22-cv-00236-ART-CLB (Nev. 2022).

Marlena Sonn v. Kendalle P. Getty, et al, No. 1:22-cv-02758-RPK-VMS (New York. 2022).

Index